Inventing Anzac

Also by Graham Seal

The Hidden Culture: Folklore in Australian Society

The Outlaw Legend: A Cultural Tradition in Britain, America and Australia

The Lingo: Listening to Australian English

The Bare Fax

Great Australian Urban Myths

Tell 'em I Died Game: The Legend of Ned Kelly

The Oxford Companion to Australian Folklore (edited with Gwenda Beed Davey)

Banjo Paterson's Old Bush Songs

Australia in the World: Perceptions and Possibilities (edited with Don Grant)

Encyclopedia of Folk Heroes

A Guide to Australian Folklore (with Gwenda Beed Davey)

Verandah Music: Roots of Australian Tradition (edited with Rob Willis)

Inventing Anzac

The Digger and National Mythology

GRAHAM SEAL

Series Editor
Richard Nile

University of Queensland Press
in association with the API Network
and Curtin University of Technology

First published 2004 by University of Queensland Press
PO Box 6042
ST LUCIA, QLD 4067
www.uqp.uq.edu.au

Edited by the API Network
Australia Research Institute
Curtin University of Technology
GPO Box U1987
PERTH WA 6845

Printed in Australia by McPherson's Printing Group

Cataloguing in Publication Data
National Library of Australia

Seal, Graham, 1950–   .
   Inventing ANZAC.

   Bibliography.
   Includes index.

   1. Australia. Army. Australian and New Zealand Army Corps.
   2. Nationalism — Australia — 20th century. 3. Heroes —
   Mythology — Australia. 4. World War, 1914–1918 — Australia
   — Anniversaries, etc. I. Title.

320.540994

ISBN 0 7022 3447 8

Contents

Preface

This book traces the origins and development of the central Australian mythology of the twentieth century — and beyond. Anzac and its essential hero, the digger, are the consequences of historical, social and cultural processes that lie at the core of Australian national identity. These processes, both official in the case of Anzac and informal in the case of the digger, have twined together, sometimes comfortably, sometimes less so, for almost a century. Over that time, they have become the focus for the most cherished custom of the civic calendar, of a national shrine, a still-influential lobby group and a continuing folklore of the volunteer civilian foot soldier. In war and, just as powerfully, in peace, the myths and legends of Anzac and the digger have continued to motivate Australians and be employed by their governments. In order to understand how these powerful cultural factors have influenced Australia in the past — and how they will be likely to influence us in the future — an appreciation of the cultural scripts that combine into the national narrative is necessary. This story, like all stories, is a construct. In the case of Anzac, the story has many authors. Some tellers of the tales have been more influential and important than others. Some have been more conscious of their ends and deliberate in their attainment. Some have even told the truth, or at least what they believed to be the truth, which comes to the same thing, in the end. All have contributed to the invention of Anzac.

The power of Anzac is its ability to connect the potent notions of community, nation and war. It is a myth, but it is a necessary myth with which all Australians are required to have a relationship, positive or negative. It is not possible to live in this country and partake of its social and cultural life without being at least grazed by Anzac and its omnipresence in our calendar, our capital city and our preconceptions. Nor is it possible to be ignorant of Anzac's accompanying cultural icon, the digger, preserved in returned organisations and celebrated in a demotic tradition substantially of his own invention.

Inventing Anzac demonstrates how the official and the unofficial, the formal and the folkloric, the institutionalised and the communal have colluded — and continue to collude — in the construction of a potent national mythology. The cultural imperatives that gave birth to the digger and Anzac are outlined, followed by the social and political processes involved in the development of these traditions up to 1929. By this time the essentials of Anzac Day, as we have continued to observe it, were established, as were the main elements of the pervasive national mythology of Anzac and the digger. The continuing power of that mythology to motivate Australians in World War Two and Vietnam is then traced through to the recent grassroots community action involved in the story of 'the lost memorial' outlined near the end of this book. Tracking these events, attitudes and actions through time reveals the ability of the national mythology to reach into Australian lives, institutions and beliefs in many ways and at many levels.

The materials, sources and insights utilised in this study are diverse. They include the usual primary and secondary sources of the historian — newspapers, reminiscences, diaries — and the more ephemeral publications of trench journals and unit reunion programs. Essential to the arguments pursued was the collection and incorporation of folklore, including story, song, verse, belief, rumour and similar materials. Insights have been derived from historical, folkloristic and anthropological interpretations and approaches. Disciplinary transgressions, dangerous though they may be, are essential to understanding the power of myth and the processes by which it operates throughout a society and its culture.

The research on which this book is based extends over many years and has been assisted by many people, including Stephen Alomes of Deakin University, who supervised the PhD thesis on which a substantial part of this work is based; Peter Stanley of the Australian War Memorial; Bill Gammage, with whom I had some brief exchanges regarding folksong; Tom Stannage, who read and commented on a draft of the manuscript; and the many individuals who responded to media or direct appeals for wartime folklore over 1980–1982.

Organisations that have assisted include the Division of Humanities at Curtin University of Technology, the Australian Folk Trust and the Australian War Memorial, both of which provided research grants (two in the case of the Memorial).

Finally, and as always, I thank my family.

CHAPTER ONE

Tradition, Myth and Legend

The first official Anzac Day observance in 1916 inspired the then-Minister for Defence, Senator Pearce, to declare:

> Nor has the thunder of the cannon been necessary to inspire Australians with a conception of their duty; and the explanation of it all is that we have inherited to the full that spirit of our forbears which enabled them, not so long ago, to tear themselves from homeland firesides to shape careers in this great island continent, and to overcome with indomitable pluck the awful hardships of a pioneering life. For generations to come the story of the entry of Australian troops to the European battlefields will ring in the ears of English-speaking nations.[1]

These words indicate the fusion that had already been made between the discourses of imperialism, pioneering and war. They also foreshadow the determination of Australian governments and the groups they represented to perpetuate such notions within a nationalistic framework. Unremarkable for the time, the place and the occasion, these words and the cultural complexities that underlay them also encapsulate the central Australian myth. That myth was formed through the intersection of two disparate cultural traditions — the folkloric tradition of the digger and the official tradition of Anzac.

The 'digger' and the nature of Anzac are subjects that have long fascinated scholars, soldiers, politicians and the general public. Since the fateful April 25 of 1915, Australians have been continually enmeshed in discourses that have included participation, celebration, commemoration, condemnation, and study of Anzac and the digger. It could be argued that everything useful on the subject has been said, usually at length.[2] But despite — and perhaps, to some extent, due to — this intense interest, the power and persistence of Anzac and the digger remain in many ways obscure. This book is an argument about the two traditions of digger and Anzac, a study of the cultural and social means by which these respective images and their imperatives have been transmitted, and an interpretation of their social meanings. It traces the development of these two traditions from 1914 and shows how, through their complementarities and their contradictions, we invented the nation's

' "Damn your explosive bullets! You've gone and bust the pocket I 'ad me cigarettes in!" ', Cecil L. Hartt, *Humorosities* [1917], Australian War Memorial, Canberra, 1985, np.

most potent mythology. A number of themes and issues recur throughout this investigation. The most important of these are introduced below.

The Digger Tradition

The 'digger tradition' is the folklore of the digger socio-military group. It is a tradition that consists of the informal, unofficial, private ethos and expressions of the diggers including the language, narratives, verse, song, customs and beliefs shared between the members of that group. Much of this lore was derived from nineteenth-century notions of the ideal Australian 'type' — the bushman and the city-bush dichotomy that is widely recognised as a foundation of Australian cultural consciousness. While the members of the digger group were of diverse ethnic, social, occupational and economic backgrounds, their membership of the First Australian Imperial Force (AIF) conferred upon them a unique status, reflected from 1917 in the title 'digger'. The title — and it is one — describes the volunteer civilian members of the First AIF. The digger is not, during the period mainly covered by this book, a professional soldier. He is a temporary bearer of arms and uneasy wearer of uniforms. He is 'an ordinary bloke' doing a job of work for a reasonable day's pay. That this work was in the interests of the Empire to which Australia belonged was a commonplace of the time.

The digger tradition is private, exclusive, small-scale/amateur, face-to-face (i.e. strongly dependent upon orality and related modes of transmission), informal, unofficial and male-dominated. Specific and easily identified aspects of the tradition are anti-authoritarianism, particularly directed against officers, especially British officers; mateship; irreverence and larrikinism; swaggering arrogance; an aggressively nationalistic and, by later standards, blatantly racist stance; sardonic, even cynical humour; and a nonchalant attitude to death and injury. But embedded within this tradition were contradictory and ambivalent elements usually overlooked — the 'soft' emotions and expressions of sentimentality, pity and fear.

The digger tradition can be characterised as a comparatively 'spontaneous', 'authentic', small-scale tradition, initially created by the AIF from materials already to hand (the bushman, the larrikin) and from the exigencies of sacrifice and suffering occasioned by Gallipoli and the Western Front. The Anzac tradition came initially out of those same circumstances, but from the beginning occupied a more formal socio-cultural position than the demotic tradition of the digger.

The Anzac Tradition

The Anzac tradition, like its obverse described above, is a complex cultural process and institution involving the formal, official apparatus of Anzac Day, war memorials — particularly the Australian War Memorial in Canberra — the army, the Returned Soldiers' and Sailors' Imperial League of Australia (RSSILA) and similar organisations, and, ultimately, the politics of nationalist and military pragmatics. The word itself was, and is, protected from misuse by legal proscription. This tradition is public, inclusive and, implicitly, authoritarian.

Along with this apparatus belongs a set of attitudes and values within which notions of honour, duty, bravery, sacrifice and salvation are central, located particularly within a militarist context. Overarching these are the imperatives of commemoration and remembrance linked with an overpowering aura of nationalism, emphasising unity, sameness, heritage, patriotism and loyalty. Underlying these elements, and so increasingly sacralising Anzac, is the impact of temporal distance from the first Anzac Day. History itself imparts ever-accumulating significance to Anzac in the form of 'sacred time', forever elapsing, forever accreting around the icons and images of the Anzac tradition. Anzac is an invented tradition; a deliberate ideological construct which, in collusion with the digger tradition, operates hegemonically within Australian society. It is a part — the dominant part — of the central and formal identity of its society, and the culture of that society.

These two traditions of digger and Anzac can be clearly and usefully conceptualised as opposing ends of the same spectrum. But while these traditions are separated here for interpretative purposes, they are not isolated from each other but flow in and out of each other. These interactions are the means by and through which the Australian national-military mythology is powered, transmitted and sustained. It is an interaction that at some points shows the two traditions to be in agreement, at others in contradiction and at yet other points to uneasily cohabit the same cultural space. This unease is effectively mediated by various individuals, events and processes in history and society. The result of these mediations is the creation of the powerful mythology of celebration, commemoration, nationalism and, ultimately, of militarism that constituted national identity during the war, in the post-war period and since.

The ongoing interaction of the digger tradition with the tradition of Anzac took place, and takes place, at many levels and in many contexts. At unit reunions, within veterans' organisations, in homes and hearts was kept alive the private digger folk tradition of anti-authoritarianism, irreverence,

Hewett, W. Otho, 'Each one doing his bit', *The Anzac Book* [1916], Sun
Books, Melbourne, 1975, p. 167.

efficiency, resourcefulness and mateship. The more public Anzac tradition was perpetuated in the populist areas of the publishing industry, given official and monumental significance through the *Official History of Australia in the War of 1914–18* and in the establishment of the Australian War Memorial, through the activities of the Returned Soldiers' and Sailors' Imperial League of Australia (RSSILA), and through the development of Anzac Day as the dominant national observance.

None of the participants in this myth making were entirely or even substantially innocent. The original diggers consciously and aggressively created their own image and folklore. Many also projected certain aspects of that tradition into the public arena, participating in and supporting the rituals and demands of the official Anzac tradition through memorial services, marches and related events. Such rituals and observances were convenient to returned diggers as a group because they assured them of a continuing moral and social power base in an uncaring and economically difficult peacetime Australia, where ex-soldiers often felt they were under-rewarded and, increasingly, discriminated against.

Military, political and other establishment elites also were glad to extract from the digger tradition whatever elements seemed appropriate to the invention of a nationalistic-militaristic mythology of great convenience. It was convenient both as an ongoing nationalistic focus for a diverse, rambling and restless country, and a useful tool for jingoistic drum-beating at wartime. All these groups, with their private and public imperatives, had intersecting motives for the creation and maintenance of this mythology from the complex of folkloric and official elements that came to hand — and which were taken in hand — from April 25, 1915.

The Language of Tradition, Myth and Legend

Writers on Anzac and the digger have found great use for the terms 'tradition', 'myth' and 'legend'.[3] The terms have been, and continue to be, used and abused because they connote the qualities that are clearly present in the cultural complexities of the digger image and the representation of Anzac. There is a definite continuity of many of the central elements of these cultural items, making the term 'tradition' especially appropriate. However, there are a number of distinctive cultural traditions involved in the digger and the Anzac representations. These include the traditions associated with the pioneering past; certain elements of military tradition; the traditions of the digger in war and peace; and the traditional civic elements of commemoration, preservation and spectacle that motivate Anzac Day and its meanings. The makers, diffusers and bearers of these various traditions are sometimes the same, sometimes not. Frequently they interact, a factor that receives considerable attention in what follows.

While tradition has been a favoured term in much of the previous work on the digger and Anzac, it is a term that can obscure as much as it reveals. As with so many other matters related to Australia's wartime past and present, the mischief can be traced back to C.E.W. Bean. At least as early as 1942 Bean used the term 'Anzac Tradition',[4] impelled, no doubt, by the exigencies of World War Two. Historians, academic and popular, have often followed Bean's terminological lead.

To make appropriate and fruitful use of the concept of 'tradition' it is necessary to discern different traditions, identify the various elements that constitute these traditions, understand when, how and why they interact and, above all, to understand the motivations of those groups who perpetuate the traditions. That is one of the aims of this book. It is also necessary to define the way that 'tradition' is used in this book. Briefly, the term 'tradition' is understood here as a cluster of identifiable cultural attitudes, expressions and practices that have a coherent persistence and meaning among a social group or groups over time and space.

'Legend' is another term that has obviously found favour with those who wish to understand the traditions associated with the digger and Anzac due to its connotations of longevity and, most importantly, of belief. While the metaphysical element is actively satirised in the traditions of the digger and only given the occasional overt obeisance in the tradition of Anzac, it is ever-present in both, nevertheless. For the diggers, it was expressed at two apparently contradictory levels: firstly, in their frequent scepticism, parody and general subversion of priests and padres in many of their folk expressions; secondly, the metaphysical is present in the digger's folk beliefs, or 'superstitions', regarding fate, life and death. In the context of Anzac, the institutionalised religious aspects are present in the sombre observances of Anzac Day itself and in the fabric and the function of the Australian War Memorial, the chief of many shrines that mark the landscape. 'Legend' is therefore a term that resonates comfortably with both the folkloric and the official manifestations of religious belief within the traditions of the digger and of Anzac.

A 'legend' is also a narrative, a meaningful progress of events from a beginning, through a series of events to a prefigured end. The traditions of the digger and Anzac are the supreme national story and, indeed, are often referred to as 'the story of Anzac'. The elements of Gallipoli and the Western Front, both historical and fictional, were rapidly woven into a narrative of heroism, sacrifice and patriotism. In accordance with the formal traditions of war and military duty, the ending of the story has the gallant dead attaining their reward for earthly sacrifice in heaven. Thus the story has further metaphysical significance, making the term 'legend' — originally meaning the story of a saint's life — particularly attractive. Peter Cochrane uses this term for the progress of the Simpson story, usefully pointing out that it is also a particular kind of legend. The Simpson story is part of the Anzac — not the digger — tradition, and is therefore properly identified as an 'institutional(ised) legend'.[5] This usefully and necessarily distinguishes Simpson (and other stories, such as Jacka's VC) from the folk legends of the diggers, including those concerning the identity of the first man ashore at Gallipoli or the numerous stories of miraculous avoidance of death, such as the enemy shell with the digger's regimental number on its base or the Bible in the breast-pocket that stopped a Turkish/German bullet/piece of shrapnel, and the like.

Myth and Mythography

'Myth' is a term much used by anthropologists, literary critics, students of popular culture and historians, as well as in popular parlance. Its meanings shift accordingly. In this work 'myth' is understood as a belief-structure fundamentally embedded in a society and its culture. Myth is at once 'true', or appearing to be so, and 'false', in the sense that it hides, disguises, or distorts (by sanitisation or enhancement), ignores or trivialises aspects of lived experience.[6] Cultural traditions, formal and informal, are the essential underpinnings of myth.

Unlike the influential Barthesian formulation and its derivatives, myth is not here considered to inevitably perpetuate dominant ideology. Rather, myth is seen as a 'neutral' process that may be convenient at different times, in different ways, to different groups in a society. Myth is available for manipulation by various, often conflicting ideologies, in the interest and for the convenience of the holders of such ideologies. The same myth may be adverted to, even hallowed, in different ways by different groups — in short, may mean different, often antagonistic things to different people. The mythology that has evolved from the intersection of the digger and Anzac traditions is an especially intriguing and important example of this proposition.

In recent years, attention has been paid to the 'construction' of the myths, legends and traditions of Anzac and the digger.[7] C.E.W. Bean emerges from these studies, along with a supporting cast of British and Australian characters, as the chief myth-maker of the entire Anzac complex.[8] Bean is everywhere: he sends crucial despatches to Australian papers; his diaries show him manipulating the spontaneous trench productions of Gallipoli and concocting *The Anzac Book*; he is the motivating force behind the establishment of the Australian War Memorial; he has a hand in the promulgation of the institutionalised legend of Simpson; he is the writer of popular works on Anzac; and is editor and part-writer of the *Official History of Australia in the War of 1914–18*. Not without justification have we become obsessed with the mythologist as hero, to the extent that attention has been diverted from more profound processes of mythologisation within Australian culture. Nevertheless, it is impossible to avoid continually bumping into Bean the mythographer and 'the great inventor', from the time of his editorship of the Gallipoli trench journal *Sniper's Shots*.

The bloody terrains of Gallipoli and the Western Front were not only battlegrounds but also sites of ideological struggle and cultural appropriation. A new kind of war involving an incomprehensible level of slaughter was in progress. However, war did not dissolve the class antagonisms and ideological divisions of Australian society, much as contemporary observers (and many since) have sought to imply. This cultural appropriation and its consequent minimisation of protest and opposition within the AIF continued throughout and after the war, with Bean's editorship of *The Anzac Book* and *The Rising Sun*, his wartime dispatches, his post-war popular writing and, of course, his activities and influence as 'Official Historian'. Bean's motivations and aspirations in all this have been the focus of considerable debate,[9] and while this is beginning to strip away the shrouds of myth that cling to Bean's figure, it has also tended to direct attention away from the more fundamental cultural processes occurring around, beneath and above Bean himself. Certainly Bean was important — indeed, all-important — as a facilitator and catalyst, but the forces and imperatives that he focused and manipulated with amazing effectiveness must be understood as originating and operating beyond one man, and as aspects of Australian society and culture.

Myths usually develop over long periods and from obscure origins. In the case of the Australian national-military myth — the product of the interacting traditions of the digger and Anzac — we know the exact historical moment when it began. We can trace its origins in the romanticisation of pioneering and bush life that took place in the later nineteenth century, in the Australian experience of the Boer War and in the broader need for an appropriate national totem. Like many myths, ours was waiting to be invented.

CHAPTER TWO

The Digger Tradition, 1914–1919

Who were the diggers? From where did the men of the first AIF come? What did they do for a living? Where did they live? Historians have sought and, to some extent, have found answers to these questions. In terms of occupation, marital status, residence, nominal religious affiliation and birthplace, the First AIF was a close reflection of the white, adult male Australian population of the time.[1] How did this affect the culture forged by the diggers in the Great War?

Maleness was the single most significant marker of the social composition and cultural formations of the AIF. With the exception of a very few nursing staff,[2] the AIF, like all armies of the period, was an exclusively male domain. However, in this particular army, masculinity was imbued with especially powerful associations derived from prevailing notions of the Australian 'character'. These notions involved the stereotypical representation of the ideal Australian as a tall, tough, laconic, hard-drinking, hard-swearing, hard-gambling, independent, resourceful, anti-authoritarian, manual labouring, itinerant, white male. This image of the ideal Australian bushman was well established as a cultural cliché by the 1890s. As Ward and others[3] have shown, the cliché was celebrated in the poetry of Adam Lindsay Gordon, Henry Lawson, A.B. 'Banjo' Paterson, Will Ogilvie and a host of other versifiers and writers, many of whom were associated with the *Bulletin* magazine. The famous and popular ballads of the period privileged the bush hero in a variety of guises: swagman, unionist, horseman, stockman and defender of the Eureka Stockade. The rural folksong and verse tradition, in some cases traceable to the pre-gold rush period, provided a popular cultural reinforcement of the composed works of the later period. The protagonists of these works were overwhelmingly male: 'Jim Jones', 'Bold Jack Donohoe', 'The Wild Colonial Boy', Ben Hall, Frank Gardiner, Ned Kelly, overlanders, gold diggers and free selectors. Correspondingly, the antagonists of these heroes were also male: the squatter on his thoroughbred, the floggers, the gaolers, the trooper police and authority figures from the licence clerk to the governor.

The existence of such popular views of Australian male identity and attributes provided a solid basis upon which the folk culture of the digger could be built in wartime. These attributes had already found a militaristic form during the Australian involvement in the Boer War.[4] Lloyd Robson convincingly locates the birth of the 'stereotypical' Australian soldier in the Boer War and then traces, in broad outline, the development of that stereotype through two world wars. The Australian colonial soldier of the Boer War, he writes, 'was material for the creation of a new folk-hero, the bushman soldier'.[5] Robson's work reveals the elements constituting this stereotype as they emerged during the Boer War. These were, in addition to — and, to a great extent, derived from — his rural background: toughness, steadfastness, egalitarianism, a tendency toward theft, looting and light fingers, a distinct lack of respect for army hierarchy and the officers who represented it, and a resulting level of indiscipline.

Apparent contradictions within the stereotype of the Australian soldier are also noted by Robson. The swaggering, belligerent larrikinism of the Australian soldier and his dislike of British officers were counterbalanced by a profound respect for the Empire, the monarch and the 'old country'. Later, in 1914–18 (though Robson does not observe this) a strong element of sentimentality was also to become a contradictory aspect of the digger's communal make-up. Robson concludes: 'A strong stereotype of the Australian serviceman was not created in South Africa, but the foundations and general outlines were established'.[6] He then continues to examine the consolidation of the stereotype in 1914–18:

> What was the stereotype or image of the Australian soldier as it emerged during the Great War and came to be elaborated as a settled part of the Anzac legend? It was that of a member of a sublime army of young Australians volunteering to go forth on a kind of crusade. These men reflected the egalitarian colonial origins of Australia and were direct and straightforward in their dealings with each other, and contemptuous of lesser breeds; they could and did fight like threshing machines when they had to; they grimly rejected on two occasions their government's wish to reinforce by conscription their grievously depleted numbers [in fact, the AIF voted in favour of conscription, but for many years left-wing or radical historians promoted the idea that the soldiers voted against it]; they showed up all other soldiers and especially the British to be lacking in initiative and go; they revealed that they were rather undisciplined when that discipline was merely a formality, but really needed no controlling when it came to the deadly business of battle — then they became highly effective, skilful and feared killers; they were a classless army; they stuck to their mates through thick and thin; their burden as soldiers was lightened by a sardonic sense of humour that sometimes took the form of practical jokes, and in their ranks abounded many wags and tough nuts who made it a rule to always outwit the authorities; they did not give a damn for anyone on earth, in heaven or in hell. Their highly distinctive tunics and hats were perhaps never cleaned and brushed as they might

have been but if a man appeared spick and span it was a sure and certain sign
that he was up to no good; they had a penchant for removing objects of value
left in their way and were expert con men; their contempt for 'Gyppos' was
notorious; though they at first hated the Turks and though they tortured prisoners,
very soon they developed a respect for Johnny Turk; their attitude to the German
soldier was not one of hate but of respect, except on those few occasions when
the enemy pretended to surrender and then produced weapons. The stereotypic
Australian soldier was very tall and sinewy and hatchet-faced. He had a great
respect for the institutions of the 'old country' and what he perceived as its
quaintness, but little time for pommy officers and men as a rule, or until they
proved themselves manly. He got on well with the Scots. The stereotype was not
formally religious but had a lot of time for the Salvation Army and some of the
'fighting' padres.[7]

Robson also notes: 'The stereotype of the Australian serviceman in the
Great War is the colonial Australian male stereotype, refined to a sharpened
cutting edge'.[8] He goes on to embellish some of the elements contained in
this quotation, particularly the racism and larrikinism of the Australian soldier,

Barker, David, 'At the landing, and here ever since', *The Anzac Book* [1916],
Sun Books, Melbourne, p. 22.

the voluntary nature of the AIF, their physical attributes, their youth and anti-authoritarianism and the distinctive uniform of the troops. The article continues by briefly examining the persistence of the digger 'tradition' (or is it a stereotype? The distinctions, if any, are not clarified) throughout the inter-war years and its reinvigoration during the 1939–1945 war, particularly in the Japanese prison camps. Taking a more restricted chronological sweep, 1899–1918, Gammage reinforces Robson's analysis of the stereotype of the Australian soldier, particularly the element of rural and so apparently 'natural' soldierly abilities. He also establishes the civilian — and therefore volunteer — nature of the Anzac tradition, tracing these to the Boer War.[9]

This is valuable work, as is Robson's. Yet a close reading of both reveals a fundamental flaw in the analytic concepts used by historians to explain the power of digger and Anzac. Robson is quoted at length for two reasons. The first is that in these sections of his article he very accurately summarises the essence of the digger 'image or stereotype'. The ambivalent deployment of these two terms, here and elsewhere, is the second reason, and indicates the shortcomings of Robson's analytic concepts. The connotation of 'image' is that of something projected from or by the object or subject under consideration. 'Stereotype', by contrast, connotes a point of view brought to an object by its beholder, an external source. Obviously the two concepts are related, but neither the distinction between the terms and their concepts, nor the nature of their relationship, is apparent in Robson's analysis. Further, the very same cultural and historical manifestation that Robson variously calls the 'stereotype' or 'image' (and occasionally the 'tradition') of the Australian soldier or 'digger' is called by Gammage 'the Anzac Tradition'.

The conflation of the self-generated culture of the digger with the invented tradition of Anzac and its unproblematic acceptance by many Australian historians has bedevilled the debate and understanding of this central cultural manifestation ever since Inglis, Serle and others first approached the topic seriously almost forty years ago. The failure — perhaps the disinclination — to distinguish between the unofficial and the official has tended to obscure the differences between the two and, more importantly, the extent and nature of the interactions between them. It is precisely the confusion or conflation of the projected 'digger' and the externally imposed concept of 'Anzac' that is central to the concerns of this book, because it is this conflation that allowed and encouraged the hegemony of 'Anzac'. The culture of the digger must be understood as distinct from, though related to, the elaboration of Anzac. It is not possible to fully comprehend one without the other.

From 1915, the embryonic cultural figure of the digger would be given a most powerful reinforcement at the official level of communication through the published works and influences of C.E.W.Bean. As official correspondent, author of numerous popular works, in his influence on the development of the Australian War Memorial and, ultimately, in his capacity as Official Historian, Bean placed himself amidst the very men and materials he would use to construct his — the Anzac — version of the digger.

The Democracy of Death

Central to the development of the culture of the digger was an extraordinary self-consciousness among the diverse body of volunteer civilian infantry who would become the diggers. From an early stage there was an awareness of distinctiveness, of a difference that was often articulated not only in the soldiers' own song, verse and narrative expressions, but also in more formal mediums, such as the reminiscence. A New Zealander, under the pen name 'Anzac', wrote of his (spurious) experiences in the First AIF in Egypt and at Gallipoli, publishing this work in 1916. The following quotation is perhaps one of the earliest examples of a genre that mindlessly and inaccurately lauds the Australian soldier at the expense of truth, and which is still the mainstay of much popular fiction and 'non-fiction':

> There has been a lot of rot written and said about the lack of discipline in the Australian and New Zealand forces. There was discipline, although not quite the same brand as that of the British army. It is true they didn't cotton on to saluting as an amusement, and you can lay a safe bet they never will. But what of it? Their own officers didn't press the point, knowing the class of men they commanded. At the same time those officers knew that the rough diamonds under their orders would play the game right to the last man; that they would fight like lions in their own devil-may-care, reckless way — and, if need be, die like men, with a careless jest or muttered oath on their lips ...[10]

'Anzac' goes on to describe the absence of cowardice among Australian and New Zealand troops and the heroism of the 3rd Light Horse at 'Quinn's Post' (presumably The Nek):

> They didn't salute much (except when in an unusually good humour — or outside a big drink), even their own officers, but they would follow those officers to certain death — and well the officers knew it. They were just big, hard-living, hard-drinking, over-grown boys: not exactly saints or respectable church-going citizens, I fear. But they were white right through — even if they sometimes did go looking for trouble! And there wasn't anything on the Gallipoli Peninsula could show them the way when it came to scrapping. They were absolutely the grandest fighting men that God ever put breath into! You saw it in the square

set of their jaws and the grim, straight-forward glance of their eyes. But parade ground soldiering wasn't much in their line, nor the cheering crowds either ...[11]

'Anzac' then describes the Gallipoli landing (at which he was clearly not present) where 'those long, lean, brown-faced men with the square jaws and fierce eyes' are said to have routed the Turkish resistance — a remarkable re-writing of the very recent past. The author inserts into this section of his work the following appreciation of the Australian 'character':

> It is difficult to understand the Australian character. He will joke even in the midst of danger, nay, death. He is, as a rule, a 'hard-doer'; and even his best friends must admit that he is often a hard, and fairly original, swearer. Nothing is safe from him when looking for a butt; very little is sacred, I fear, and his humour takes a queer bent sometimes ...[12]

The colonials are described pursuing the Turks up the cliffs of Gallipoli, uttering 'ear-splitting coo-ees, wild bush oaths, and a running fire of blasphemy'. Immediately after these evocations of the distinctive and heroic character of the Australians (and their New Zealand companions), 'Anzac' strikes the usual note of Empire jingoism fashionable at the time.[13]

Although most of the Australian troops no doubt felt this way about their place in the Empire, it became increasingly difficult to reconcile Imperial loyalty with what the Australians very quickly came to see as the manifold failings of the British soldier and particularly of those who commanded him. This contradiction, never resolved, underlies the considerable folklore regarding the British and, of course, the persistent Australian belief that Gallipoli was an inevitable, if glorious failure, due to British military bungling. In the following passage, 'Anzac', unwittingly, articulates the ideology that at once purported to explain the character of the Australian soldier, yet at the same time conflicted with and contradicted the concurrent emergence of a *distinctively* Australian type. The landing, at least in 'Anzac's' version:

> ... was the personification of grandeur: it was the apotheosis of the ludicrous. In a word it was the old reckless, dare-devil spirit of their ancestors — the men who carved out the British Empire — re-born in those virile youths and young men from that bigger and fresher and brighter Britain overseas.[14]

These passages make clear the relationship of the jingoistic nationalism of the moment to the Australian 'type' promoted in so much literature and rural folklore. They also explain the contradictory duality inherent in that image and the persistent problem identified by A.A. Phillips as 'the cultural cringe'. Australians were really swapping one set of contradictions for another. The ideal bushman and his urban progeny, the larrikin, had been an amalgam of both desirable and undesirable elements. Yes, the independence, resource-fulness and toughness were admirable, but there were also the potentially dangerous traits of anti-authoritarianism, alcoholism, crudity and criminality. Now, these worrying traits could be given an ideologically sanctioned role in the figure of the heroic, if rough diamond, soldier. However, there was the problem of Britishness to be faced — literally — far from Australian home ground where the English, Irish, Scots and Welsh could be conveniently and scornfully categorised as 'new chums'. The British, their power, prestige and assumed cultural superiority over the 'colonials' had to be dealt with, at best, on the neutral ground of no-man's land and, at worst, 'at home' in 'Blighty'. The processes evolved by the digger to deal with this were a fundamental, if generally unarticulated, element of digger culture.

Important in the construction of an archetypal Australian wartime character was the stereotyping of 'others', the categorisation of all those groups that were outside the ambit of the Australian soldier. The men of the AIF took up this challenge with alacrity, speedily developing a culture that simultane-ously brought the Australians (and their like) together and distinguished them from others who were not (from 1917) 'digger': but civilians, allies, enemies, the British army, officers and 'Gyppos'.[15] It is too simplistic to see Bean as a kind of one-man conspiracy for constructing an official image for the Australian soldier — others were busy at the same task, if rather less ably. Most importantly, the subjects themselves were deeply involved in the cultural processes that projected the digger onto the national consciousness and the international wartime stage.

As discussed, Robson has outlined the essential characteristics of the digger. To these can be added some refinements. The Australian soldier of the tradition (the inclusive term 'digger' is anachronistic until early 1917) was also brash, cocky, resourceful, innovative, a larrikin, drinker, womaniser, scorn-ful of book-learning, unless it could be shown to have some practical application, and suspicious of 'side' or any kind of pretence or affectation, whether observed in British officers or the diggers' own ranks. Some of these characteristics were recognised by the British. According to an un-identified English girl quoted in the London-produced *Anzac Bulletin*, 'the Englishman's idea of an Australian' was encapsulated in this rhyme, the first part only of which has become traditional in Australia, possibly because the second half is rather too perceptive:

> Australian born, Australian bred;
> Long in the legs and thick in the head;

Terribly funny, awfully rude
Beastly familiar, confoundedly shrewd.[16]

It is difficult to keep the romance and the reality separate, a difficulty that at once accounts for previous analytical problems and indicates the importance of the interaction between fact and fiction. Those aspects that are left out of the common representation of the digger include the fact that diggers were also sentimental: they were poets, artists and parents, they wrote heart-rending letters home and diary entries about their mothers, and were often keen cultural tourists. They were also frightened, cowards, murderers of prisoners, businessmen, con-artists willing to swindle their 'mates' and a host of other less romantic things unsurprising in so large a body of persons as the AIF.

The selection of only certain characteristics, both by diggers themselves and the wider public, to project and identify the typical digger is related to persistent Australian stereotypes about male roles in a new and pioneering society with a heavy economic reliance on primary industry and an apparently contradictory demography of urban concentration. Also involved is the ambivalent position of the colony and, later, Commonwealth federation: the close ties to the 'motherland' through heritage and persistent immigration, imperial economic and political power, and the consequent 'colonial cringe'. These combined to give the emergent nationalism of the diggers an aggressive, even pugnacious edge, especially when exercised against the British, or aspects of 'Britishness' perceived as unattractive by the digger. This aggressiveness may well have been sharpened by the isolation of Australian soldiers from family and friends. A digger was asked in Britain how often he had leave back home in Australia: 'Once every war', came the answer, 'at the end of it'.[17]

The link between the pioneering bushman hero and the digger was recognised and promulgated by contemporaries. Herbert Nicholls, writing in the 1917 *Anzac Memorial* (a substantial commemorative volume produced by the New South Wales Returned Soldiers' Association), celebrated the success of the 'young Australian' being 'worthy of his breed'. 'We used not to feel that we were really any kind of people at all', wrote Nicholls, and went on to describe the larrikin as 'a wee bit of an outlaw', but asserted 'that the larrikin, when disciplined, would make the finest soldier in the world'. Not only was the larrikin the progenitor of the Anzac, so were the children of the pioneers: 'Our Anzacs in Gallipoli and France are worthy sons of the pioneers. Their very don't-care-a-damness is typical of the old Colonial days'.[18] War artist Will Dyson gave this link visual representation in his wash drawing depicting a dead digger on a French battlefield. Dyson titled the work 'The Wild Colonial Boy' and beneath it quoted a famous line from the ballad of 'The Wild Colonial Boy' — 'Sooner than live in slavery/bowed down by iron chains'.[19]

Powerful ideological forces interacted to forge the persona of the digger and all that he stood for and against. In time, this persona would also come to be a central defining image of 'Australian-ness' for the whole country and for subsequent generations. The fact that the persona effectively shut out large and/or important segments of the population, including women, Indigenous Australians and migrants (particularly, though not exclusively, those of non-British backgrounds), as well as those males unwilling or unable to conform to it, was largely unrecognised and generally unlamented until quite recently. The all-pervasiveness, the seeming naturalness and normality of this stereotype has had a significant impact upon the conceptualisation of Australian-ness and national identity, as well as the self-identity of Australian soldiers, for most of the twentieth century. A single word focuses the potency of this cultural complex.

'Digger'

The defining characteristics of the Australian volunteer foot soldier were well established, both within digger culture and within popular mythology, long before the word 'digger' came into general use to describe and define the Australian and New Zealand volunteer infantryman. But it was not until the third year of the four-year conflict that this bundle of elements became solidified and concentrated into one general term. This term, once it had become accepted, was one of extreme potency for its bearers and users, as demonstrated and reinforced by the debate about its origins that was touched off almost as soon as 'digger' became canonised. The already mentioned double need of internal self-identification and external distinctiveness underlay the almost frenzied debate about the origins and ownership of the term 'digger'. Even as the worst battles of the war raged, so Australian and New Zealand troops conducted a war of words within their various publications about the six letters that subsumed all the various elements of the ethos of the civilian volunteer foot (and horse) soldiers from the distant rim of Empire. As a result of this central significance, the arguments over origins and ownership of the term achieved a folkloric status of their own and are valuable sources of insight into the culture and traditions of the digger, not only in World War One but also during the post-war years to 1929, and after.

The term 'digger' first appears in Australian parlance in the late 1840s as a term for an individual gold miner. It was used in America with the same sense, before its transference to the Australian diggings.[20] The term, in this context, is unambiguous, and although this was often given as the source of the wartime use of the word in folk etymologies, it does not appear to have been the origin of the folk descriptor for the volunteer Australian foot soldier. Despite this, it is the connotations of hard work in a rural setting, the struggle for democratic representation as transmitted through the mythology of the Eureka Stockade and the perceived virtues of the pioneering past, that motivate the appeal of 'digger'. The 'diggers' of the gold rush era have a resonance in the development of the wartime digger culture that is directly related to the precedents of that culture in the myths of the bush hero. Nevertheless, the etymology of the wartime use of the term is not directly related to its previous Australian usage.

The earliest reference given for the use of the term digger in its wartime rather than its goldfields sense is in the diary of C.A. Hemsley, August 12, 1916, where an Australian soldier spoke the word in jest to (ironically) an officer addressing a parade.[21] An article in the Bulletin's 'Red Page' of June 8, 1922 claims that: 'there were no Diggers at Gallipoli where we dug most — the word had not come then!'

Examination of the hand-written newspapers produced by Australian and New Zealand troops at Gallipoli and elsewhere, as well as a substantial selection of their letters and diaries, confirms this statement. Soldiers are referred to as 'privates', 'Australians', 'men' or 'troops', sometimes as 'Billjims'. The 1915 issues of the 5th Corps Ammunition Park journal, Honk!, published in France, also do not use the term 'digger'. Indeed, a January, 1917 issue of the continuation of Honk! edited by Bean and called The Rising Sun,[22] carries a reply to a query in the January 1 issue from 'B.P.' asking 'What is an Anzac?' The reply from 'A.E.', apart from indicating the absence of the term 'digger' from the Australian foot soldiers' vocabulary, is also most revealing of attitudes towards the term 'Anzac' which had become glorified by the popular press in Australia and Britain. This elevation of the Gallipoli Anzacs was often resented by the troops who either did not serve at Gallipoli, having been posted to France, or who came after December, 1915. It may also be read as one reason for the development of the term, in order to replace the exclusive 'Anzac' with the inclusive 'digger'.

> An 'Anzac' ... is a resident of England or of a Base Camp. It wears an Australian uniform, but the habitat of the English variety is mostly in London. It invariably insults men on leave from France, by asking to which camp they belong; and feels insulted when the 'bloke' spoken to replies, The Somme. It wears kiwi

leggings, an Officer's tunic, a wounded soldier's face, about 8 gold stripes, and a 'G.S.' [General Stores] wagon load of Ostrich plumes in it's [sic] hat. Also generally wears the battalion colours of some unit which is doing it's [sic] bit, but has long since forgotten that he existed.[23]

In a printed version of a letter dated December 1, 1916, (though not published until c1919), W.F. Adcock has one Australian saying to another: 'Where are we now, Dig?'[24] It is reasonable to assume from this evidence that the term 'digger' (and its contraction) was initially employed as a general mode of address, rather as 'mate' is used in Australian vernacular speech.

'Digger', then, was not a commonly used descriptor of Australian foot soldiers in January 1917. However, in the February 12 issue of *The Rising Sun*, the following typical humorous anecdote appears:

Do the Sappers Wish They Did?

Returning to Camp on Christmas Eve from the trenches, a voice was heard inquiring: 'Hey, Digger, do yer know the duck walks down to the Engineer's Camp?' Came the answer out of the dark, 'Tres bon, tres bon; I'll tell old Tom, our cook, about that'. Result, mystified look on face of inquirer.[25]

Here the term is clearly used in its familiar denotation and appears to fit well with lexicographer Eric Partridge's personal observation that Australians used the term in conversation with each other, to describe others, and that others called Australians 'digger'. However, Partridge implies that the term was not used generically to describe Australian private soldiers.[26] And even in March 1918 it was still possible for an unnamed writer in the London-produced *Anzac Bulletin* to write, belatedly: ' "Digger" has almost entirely supplanted "cobber" among the Australians overseas'.[27]

The centrality of the term in digger culture is emphasised in the *Official History*, where Bean writes:

It was at this stage [June–August, 1917] that Australian soldiers — in particular the infantry — came to be known as 'diggers', together with the New Zealanders, who are said to have inherited it from the gum-diggers in their country. It carried so rich an implication of the Anzac infantryman's own view of his functions and character, that it spread like fire through the AIF, and by the end of the year was the general term of address for Australian and New Zealand soldiers.[28]

Consequently, it seems reasonable to suggest that the term 'digger' came into general use as the preferred description of the Australian soldier and all he stood for, probably a little before Bean's estimate, in early 1917. Bean was certainly unaware of it in November of 1916, when he penned a reasonably extensive discussion of the term 'Anzac' and the importance of what Australian (and New Zealand) soldiers called themselves for the London-produced

Anzac Bulletin of December 6. The term 'digger' does not appear in this discussion, an inconceivable omission if the term had by then achieved its defining symbolic status.[29]

By mid-1918 the word had progressed from its place in the informal oral culture to the masthead of the weekly newspaper *The Digger*, which was 'published with [the] authority' of the Australian Bases in France. This very official organ even included a verse in its September 29, 1918 edition that summed up one central element of digger philosophy and activity:

> THE DIGGERS' TOAST
> The Frenchman likes his sparkling wine,
> The German likes his beer,
> The Tommie likes his half and half
> Because it brings good cheer.
> The Scotsman likes his whisky,
> And Paddy likes his pot,
> But the Digger has no national drink,
> So he drinks the blanky lot.

Here is the characteristic blend of nationalism, distinctiveness and fond self-image that by this time was well established as the stance of the digger. Making a virtue of necessity — having no national drink and being, therefore, at something of a disadvantage in relation to the allies of other nations, the digger solves the problem in accordance with his own imperatives — a kind of neat one-upsmanship that at once recognises and overcomes what is considered as a failing of national character. This economical solution to similar problems is repeated again and again in the folklore and informal culture of the digger.

The extent to which the word became the accepted term for the Australian soldier can be gauged by the folk etymologies that were almost immediately proposed and deposed. The newspaper *Aussie* began at the front in January 1918 and, from its second issue in February, carried impassioned correspondence on the origins and ownership of 'digger'. Claims for a Western Australian origin were put forward; that it originated on the Salient; or that it derived from the necessity of 'digging in'. A poem titled, predictably, 'The Dinkum Oil About "Digger" ' appeared in issue number four, and correspondence wound on through subsequent issues into 1919. The folklore of the term also included its linguistic origins in New Zealand (as Bean and others suggest).[30]

The *Digger* in France also carried extensive correspondence about its namesake, including claims for a New Zealand origin.[31] The issue was frequently addressed in the columns of the post-war *Aussie* and other Australian publications, such as the *Bulletin, Smith's Weekly* ('the Diggers' Bible'), and numerous returned soldiers' newspapers and journals like the *Digger's Gazette* (Official Organ of the RSSILA, SA Branch), and the *Listening Post* in Western Australia. For example, in the 'Digger's Diary' column of the *Western Mail* for January 9, 1930, Longmore put forward a convincing claim for the origin of the term amongst members of the 3rd Division's 11th Brigade as they trained on Salisbury Plain in September and October, 1916.[32]

That debate on the term is still raised from time to time[33] is an indication of its importance in Australian culture.[34] It is the focusing concept, the keyword, for the wartime and post-war culture of the Australian civilian infantryman of no rank or low rank.[35] Encapsulating in its two syllables the total mentality and experience of a substantial segment of the Australian population from 1915 to 1919, it is appropriate to use the word in combination with 'tradition' to denote an interrelated set of values, attitudes and relationships that has persisted through more than one generation.

Oral Culture

The digger tradition is the articulation of the informal, unofficial, private (with the exception of certain public manifestations discussed later) culture of the digger. Much of that culture is, or was, oral in nature.[36] However, the oral aspects of the culture intersected with the written and printed 'media' of the war. Consequently, it is possible to correlate oral materials retrieved years or even generations after the events that gave them birth with the written records of the time. Using this approach provides some glimpses of the digger's World War One culture and, consequently, the formation of the continuing digger tradition. The major components of digger culture were language, song, verse, story, joke and belief, expressed in various narrative forms such as the legend and, especially, the rumour or 'furphy', as documented later.

Digger culture is described as the 'authentic' articulation of the digger for a number of reasons. Firstly, the artistic and expressive forms that voiced and reinforced the culture of the digger were produced at the time and in the place of the events to which they refer. Secondly, they were produced by men who experienced those events. Thirdly, they are not the articulations of individuals but are the anonymous creations and re-creations of the diggers' own culture, and are transmitted either orally or otherwise informally from man to man within the group. They are thus the expressions of communal rather than individual attitudes and points of view. This distinguishes these expressions both from the individually authored items that made up the bulk of *The Anzac Book* and trench journals, and also from the commercial productions of the popular music and literature industries.

The recognition of these distinctions, however, should not lead to the erroneous conclusion that such folk expressions are created and transmitted in a vacuum. There is a close interrelationship between the folkloric, the 'popular' and the individual. Each flows into the other and there are no hard and fast borders or boundaries. Discussion here concentrates upon the folkloric because these songs and verse, along with the language and the yarns of the digger, are the reclaimable 'documents', the sources from which some understanding of the development of digger culture may be gained. Together with what can be found in more or less incidental lodgements in official, semi-official and personal publications and papers, as well as some ephemera, they are the only sources for studying the oral culture of the digger.

A fourth point in support of the characterisation of these materials as 'authentic' is that most of the texts presented here have persisted in memory long after the events that produced them have become footnotes in military histories. Nor have these items stayed only in the memories of the generations who experienced World War One but have, in some cases, been passed on to subsequent generations to do service again in World War Two and in Vietnam, as outlined in chapter nine of this volume. During this process, many of these items kept alive digger culture in the inter-war years, having a central nostalgic function to perform at unit reunions, smoke nights and Anzac Day festivities.

This process, often referred to as 'popular memory', has been traced in Alistair Thomson's *Anzac Memories*.[37] Thomson shows how, through the reminiscences of selected World War One diggers, memory, subsequent experiences and attitudes each shape the other, though it is important to note that Thomson's interviews concentrated mainly on the pre-war, wartime and immediate post-war experiences of those interviewed; that is, mainly until the mid-1930s.[38] Most importantly, Thomson also illuminates the ways in which private memories are composed and recomposed to complement 'the public myths', a process intimately related to personal identity and the individual's need for community affirmation. Thomson's twenty-one diggers, of whom three form the focus of his book, articulated the 'typical' digger persona, expressed in verbal forms that resounded with the tenets of digger culture — 'they recited familiar anecdotes about the egalitarian Anzacs and

AIF'.[39] The common and communal elements of each individual's oral identity were those described here as the 'authentic' digger culture.

Just as the expressions of each individual are a 'composure' (Thomson's useful term) of the public and the private, the communal and the personal, so the construction of digger culture is a melding of the invented and the spontaneous. There is no hard and fast division between invention and spontaneity. Both are present in the processes by which a new social organism, the AIF, developed its own culture. While some facets of this culture were derived from already existing stereotypes of nationality, others arose from the specific and, in many cases, unprecedented experiences of the diggers. Regardless of the origins of digger culture, the fact that it was created and re-created ('composed') by the members of this new social group from their own communal experiences and perceptions, was circulated by them and among them and was preserved by them after the war, justifies the description 'authentic'. Just as Thomson's diggers preserved their sense of self by adjusting their memories of the war with their subsequent experiences of peace, so the group of which they were a part created its sense of self by adjusting the cultural baggage brought with them from civilian life against the experiences of the war. This process emphasised the communal. The process identified by Thomson emphasises the personal. Nevertheless, in all cases there is continual interaction and interchange between the invented and the spontaneous, between the communal and the personal. Few would argue that the perceptions (and their expression) of Thomson's individual diggers were 'unauthentic'. Nor were those of the community to which those men, and tens of thousands more, belonged.

'Diggerese'

The language of the diggers was their means of expressing a sense of coherence and self-identification as members of a social group distinctive from all other groups, particularly other Empire troops and civilians. Long before the term 'digger' became the accepted description of the Australian soldier, he had developed a language, a 'lingo' of his own. This language, part occupational jargon, part in-group argot, was derived from various sources. Some terms and expressions came from the rich vocabulary of nineteenth-century rural occupational speech (for example, 'prad', meaning 'horse'), some were derived from the street-slang of the larrikin pushes (for example, 'stoush', meaning 'fight'), but most were developed from the experiences of the war itself. A number of terms were immediately adapted by the AIF from Arabic, for instance, 'saida' (goodday, goodbye), 'mafeesh' (finished, gone), 'imshi' (go, move), to mention only some. Likewise, some terms were appropriated from the French, such as 'tray bon',[40] 'compree' (understand) and 'mongy' (to eat, to be hungry). Terms were also borrowed from British soldier slang, including 'Blighty' (England, Britain), and 'na(i)poo' (nothing doing, finished).[41]

In order to become a member of the digger group, it was necessary to speak and understand the language. Recruits ('Reo's' or 'reinstoushments') were initiated into the mysteries of 'digger-ese' (or 'Anzacal', as one Gallipoli soldier described the speech on Gallipoli in a letter home) through usage, of course, but also through the venerable folk device of the 'alphabet'.

ANOTHER ALPHABET
(*From the Anzac Book MSS*)
A is for Anzac, removed evermore,
B is for Beachy who busts on the shore.
C is for Colic, which follows directly,
D is the Dose taken paregorectly.
E is for Exercise climbing the hills,
F for Fatigues that come faster than bills.
G is the German who made the Turk fight,
May H____ be his portion or serve him well right.
I is for Indian, excellent fellow,
J is for the jaundice which makes us so yellow.
K is for Kobber, Australian for friend,
L is the Last Post, which comes right at the end.
M is the Mule who's game as a sparrow,
N is the Nuisance with saps much too narrow.
O is the Oaths, some of which are fair snorters.
P is the pain they produce at headquarters.
Q is the Quiver which runs down your back,
When R a big Rooster comes plunk from Chanak.
S is the Soft Jobs you get back at the base,
T is the Turk and a pretty tough case.
V is for Vickers, that man-killing pest.
W's the Whisky we sigh for in vain,
X is for Xcitement, 'The mail's in again'.
Y is for Yes, if we're asked to go home,
Z is for Zero — I'm chilled to the bone.

L.F.S.H. 8th L.H.R.
Anzac, Dec. 1915.[42]

AN ANZAC ALPHABET

By J. W. S. HENDERSON, R.G.A.

A is the Aeroplane buzzing above,
Sending us tokens of friendship and love.

B's Beachy Bill, such a marvel of cunning,
A message from whom sends the best of
us running.

C is the Chilliness felt in the feet
When bullets commence to invade our
retreat.

D is the Dug-out we've spent so much time
at,
Working in hopes of defeating the climate.

E is for Eye-wash, a wonderful lotion,
Employed by the man who is keen on promotion.

F is the Fool who got caught in a trap,
By pulling the tail of a mule in a sap.

Henderson, J.W.S., 'An Anzac Alphabet', *The Anzac Book* [1916], Sun Books, Melbourne, 1975, p. 115.

From time to time the trench papers published lists of digger terms, of greater or lesser extent. The inaugural issue of *Aussie* in January of 1918 provided a glossary of AIF slang, and defined 'digger' as 'a friend, pal, or comrade, synonymous with cobber; a white man who runs straight'.[43]

As well as ensuring communication and confidentiality, such language also allowed the diggers to trumpet their distinctiveness. There is a definite awareness of difference embedded in the vocabulary and the use of this language; a flaunting of linguistic and cultural distinctiveness. Frequently this was allied with a belligerent nationalism, as in this anecdote with its inevitable taking-down of the Englishmen perceived to be 'swanking' by speaking French:

> Two English privates were sitting in an estaminet t'other evening conversing loudly in French. A couple of Australians at an adjoining table decided that they were not going to allow themselves to be out-swanked. So one, who came from NSW, remarked excitedly to his companion:
>
> 'Wagga Wagga walgett, woolloomooloo wee waa wallerawang woolgoolga yarramalong.'
>
> 'Woollongabba,' replied his comrade, who came from Queensland, 'Cunnamulla toowoomba toowong thargomindah indooropilly camooweal goondiwindi.'
>
> 'Bondi coogee maroubra,' said the other, with great determination.
>
> It made the Englishmen slew round and take notice.
>
> 'Excuse me,' said one, 'but what language is that you're speaking?'
>
> 'Oh, that's our Australian language,' he was told. 'We learned English before we came away, but we always prefer to speak our own language among ourselves.'[44]

An essential component of digger speech was swearing. The use of 'bad' language was considered the identifying characteristic of the Australian foot soldier. In volume six of the *Official History*, Bean provides an uncharacteristic (for him) view of the everyday life of the digger. Quoting (apparently) from his notes taken at the time,[45] Bean provides an extended description of an Australian unit out of the line in May 1918, which includes evidence of digger discourse:

> The language in the yard [of the building in which the troops were billeted] is such that you'ld [sic] think there was going to be a knifing every two minutes. 'Ah____ you, you lazy bastard.' 'Go to b_____, to hell wid yer.' 'Would yer, yer bastard!' — and you look out of the window and find that it is all spoken with a grin. The most ferocious oaths are flung between the passing men ...[46]

Furphies

Perhaps one of the earliest digger neologisms was that for a rumour — the 'furphy' (furphie, furfey, furf). The first written record of the term appears to be a mention in Bean's Gallipoli diaries for June 7, 1915.[47] C.F. Laseron in *From Australia to the Dardanelles* uses the word to describe rumours aboard ship during the convoy carrying the First AIF to Egypt in December, 1914.[48] However, although based on his diaries, Laseron's book was published in 1916 and must be treated as a likely use of the term in hindsight.

The word 'furphy' derives from the brand name clearly displayed on water and sanitation carts used by the First AIF, 'J. Furphy and Sons'. These carts were in use in Egypt before the Australians departed for Gallipoli, and the term probably originated there in reference to the fact that the carts (the water rather than the sanitation variety) provided a meeting point where men swapped 'information' in the form of gossip and rumour. Another possible reason is that the drivers of these carts had access to the world outside Mena and other camps, so brought back 'news' believed by the troops to be more reliable than that available to them through official channels. Either or, more likely, both of these explanations may lie behind the genesis of the term.

What both these explanations indicate is the central importance of informal communication to the diggers (and, as we shall see, to those who commanded them). Rumours or furphies were often *the* topic of conversation within the oral culture of the digger, of his prose, of his trench newspapers and even of his versifying. 'The Furphyite' appeared in the third number of *First Aid Post*, August 11, 1915, a 2nd Field Ambulance journal printed on Gallipoli:

> Who gives us all a sleepless night
> With his blooming infernal skite,
> Brings us joy which turns to fright?
> Why, don't you know — 'The Furphyite'.
> If we could catch the Furphyite,
> The mob would end his silly skite;
> His death would be so expedite
> That peace would reign and all be quiet.[49]

Furphies abounded in great variety, each being rapidly superseded. There were rumours about the end of the war, about going home, about not going home, about victories, defeats, the coming 'big push', and about enemy spies within the Australian ranks. 'Anzac', in his *On the Anzac Trail*, provides a characteristic description of rumour-mongering in Egypt:

> ... rumours were in the air; true, these 'wireless messages', it was proved, almost all emanated from a rather unsavoury source (the Anzacs will recognise the

locality), [a reference to the belief that furphies derived from Egyptian brothels. G.S.] but they travelled round the whole camp with most disconcerting frequency until one never knew what to believe and what not.[50]

Alexander Vennard (under the name 'Frank Reid') edited *The Kia Ora Coo-ee* soldier's newspaper in Egypt in 1918. In the September edition (under his other pen name, 'Bill Bowyang') he published an article titled 'Furphies'. He points out that rumours are manufactured and initially transmitted by individuals with a particular ability for such concoctions. Vennard admits to having sent a few furphies of his own devising on their way in Egypt towards the end of 1915. One of these was that his Division was about to leave for France. The 'rumour' was told to one group in the morning and was repeated to him as fact by an Egyptian tour guide at the Pyramids the evening of the same day.[51]

The role and importance of rumour and belief in wartime has been the subject of considerable research and theorisation by social scientists. Psychologists, social psychologists, sociologists and folklorists have generated an extensive literature on this subject, involving numerous wartime situations, both small- and large-scale. In addition, a number of studies have been made of the origins, transmission and effects of rumour in peacetime.

The most influential social psychological study of rumour is that conducted by Allport and Postman for the American government during World War Two.[52] They produced a formula for better understanding the origins and spread of rumours and their intensity that highlights the environing conditions in which rumours originate and are diffused. Allport and Postman suggest that the degree of importance of the subject matter to the hearers is one of the main reasons for rumour-mongering. The second main requirement is the degree of ambiguity (or absence of 'hard' information) available to the group. These essentials have been generally confirmed by subsequent researchers, all of whom agree that situations where crisis, conflict, confusion and catastrophe are present are the classic circumstances for rumour-generation. Clearly, wars are just such circumstances,[53] though when uncertainty was largely removed, as was the case in Egypt by late 1918, rumours decreased. 'Bill Bowyang' supports this correlation between rumour and lack of 'hard' information:

> Just at present there is a scarcity of good solid 'furphies', but wait until Peace comes and we are waiting to return home. That boat which is going to convey us to Australia will arrive at Port Said about fourteen times a week. It is then the 'furphy' manufacturer will come into his own. He will issue 'special editions' daily, each one contradicting the 'dinkum oil' contained in its predecessor.[54]

As well as the circumstances in which furphies were generated, also important was the means by which furphies were transmitted. Researchers have identified 'rumour chains'[55] in which individuals with a common interest or concern hear and, subsequently, pass on to other like-minded individuals messages that contain information relevant to their needs or desires. The closed group of an army in combat in a foreign land is obviously quite close to the theoretical ideal. When the other elements that rumour analysts have identified as significant are examined,[56] it can be seen that the AIF, in common with other armies, would be a fertile ground for rumour-mongering. Casualty figures for the AIF indicate that sixty-five per cent of its members were killed or wounded.[57] These retrospective figures confirm the folk perception of the time that being in the AIF was an extremely high-risk circumstance. The threat of death or maiming was therefore a very real one and this further contributed to an atmosphere appropriate to the genesis and transmission of rumours.

The desire for 'news' or hard information is a primary characteristic of situations that foster rumours. The AIF, particularly in Egypt and at Gallipoli, was continually starved of information, both news from home in the form of letters and papers, and news from those parts of the European world outside the various theatres of war. This was exacerbated by a lack of official information about upcoming orders or military moves, the knowledge that military censorship would be applied to any news, and a folk suspicion that the generals and politicians did not know their true situation either. The resulting information vacuum was filled with incessant furphies about enemy spies, going home, being sent elsewhere, fierce battles, decisive victories and equally devastating defeats. Many of the early trench papers, such as the *Dinkum Oil*, were basically rumour-sheets spiced with a few crude cartoons and jokes. The *Dinkum Oil* eschewed verse in favour of a 'Serial Story' and satirical parodies of advertisements ('To Let — Nice dugout on the skyline. Owner leaving for field hospital'), though also included sections called 'War News' and 'The Reason Why', which mongered furphies and provided humorous parodies of war news.

The concentration of *The Dinkum Oil* and other trench newspapers on rumour and humour indicates their close relation to the oral communication of the diggers on Gallipoli. This informal communication network revolved around furphies. Furphies regarding Turkish or German spies and infiltrators; good or bad news of the war on other fronts; the sinking of ships, either allied or enemy; impending evacuation or advance, and so on, were a continuing preoccupation, even an obsession, in most of the trench papers, regardless of the paper's level of crudeness or refinement. Under the headline:

WAR NEWS
NATIONAL CRISIS
Lord Kitchener's Desertion
(cable from Kerguelen Island)

The Dinkum Oil of June 11, 1915, printed a handwritten item:

The recent activity of the destroyers is now explained. They say that, on account of the failure of the allies to advance, Lord Kitchener has deserted and is coming to assist the Turks in an Austrian submarine. He has the plans of Buckingham Palace with him.[58]

Further down the page:

A major's batman states that the second brigade is leaving by the *Mauretania* on Sunday night at 7.20 to garrison the captured German seaport of Tsing Tau in China.[59]

The trench papers can be seen as attempts to crystallise these aspects of talk and belief (or disbelief) into a slightly more formal mode designed to provide light relief and, consequently, some release from the desperate circumstances in which the diggers found themselves. They also provided a means of mildly criticising and condemning the attitudes and actions of certain officers in an approved forum very much like that of the oral communication network. Under headings such as 'Things People Are Talking About' could be printed items of all kinds:

The dinner given by the 29th Bty Officers to the 107th Officers.

★ ★ ★

At this the 'Baptism' of Lieut. Venn-Brown made quite a splash.[60]

The advantage of the published version, of course, was that those expressions of discontent that could be communicated between equals but not to officers could be included in the printed form with some degree of safety, avoiding charges of insubordination. Even if the supervising officer/censor who generally oversaw these publications would not allow a particular item to be published, he was nevertheless informed of dissatisfaction or criticism from below. As well as mongering furphies and, as the publications were appropriated by officialdom, of controlling them, trench publications monitored morale from the perspective of the officers and provided a safety-valve for gripes and whinges from the lower ranks.

An important facet of furphies was their diversionary value. While active duty is a highly stressful situation in which death or serious injury may occur imminently, it is also an experience that includes lengthy periods of

BEACH THEATRE

of Varieties, Anzac.

TO-DAY!!   TO-DAY!!

Celebrated Pair of High Kickers and Whistling Wonders

Miss ANNA FARTA
(Soprano)

AND

Miss OLIVE GROVE
(Contralto)

Also FIRST APPEARANCE AT ANZAC of the
world-renowned

JACK JOHNSON

For One Night Only

TIRED TIM, the Juvenile Acrobat,

AND

KABA TEPE, the Turkish Juggler,

will combine in their

ASTONISHING DISAPPEARING TRICK

 N.B.—The Anzac Artillery guarantees that this is positively the last appearance of the above artists.

Advertisement, 'Beach Theatre of Varieties, Anzac', *The Anzac Book* [1916], Sun Books, Melbourne, 1975, p. 166.

boredom. Repetitious, basic tasks involving survival, the maintenance of equipment and other aspects of day-to-day routine were likely to be punctured by moments of extreme danger. Diaries and other accounts of Australian soldiers frequently paint a picture of deadly monotony rather than deadly combat. Gunner Stoppard wrote of his Egyptian experience in January, 1915:

6th Gun drill again.

7th. Camp life, nothing but sand and niggers.

8th. Battery for duty, more work as [?] Canteen Orderly. Very easy work, did nothing but write letters,

9th. Church Parade, review and Communion. Came back and put under open arrest for speaking to an officer without being paraded by a sergeant (result tomorrow),

10th case dismissed, all a farce.[61]

Both as a reaction to the dreariness of routine such as that described by Stoppard, and as a relief from the danger or apprehension of combat, the furphy was a useful means of taking one's mind off the monotony of everyday army life. 'Bill Bowyang' in his *Kia Ora Coo-ee* article on the furphy writes of Padre Murphy cheering up the often despondent men in the trenches at Gallipoli by spreading rumours, such as 'Achi baba's going to fall this week and our ships will then dash through the narrows. It's all fixed up, and we'll be in Constantinople sometime next week'. Bowyang points out that such 'dinkum news' brightened a life that 'was just a drab existence of "bully", biscuits and "stand-to". Bowyang also gives evidence of the speed with which such rumours travelled by word-of-mouth — 'The Padre would have scarcely left the trench before the "furphy" would be flying along it at express speed'.[62]

Psychologists have demonstrated that individuals and groups subjected to the apparently unexplainable will seek some form of causation, some sort of explanation — no matter how implausible — to make sense of their circumstances. A structure of meaning must be imposed, a reason or reasons must be found for the unreasonable. In the palpable unreasonableness of Gallipoli and the Western Front, it is not surprising that almost any piece of 'information' would be given credence and perpetuated.

Belief

Closely related to 'rumour' are 'legends'. Sometimes described as 'solidified rumour', these are apparently true stories, though usually about improbable or supernatural events. A classic wartime example is the 'Angels of Mons' incident where thousands of retreating British troops claimed to have seen one or more 'angels', cavalry, bowmen or other figures in the sky above the battlefield in August of 1914. This case has been extremely well documented and discussed,[63] but represents only one particularly spectacular manifestation of a phenomenon of oral culture. A less dramatic Australian micro-example of the same process is the persistent story that an unknown Queenslander was the first man ashore at Gallipoli. He hit the beach and disappeared into the dark inferno of Turkish fire, never to be seen again.[64]

Into the same category can be placed the deeds attributed to heroes such as Simpson and his donkey, around whom a complex and contradictory legend has developed. As well must be mentioned the attributed humorous sayings and doings of lesser lights, known mainly to members of their immediate units by a variety of nick-names. Typically such legends involved attempts to fake illness or injury in order to escape unpleasant tasks or to be shipped home. Usually they end in the failure of the ploy, with the hapless one returned to his proper place and the structure and function of authority intact, as in this example, titled 'Coming a Proverbial':

> 'What's the matter with you, my man?' said the MO, at the Medical Board. 'Oh, bad sight, is it? Well, what's this?' (holding up a two-franc piece).
> 'Please, sir, I can't see it.'
> 'Can't see it, eh? That's bad, very bad. Can you see this?' (holding up a tin plate).
> 'Yes, sir, I can see that; it's 'alf a franc.'
> 'You'll do,' smiled the MO. 'If you take that for half a franc you'll take the Prussian Guards for bantams.'[65]

In the circumstances of active duty, belief in all manner of likely and unlikely eventualities was not only possible, but magnified. Superstitions were rife on the battlefield, including the widespread fear of the number thirteen; the taboo upon lighting three cigarettes from the same match[66] and the touching of various objects — including rusty pistols and the hand of a corpse protruding from the side of a trench — for luck. No matter how uncomfortable the sleeping arrangements, Australian soldiers would rarely make their beds on a medical stretcher, fearing they would come to occupy such a stretcher, thereby manifesting a belief in 'sympathetic magic'.[67] Mascots and totems of various kinds were also widespread as bringers of luck or, at least, the avoidance of 'bad' luck.[68] Beliefs in omens, charms and other symbols, objects or acts of 'luck' were extremely prevalent during the war, imparting a sense of personal control over one's fate. As Eric Leed points out in his study of individual identity in World War One, 'Men became superstitious in war. Their use of magic, ritual, spell, and omen seemed to be an unavoidable response to the total loss of individual control over the conditions of life and death'.[69] Animal mascots were also frequently invested with miraculous powers for avoiding death or injury, as was the case with Simpson's donkey and numerous other animals on Gallipoli.[70]

One widespread aspect of folk belief or superstition was the fatalistic certainty that one would not die until one's number was up, or the bullet with one's name on it arrived. George Cuttriss, writing of his experiences in France with the 3rd Division, retails the story of a soldier he allegedly spoke to about the dangers of trench warfare: the soldier replied that he would be all right unless the shell with his number on it arrived. A few days later, the soldier was lucky to escape extinction as a 'dud' dropped near him. Upon examining the base of the defective shell, the soldier discovered that it bore his regimental number.[71] True or otherwise, such incidents were integral to the culture of the digger, endlessly recycled through the informal channels of belief, furphy and anecdote.

CHAPTER THREE

The Anecdotal Republic

The anecdote belongs to that facet of the diggers' oral culture that can best be described as the 'yarn', the apocryphal, humorous, moralistic and even cautionary narrative. Such stories were told to teach a 'truth' and so bolster individual and group morale. They were also told to reflect and so reinforce the assumptions and attitudes to life and death that underpinned the culture of the digger. Frequently such anecdotes were humorous, having the additional value of raising a laugh in decidedly humourless situations. Yarns were — and are — almost infinite in variety, variation and intent. They are also, by their nature, very difficult to excavate from a bygone oral existence. However, persistent examination of written and printed sources, correlated with versions retrieved from oral tradition, does allow some reasonably confident categorisation and analysis of the diggers' yarns.

Study of the provenance of digger yarns, and of their persistent themes and concerns, also provides insight into the self-image of the digger, during and after the war. While most of the yarns included have been sourced to World War One or earlier, their provenance frequently exceeds the period of the war. The typical modes of transmission of this material include privately circulated typescripts and manuscripts, limited-circulation publications and periodicals of various kinds, as well as oral transmission. In order to show this continuation it has been necessary to survey such sources over a broad chronological sweep.

Spinning the Yarns

One important aspect of this type of research lies in defining the genre of the yarn. There is no agreed definition of this diffuse form of folk narrative and the very term itself is open to a wide variety of linguistic usages. One may 'have a yarn', meaning to have an informal conversation on almost any topic with one or more other persons. One may 'spin a yarn', a usage which often implies a level of falsehood or at least exaggeration in the content of the 'yarn'. Or one can tell, say, a 'bush' or other sub-genre of the yarn. Contrary to the previous two usages of the term 'yarn', this usage implies firstly that there is a level of narrative structure in the 'story' and that there is also a degree of 'truth' or at least verisimilitude in the story, even if this 'truth' is often seen to be more metaphorical than literal. The term 'yarn' is therefore frequently used with considerable imprecision and, as suggested, even contradiction. Attempts, mainly by Ron Edwards,[1] to define and describe the yarn, have been less than successful. One particular problem with Edwards's argument is that he wishes to see the yarn as a typically, even uniquely 'Australian' mode of folk articulation. As the term 'yarn' is also used in similar ways in other Anglophone cultures, such nationalistic interpretations are of limited value in defining the yarn. They are, however, most revealing of the continuation of the same attitudes that underlay the digger's relish for this particular form of expression. Taking their cue from the earlier nationalistic literary popularisation of the yarn in the 1890s and after, the diggers themselves perceived the yarn as an authentically Australian mode of expression and used it in exactly that way, a point reinforced by the often aggressive nationalism that bares its teeth in digger yarns.

The term 'yarn' is used here to describe the usually humorous, often (though not necessarily) apocryphal anecdotes that show the digger in accordance with his own self-image. These frequently make an implicit or explicit moral point about that image and its culture. Major themes of digger yarns are digger nonchalance under fire, General William Birdwood, anti-authoritarianism, contempt for Tommies, attitudes towards British officers, Australianism, self-deprecation, and emblematic, colourful Australian speech. As with other areas of digger expression, such as verse and song, there are some significant absences from the themes of digger yarns. Generally the favourite yarns are silent on the topic of mateship, sacrifice, duty, loyalty (unless satirised) and tales about Simpson and his donkey. These absences are discussed elsewhere, but it is worth noting at this point the significant fact that they often relate more strongly to the Anzac tradition than they do to other aspects of digger folklore.

Yarns also frequently deal with situations and personalities that in some way mediate between antagonistic or otherwise contrasting points of view or attitudes. Problem areas such as the imposition of authority within the AIF are dealt with in a number of yarns, but nowhere more strongly than in those revolving around the figure of General William Birdwood. His apparent ability to relate to the everyday lives and problems of his troops is, in the yarns concerning him, embellished to present him as a mediator between the demotic, egalitarian impulses of the diggers and the official necessity for authority and discipline within a large body of soldiery. The sometimes naive, sometimes knowing failure of the common foot soldier to acknowledge the rank of Birdwood simultaneously allows both the recognition of authority and its containment into those arenas approved by the worldview of the digger: official authority is permissible in military strategy and official observance, but <u>not</u> on the battlefield or other sites of digger ascendancy like the camp, the track to the lines, or during leisure time.

Similar observations apply to the numerous yarns concerning British officers and their relationship with the British equivalent of the digger, the Tommy. In these yarns, British officers are portrayed as blustering nincompoops and incompetents with an obsession for the observance of military decorum. Again, the problem of authority and control is implicated here, as is the nationalistic impulse of differentiating the Australian from the British.

The peculiarly male problem of conducting oneself under fire in such a way as to avoid dishonour or, even worse, the disapprobation of comrades, is treated in yarns dealing with the supposed coolness and nonchalance of the digger in battle. It is not simply a matter of bravery — all soldiers are expected to be brave — but it is a matter of ignoring the imminent possibility of injury or death. This accords well with existing notions of resolute calmness in the face of adversity that were already well entrenched in Australian society through the myths of the pioneer and the bushman.

The very pressing problem of defining Australians as members of a new and distinct nation within the Empire is dealt with in a number of yarn genres, including those related to Australian-ness, colourful language and self-deprecating humour. Perceived or desired differences of attitude and action are privileged in these yarns. The frequently criticised Australian 'colonial' fondness for what (the diggers believed) the British middle classes considered to be reprehensible language is the pivotal difference in a number of yarns, where swearing identifies the speaker(s) as 'Australian'. The same need to project a distinctive national image in order to contrast oneself to 'others' (mostly the British; less frequently the French and Americans) is clearly satisfied in a number of yarns.

Unravelling the Yarns

An important group of yarns are those involving British officers. These typically revolve around the refusal of Australians to recognise the officers and their rank through the traditional and, as far as the professional officer corps were concerned, mandatory salute. Such yarns were, and are, legion, the following being representative of the genre: Two diggers on leave in London fail to salute a passing British officer. The outraged officer demands of the diggers: 'Do you know who I am?' One digger turns to the other

'Sub: — "Don't you know what to do when you pass an officer? — You're a soldier, are you not?" Private Anzac: — "No — I'm a farmer!" ', Cecil L. Hartt, *Humorosities* [1917] Australian War Memorial, Canberra, 1985, np.

and says, casually: 'Did you hear that, Dig? He doesn't even know who he is'.[2]

Another yarn on the same theme involves a digger travelling on a train with two English officers. The officers are discussing their family backgrounds, relationships and pedigrees. After listening to this conversation for a while, the digger introduces himself to the officers as 'Bluey Johnson — not married, two sons — both Majors in the British army'.[3]

An old favourite is also retold by Albert Facey in his *A Fortunate Life*, and involves a high-ranking British officer who visits the trenches at Gallipoli and is offended by stench of the dead. Asking why they can't be buried, he is told by the Australian commanding officer that it is too dangerous to send men out to get bodies. 'What is a few men', is his reply. Facey says that the Australians referred to the officer as 'Lord Kitchener' from then on.[4] The obverse of this story is well known to military historians as the 'Kiggell anecdote': on being shown the Ypres (or other) battlefield, a high-ranking, usually British, officer says: 'My God, did we really send men to fight in that', or similar. The officer has been identified as Major General Sir Lancelot Kiggell, Chief of Haig's General Staff, hence the use of this generic title by historians.[5]

An especially popular yarn type was the story that revelled in various distinctively Australian traits, usually played off against the Tommy rather than his officers. The earlier anecdote quoted in the previous chapter involving the diggers speaking 'Australian' is one example of this type of yarn.[6] Anecdotes emphasising aspects of 'Australian-ness' were quite common, not only in the aggressively anti-British modes categorised elsewhere here, but also in the less tribal forms instanced below. Such yarns involved characters like the pre-World War One 'roo shooter who refused to snipe men. The hard-bitten Sergeant then says he'll ask Fritz to hop for him.[7] Another yarn concerns the digger who appears on parade poorly shaved and is reprimanded. He responds by explaining that his rough shave is due to having to use an army razor because he lost his penknife.[8] One well-known yarn, usually called 'The scrap of paper', tells the story of a digger who, through a variety of clever ruses, convinces the MO (Medical Officer) that he is mentally disturbed and receives his discharge certificate.[9] Some other examples of this type of yarn are more detailed and portray a direct confrontation between Australians and other nationalities. In many of these, the Australian outwits the American in the telling of a tall tale, a genre of folk anecdote still popular in Australia.[10]

One particularly popular type of the yarn genre were stories dealing with the real or apocryphal activities of General William Birdwood, commanding officer on Gallipoli and known fondly to diggers as 'Birdie'. Birdwood yarns typically deal with three facets of the digger's self-image: refusal to be impressed by rank, quick-witted humour, and deflating the pomposity of the British, as the following example illustrates:

> He [Birdwood] was nearing a dangerous gap in a sap on Gallipoli when the sentry called out: 'Duck, Birdie; you'd better — — well duck!' 'What did you do?' asked the outraged generals to whom Birdwood told the story. 'Do? Why, I — — well ducked!'[11]

In other versions of this yarn, the outraged officers are specified as being British.

While this group of stories revolves around a person rather than a theme, as with the other categories here, the Birdwood yarns form a coherent cycle of anecdotes in themselves. Most of these yarns present Birdwood as a 'digger with stripes', a leader who recognises and accepts those qualities of his soldiers that the men themselves value highly. Birdwood's acknowledgment of and acquiescence in the values of the digger are held up for admiration in these narratives. The themes of a number of these yarns could, of course, place them appropriately under the other categories identified here, as in this example which neatly combines the cherished Australian anti-authoritarianism with the equally cherished anti-Englishness:

> Whilst General Birdwood was chatting in the Strand (London) with two or three Tommy officers, an Aussie strolled by, characteristically omitting the salute.
> 'Notice that Digger go by, Birdwood?' asked a Tommy officer.
> 'Yes, why?'
> 'Well, he didn't salute. Why didn't you pull him up for it?'
> 'Look here', said Birdie, 'if you want to be told off in the Strand, I don't.'[12]

A number of the Birdwood yarns play upon the General's ordinariness and ability to be 'the common man'. This is managed through the device of a digger failing to recognise Birdwood as a high-ranking officer, being non-plussed when he discovers his mistake and Birdwood being jovially accepting of the mistake. One such involves General Birdwood shaking hands with the naive sentry who fails to recognise him and challenges his identity.[13] Another makes much of Birdwood's reluctance on Gallipoli to wear his badges of rank. He speaks to a digger who doesn't realise who he is:

> 'Do you know who I am?' asks the surprised Birdwood.
> 'No', says digger, 'who are you?'
> 'I'm General Birdwood'.
> 'Struth', says digger, springing to attention; 'why don't you wear your feathers the same as any other bird would?'[14]

Further, there is the story of the Gallipoli reinforcement who mistakes the General for a cook, again because he is not wearing his badges of rank,[15] and the digger who, upon being told the identity of Birdwood by other officers, invites him to 'ave a cup o' tea, Mr Birdwood'.[16]

Some Birdwood narratives involve diggers recognising Birdwood, yet responding to him as they would to an equal in rank. For example, on Gallipoli General Birdwood sees an Anzac pushing a wheelbarrow, an unusual sight at that time and place. 'Did you make it yourself?' queried the General. 'No Mr Birdwood, I bloody-well didn't', panted the exhausted digger, 'but I'd like to find the bastard who did!'[17] Another example is located on the Western Front. General Birdwood goes for an early morning run and invites a stray digger to join him. 'Come on, let's go for a run'. 'Too right', replies digger, and off they go. After a while, the panting digger draws level with Birdwood. 'Hey, where's that bloody rum you promised me?'[18] Other such yarns include:

'Having a good bath?' Birdwood asks Anzac digger trying to wash in a cigarette-tin half-full of water.

'Yes', says digger, 'but I could do much better if I was a blinking canary'.[19]

Birdwood's supposed ability and willingness to act like the men he commanded is highlighted in this yarn:

A digger was lying in camp dead broke, so irreverently decided to write to God for a tenner. He addressed the letter 'per General Birdwood, Headquarters'. When the General got it, he was much amused. He took it into the officers' mess, and all the officers entered into the humour of the joke. The General said: 'We will collect amongst us and raise the tenner for this fellow', but all he could raise was seven pounds; so he sent it to the Digger. Next day the receipt came to hand as follows:-

'Dear God, — Thanks for sending me the tenner; but the next lot you send don't send it through Headquarters, as Birdie and his mob pinched three quid of it'.[20]

Other significant groups of digger yarning involve the toughness and nonchalance of the digger under fire, as in this example:

Four Aussies had settled down to a game of cards in a quiet corner of the trenches. Suddenly a great commotion was heard and one of the players jumped up to the look-out step.

'Hi, you fellows!' he shouted. 'A whole enemy division coming over!'

Another Aussie got up with a bored look on his face.

'All right,' he said. 'You get on with the game. I'm dummy this hand; I'll go.'[21]

A similar story is told of the diggers who are so little worried by enemy fire that they play two-up by the light of the barrage-flares.[22] Related to this yarn are those that have Australian troops playing two-up during enemy attack so fervently and oblivious to the danger that they are mistaken for believers at prayer.[23] Other examples include the one about the diggers shooting and bombing an enemy position from whence no resistance comes, only to discover another digger inside nonchalantly cooking a meal and wondering what all the noise is about,[24] the VC-winning digger who cannot understand what all the fuss is about and says 'you'd have thought I'd won a medal in the Olympic Games',[25] and one titled 'The Price of Glory':

> A wounded soldier was being carried across No Man's land on the back of a perspiring comrade. Rifle and machine gun fire was heavy.
>
> 'Ere', suddenly exclaimed the wounded soldier, 'what about turning round and walking backwards for a spell. You're getting the VC, but I'm getting all the blinkin' bullets'.[26]

A migratory legend told in many cultures, when rendered in Australian versions, emphasises the nonchalance of those involved in the face of bizarrely bad conditions. The story goes that a unit is walking across a duckboard somewhere in France, when a slouch hat is sighted sitting in the mud. On examination they discover that there is a digger underneath the hat, buried in the mud. When the digger is asked how deep the mud is, he replies that he is actually sitting on a horse.[27] The digger's casual iconoclasm also features in some yarns, such as one where a digger is taken by a local (usually an Arab) guide to see the sacred flame (usually of Bethlehem) that has burned for two thousand years. Digger looks at it for a moment and blows out the flame, saying that it's about time someone put it out.[28]

Another group of yarns provides an indication of the linkage between digger culture and the bush tradition of manual labour, masculinity, toughness and its sardonic humour. The figure of the bush cook was, and is, a staple of Australian (and other) rural traditions. The cook was generally referred to as the 'babbler', a contraction of the rhyming slang term 'babbling brook', and as such, features in a number of digger yarns. Probably the best known of these yarns is 'Who called the cook a bastard?' This yarn is known in numerous variants, though the following is the most usually encountered:

> I came out of my dugout one morning attracted by a terrible outburst of Aussie slanguage in the trench. The company dag was standing in about three feet of mud, holding his mess tin in front of him and gazing contemptuously at a piece of badly cooked bacon, while he made a few heated remarks concerning one known as Bolo, the babbling brook. He concluded an earnest and powerful

address thus:

'An' if the _____ that cooked this bacon ever gets hung for bein' a cook, the poor_____ will be innocent'.[29]

Bean provides an insight into the dual role of the cook in digger culture. This individual was both a provider of sustenance and the (mostly) willing butt of humour within the military group with which he was affiliated, bearing the 'oaths and good-natured sarcasm' of those who had no option but to consume his offerings with equanimity and humorous forbearance.[30]

Closely connected to such yarns are those that emphasise the marker of crudity in Australian vernacular speech. The so-called vulgarity of everyday Australian discourse had frequently been commented upon — usually unfavourably — by visitors from Britain in the nineteenth and early twentieth centuries. This topic became a popular theme of digger yarns, allowing the simultaneous articulation of a unique, therefore authentic, Australian vernacular, as well as a tilt at perceived British pretensions. Neither the observers who rated Australian vernacular as worse than that of their own working classes, nor the Australians who considered their vernacular to be unique, were correct. Nonetheless, such beliefs impelled many yarns on this theme:

> An officer, inspecting first line of resistance: 'What soldiers are in this trench, my man?'
> 'First Sussex Regiment, sir.'
> After going along a little further, he questions again: 'What soldiers are in this trench, my man?'
> 'What the _____ has it got to do with you?'
> 'Oh, this is the Australian trench,' the officer said, quite surprised.[31]

This theme persists in many other yarns:

> Sentry: 'Halt! Who goes there?'
> Answer: 'Ceylon Planters [sic] Rifle Club'.
> Sentry: 'Pass, friend'.
> A little later — 'Halt, who goes there?'
> Answer: 'Auckland Mounted Rifles'.
> Sentry: 'Pass, friend'.
> As the next person arrives — 'Halt, Who goes there?'
> Answer: 'What the __ has that got to do with you?'
> Sentry: 'Pass, Australian'.[32]

In another group of yarns the British equivalent of the digger, the Tommy, is portrayed as an object of amusement or contempt. One example of this category, in which Australians confound Tommies by speaking in 'Australian' has already been quoted. Another, in which a digger drinks water despite being told by a Tommy of a dead dog in the waterhole,[33] is meant to show the contemptuous defiance of the digger for the namby–pamby concerns of the British soldier.

Related to this form of expressing superiority are those yarns that are, ostensibly, self-deprecating. These stories present Australians in less-than-favourable circumstances, yet generally manage to be sardonically self-congratulatory, despite their manifest content. One of these anecdotes involves the bullets that are heard twice by the diggers — once as they advance and a second time as they are overtaken in retreat.[34] The previously mentioned digger who blows out the flame that has burned at Bethlehem is another example of this type, as is the cook who is so greasy that a five-nine shell glances off him.[35] The best known of all such yarns is that usually titled 'The World's Greatest Whinger' or 'How Would I Be?' While it is said to derive from a Boer War original[36] and to have been widely told during World War One, the only recoverable versions of this yarn date from World War Two.[37] Too long to quote here (an indication of a considerable period of literary polishing), the yarn shows how the prodigious complaining of the digger continues into heaven, where he complains about the noise of the angels playing their harps, among other irritations. The point, and presumably the long and broad appeal of this anecdote, is to show that absolutely nothing, whether it be the military, the enemy shelling or even the domain of God, will alter the character of this particular digger nor, by implication, that of any other digger.

The 'defiant whinger' is a close cousin to the diggers who feature in yarns celebrating the fabled anti-authoritarianism of the digger. These range from the simply cheeky, as is the case with the digger who translates a Brigadier's 'de-lay' into the French for 'milk',[38] to the insubordination of the sentry who swears at a major and threatens to give him 'a bit of a __ present!'[39] Other stories on this theme include the captain who cannot give the correct password to a sentry — the ensuing dialogue elicits the hoarse cry from a nearby tent: 'Don't stand there argufying all night, Dig, shoot the blighter';[40] the General, naked after swimming, who goes along with an officious lower ranker's assumption that he is of lower rank than himself;[41] and the scruffily uniformed bush digger who enthusiastically shakes the Colonel inspecting the parade by hand, mistaking him for an old shearing mate.[42] Another well-known example involves Lord Kitchener at Anzac[43] telling the diggers how proud they should be of their accomplishment, only to have a digger call out 'My oath we are, Steve'.[44]

These apparently banal and trivial narratives figured prominently in digger interaction and publications. They were integral aspects of all things digger, lovingly remembered and retold at every opportunity, during and after the war. Yarns also formed a staple of all kinds of post-war digger ephemera, such as reunion souvenir programs and the large but under-researched publishing industry specialising in cheap anthologies of verse, song, anecdote and cartoon. These narratives encapsulate fundamental aspects of the digger self-perception and functioned to continually reinforce that perception through mutually complementary oral and print transmission.

Disrespect for British officers, the bellicose trumpeting of Australian distinctiveness and its associated inference of superiority over the Tommy, and the daring and nonchalance of the digger were all part of the digger persona. The digger's need to balance his decidedly negative view of the British soldier and his officers was satisfied in the Birdwood cycle, where an extremely high-ranking Australian officer is shown to be a 'soldier's soldier', a digger with braid. Linked with this, of course, is the essential imputation of egalitarianism, the democratic impulse fondly believed, then and since, to be the unique attribute of Australian society, and hence of its projection: the young, male, tough, casual, democratic AIF.

There were many other yarns in circulation, especially those relating to 'characters' in particular units. While these are obviously of interest, they do not relate to the broader themes discussed here.[45] Those themes provide an insight into the values, the prejudices and the ideals of digger oral culture. The telling and retelling of these yarns, their printing and reprinting, provides evidence of the significance of these narratives for those who told them, heard them and read them.

As well as 'diggerese', a self-defining belief-system, furphies and yarns, the diggers also created their own song and verse expressions. These originally circulated within their oral culture, and have been retrieved by folklorists in later years and, in some cases, have been passed on to subsequent generations of diggers. The attitudes and values that these expressions articulate were a highly valued facet of the digger tradition.

CHAPTER FOUR

The Singing Soldiers

The men of the First AIF created and re-created a body of songs unique to that particular group — ditties, marching songs, squibs and parodies of popular songs. These expressions were an important dimension of the digger wartime culture and became one of the main vehicles by which the values and attitudes of the diggers were transmitted into the post-war period. Embedded in the texts and melodies of authentic or folk soldier songs are many of the motifs and concerns specific to the soldiers' experience of World War One. These apparently trivial ditties would continue to motivate the digger ethos through post-war nostalgia, as discussed in chapter six of this volume.

'We're here because we're here ...'

The characteristic tone and content of the diggers' song sets them apart from the literary and popular effusions of the war and post-war period. The dominant mood of the folk pieces is humorous, utilising various devices. The ditty 'We're Here Because We're Here', for instance, depends on the circular inanity of those words, incessantly repeated to the tune of 'Auld Lang Syne'.[1] The song reflects the frequent monotony of AIF life and what often seemed to the diggers to be its pointlessness, implicitly commenting upon those perceptions and experiences.

There were also more explicitly critical songs, including the bitingly sardonic 'Purple Platoon':

> Our officer's out on his favourite stunt,
> Taking us out for a souvenir hunt
> Taking us out in front of the wire,
> Getting us killed by our own rifle fire.
> We used to be fifty-odd non-coms and men,
> We used to be fifty but now we are ten,
> And if this cross-eyed war doesn't end ruddy soon,
> There'll be no Aussies left in our purple platoon.[2]

In the same vein were the parodies of the war's most widely sung popular song, 'Tipperary', sung by the 4th and 5th Divisions of the AIF on their departure from Egypt in 1916. From the very earliest days, 'Tipperary' had been the theme song of the war, both in Britain and Australia.[3] Its anthemic status was comparable to that of 'Soldiers of the Queen' during the Boer War of 1899–1902, or of 'Bless 'em All' during the World War Two. It generated many other parodies:

> We have written letters to our folk in Aussie land,
> Saying we are leaving Gyppo's s__... and sin and sand;
> We are off to France to fight a much more worthy foe
> Than the Gyppo — from whom we are mighty glad to go.
> It's a long way to fight the Fritzie,
> Where we might stop a shell;
> But before we leave you spielers,
> Here's a soldier's last farewell.
> And [to?] all your rotten crew;
> It's a long, long way to hang the Kaiser,
> Goodbye, and ...__... you![4]

Many of the digger songs were attempts to humanise the inhuman through comic treatments of fear, maiming and death, such as 'We're All Waiting For a Shell'. Like many such verses, it is a parody of a popular romantic song:

> We're all waiting for a shell
> (Send us a Whizz-bang) —
> We're all waiting for a shell
> (Send us a five-nine) —
> We don't care whether it's round or square,
> Whether it bursts on the parapet or in the air,
> We're all waiting for a shell
> (Send us a nine-two) —
> Please don't keep us waiting long,
> For we want to go to Blighty,
> Where the Nurses change our nighties,
> When the right shell comes along.[5]

'I Want to Go Home' was another parody popular with the Australians. At the battle of Pozieres during the Somme offensive, Australian Private Barwick wrote in his diary:

The shellfire was now hellish and the noise deafening, but just to show you how

'Bill — on leave from the trenches — meets a pal on the staff in
London — which is which?', Cecil L. Hartt *Humorosities* [1917],
Australian War Memorial, Canberra, 1985, np.

cool the boys were, why, some of them were walking up [toward the German lines] with rifles at the slope and singing 'I Want To Go Home'.[6]

This is a representative version of this very popular song:

> I want to go home, I want to go home,
> I don't want to go to the trenches no more,
> Where the Minnies and Whizz-bangs they whistle and roar;
> Take me over the sea,
> Where the Germans can't snipe at me;
> Oh my, I'm too young to die,
> I want to go home.[7]

This song retained its popularity in the post-war years, appearing frequently in reunion songbooks.[8] It was one of a number of digger songs that expressed the strong desire to be 'out of it', preferably at home. 'Down in the Old Front Line' develops this theme at more length and, with the rueful suggestion that the war might go on for many years, projects the hoped-for homecoming far into the future:

> In Nineteen Twenty Three
> Just try to picture me.
> Down where I'd like to be,
> In — Aussie — o'er the sea.
> All I can think of tonight
> Is another five years fight.
> Machine guns going …
> Freezing! Snowing!
> Berlin! — out of sight!
> The Fritzies in the trench
> Behind them leave a stench,
> I want to see my wench,
> (Not the one that parleys French),
> She'll be right there to meet me
> If she's not too old she'll meet me,
> When I get back, when I get back,
> In the year One Nine Two Three.[9]

A number of the songs contain criticisms of or satirical observations on the army hierarchy, such as 'Bread and Tinker's Jam', 'One For His Knob' or 'Horseferry Road':

He landed in London and straight away strode
Direct to Headquarters in Horseferry Road.
A Buckshee Corporal said 'Pardon me, please,
But there's dust on your tunic and dirt on your knees.
You look so disgraceful that people will laugh',
Said the cold-footed coward that works on the staff.
The Aussie just gave him a murderous glance,
And said, 'I've just come from the trenches in France,
Where shrapnel is falling and comforts are few,
And Aussies are fighting for cowards like you.
I wonder, old shirker, if your mother e'er knew,
That her son is a waster and afraid of the strafe,
But holds a soft snap on the Horseferry staff?'[10]

Other songs critical of military hierarchy include the song titled 'Hanging on the Old Barbed Wire'. This song, like most other digger songs, is known in various versions:

If you want to find the Sergeant-Major, I know where he is,
I know where he is, I know where he is,
If you want to find the Sergeant-Major, I know where he is,
He's lying 'neath the dugout floor.
Chorus:
We've seen him, we've seen him,
Lying 'neath the dugout floor,
We've seen him, we've seen him,
He's lying 'neath the dugout floor.[11]

Complaints about conditions in general were common topics of digger songs, as in 'My Little Wet Home in the Trench' and 'Lord, We Are Lousy':

Oh Lord, we are lousy,
We've CHATS in galore;
We're all the time scratching,
Till we are sore.
When it comes on night time
They start to roam;
It starts us all thinking —
There's no place like HOME![12]

'My Little Wet Home in the Trench' is one of the earliest-known digger folksongs:

> I've a little wet home in the trench,
> Which the rain storms continually drench;
> There's a dead Turk close by
> With his feet to the sky,
> And he gives off a beautiful stench.
> Underneath in the place of a floor
> Is a mass of wet mud and some straw,
> And the Jack Johnstons tear
> Through the rain-sodden air,
> O'er my little wet home in the trench.
> There are snipers who keep on the go,
> So you must keep your nappers down low,
> And the star shells at night
> Make a deuce of a light,
> Which causes the language to flow.
> Then bully and biscuits we chew,
> For it's days since we tasted a stew;
> But with shells dropping there,
> There's no place to compare
> With my little wet home in the trench.[13]

Reflected in these songs is a self-deprecatingly humorous treatment of the fighting and disciplinary attributes of the AIF. In fact, this humour masked an almost arrogant belief in the superiority of the digger as a fighter in comparison with the British and French infantrymen. This was, as has been shown, an element of the digger's self-image, and can also be found in songs like 'The Ragtime Army' and in some of the letters and anecdotes published in trench journals, where the soldierly abilities of allies were often questioned, usually in terms of ethnic stereotypes held by many of the AIF.

> We are the Ragtime Army
> The ANZACs,
> We cannot shoot, we won't salute,
> What bloody good are we?
> And when we get to Berlin,
> The Kaiser he will say,
> 'Hoch! Hoch! mein Gott!'

What a bloody rotten lot
To get six bob a day.
We are the only heroes
Who stormed the Dardanelles,
And when we get to Berlin
They'll say, 'What bloody sells'.
You boast and skite from morn to night
And think you're very brave,
But the men who really did the job
Are dead and in their graves.[14]

Rarely do these items of digger expression directly address the prospect of death or injury in the manner of some wartime versification. The topic is usually elided through humour and a focus on the apparently banal. Nor are these items elegiac. The final two lines of the second verse of 'The Ragtime Army', for instance, approach the realistic and the mournful. It is not without significance that this verse has disappeared from the folkloric versions. These are much more likely to be along the lines of this early text of the same song:

Onward ragtime soldiers,
Fed on bread and jam,
For our bally colonel
We don't give a damn!
See our gallant major
Strutting on ahead,
And our only prayer is
'Something strike him red'.[15]

Clearly, the primary function of such songs was not elegiac or even commemorative; such tasks were reserved for more formal genres of versification, the more literary mode, as a glance at any collection of wartime soldier poetry will indicate.

Stylistically, the diggers' folksongs can be distinguished from literary verses and popular songs of the period. The language of individually authored war verse is mostly of the imitation C.J. Dennis variety, as popularised in *The Songs of A Sentimental Bloke* (1915) and *The Moods of Ginger Mick* (1916), or in 'high' literary style.[16] A good deal of authored verse is in the mode of the bush ballad. While this balladry is often closer to the folk style, the folk songs of the diggers are most typically the rough and ready parody of popular song and hymn tunes. Even more importantly, of course, most of these items were intended to be sung (or, occasionally, recited), and so follow a different set of rules than those applying to printed verse of any kind. The singers of these songs distinguished between the commercial popular song hits — 'sentimental songs' as songs like 'Mother Macree' and 'The Long, Long Trail', among others, were usually called — and their own, private musical expressions. Writing from Palestine in *The Kia Ora Coo-ee* in 1918, a 'Corporal Geebung' discusses his and others' dozen favourite popular songs of the war. Geebung favoured the two mentioned above, together with 'My Little Grey Home in the West' (parodied by the diggers as 'My Little Wet Home in the Trench'), 'The Great Big World', 'Perfect Day', 'If You Were the Only Girl', 'When Irish Eyes are Gleaming' [sic — 'Smiling'?], 'Broken Doll', 'My Home in Tennessee' (also parodied by the diggers as 'Down in the Old Front Line'), 'The Rag Picker', 'Because' and 'Cameela Camyum' '(a bonzer song this ...)'.[17] Most importantly, 'Geebung' makes the distinction between these works and 'camp songs proper, "Good Soldiers Never Die"[18] and the rest of them'. Unfortunately, 'Geebung' does not give us any further information about such songs, probably because he does not a have a very high opinion of them — 'They're all right in their way, but no one will be very sorrowful when they go west'.[19] 'Geebung' was wrong. Such songs were to become treasured icons of returned diggers during peacetime, nostalgic reminders of the wartime years.

'Singin' to the gates uv Paradise'

The tunes of the digger songs are generally those of popular songs from the immediate pre-war and war period. Being 'popular', they act as a communally known vehicle for the revised words. Additionally, some use well-known melodies from other sources, primarily hymn tunes. Many are direct parodies, a common mode of folkloric re-creation and adaptation, the significance of which is discussed below.

The centrality of song and, to a lesser extent, instrumental music is often attested to in contemporary records of the war, memoirs and other post-war reminiscences. The diary and letters of Western Australian Private H. Demasson speak of the singing, versification and recitation aboard his outward-bound transport in 1916.[20] During the advance along the Somme in August 1918 one soldier wrote home that: 'Our chaps are as happy as Larry and simply singing at the top of their voices'.[21] Earlier the same year, another digger had written:

It makes one proud to be an Australian to see our boys after all this, pass through a village singing. They are magnificent and wherever they go they inspire confidence, both in the Tommies and the French civilians.[22]

The diggers had a reputation as singers, a point that the poet C.J. Dennis exploited in *The Moods of Ginger Mick*,[23] particularly in the poem 'The Singing Soldiers'. After detailing with extraordinary prescience the circumstances and emotions involved in soldiers' vocalising, the poem concludes with this stanza:

> They wus singin' on the troopship, they was singin' in the train;
> When they left their land be'ind 'em they wus shoutin' a refrain,
> An I'll bet they 'ave a chorus, gay an' glad in greetin' for us,
> When this bit uv scrappin's over, an' they lob back 'ome again ...
> An' the blokes that ain't returnin' — blokes that's paid the biggest
> price,
> They go singin', singin', singin' to the gates uv Paradise.[24]

Mawkish and sentimental, yet — judging by the enormous popularity of *The Moods of Ginger Mick* amongst the AIF and the numerous accounts of soldier singing, as well as the songs themselves — it seems that many Australians may have gone to their deaths in just the way depicted here. Certainly the singing of 'This Bit of the World Belongs to Us' by Australians and New Zealanders advancing across the beach and up the slopes of Anzac Cove is well documented.[25]

Singing — and alcohol — also had an important morale-maintaining function, as a digger wrote home to Sydney:

At Vimy the tonic [rum] got bushed an' didn't appear in time. Half the battalion got some and the other half went dry. The blokes that got a nip went into the scrap singing like true soldiers. My end of the battalion that missed the rum sulked through the fight like a lot of curates.[26]

Similar observations about song were made by survivors, in retrospect, and it is worth quoting at some length from 'Why the Soldiers Sang':

Soldiers sang in the last war for the same reasons as their counterparts in history — and mainly for the same reason as a bird in healthy condition sings. Probably at no time in their lives were they so physically fit, and they sang to express this physical elation. Some who had never sung before joined in the chorus. Others ... were God-sends in the fact that they lightened many a lagging footstep on the march and chased away the bogie of depression in the cheerless trench and hut. They sang, too, to express in an indirect way, their feelings and sentiments. The open expression of sentiment regarding wives, families and sweethearts, would court trouble. Singing expressed these feelings in an impersonal way. Indeed, there were songs for all occasions. The War, with it's [sic] mock heroics, it's [sic] flag-waving and speech making were the subject of some bitter ditties. The Military System with its 'full dress parade', saluting and punctiliousness in trifles came in for its share of humorous banter.[27]

This extract reinforces the earlier point regarding the expressive function of such songs for individuals, as well as their more communal purpose of lightening the monotonous, difficult or depressive nature of particular tasks. The terms 'impersonal' and 'indirect' provide clues to function: because the individual was unable to express emotions of love, fear or pity due to the male codes that underlay the digger persona, bleak, black-humoured lyrics were fused with the sentimental melodies of the Victorian parlour, the music hall and the developing popular music industry to perfectly reflect the conflicting values of war and peace, bravery and fear. This reflection allowed the individual expression through communal articulations, but only in forms that denoted the dominant moral codes, while connoting a more personal set of values and emotions in their music, resonating as the tunes did of home, peace, safety, familial and romantic love, and religious solace.

Another mechanism by and through which artistic expressions allowed the articulation of sentiment was compartmentalisation. There was a time and a place for sentiment: the time was short and the place was small, but, nevertheless, both existed. It was possible to express emotions of sorrow, pity and, perhaps, aesthetic appreciation within the bounded form of the verse or song. It was also possible to express appreciation of such matters within the equally bounded and therefore safe literary genre of the letter home. Both these complementary aspects are found in a letter from Charles Sullivan to his brother, Edward:

> There is a grave outside our trenches, and this is the inscription on the cross:
>> We buried him just where we found him,
>> And now he is sleeping alone,
>> We wrapped his blanket around him,
>> And just wrote one word, Unknown.
> The verses strike me as being beautiful, and it proves that our boys have hearts as soft as women as well as stout as steel. The cross was erected by the 1st. Bat. Anzacs. Well, I must get away from sentiment and tell you of one funny sight here …[28]

To this must be added the obvious but important function of group solidarity and calming that such musical activity has historically played in military encounters.

'When this bloody war is over' — Parody and Bawdry

Related to all this is the significance that the act of parody has for parodists and their audiences. While it is not necessary to know the original work to enjoy a parody, it certainly heightens the irony if both singer(s) and listeners are familiar with the work being parodied. As most of the songs in this collection parody what were very well-known songs of the period, it seems reasonable to assume that all involved could savour the ironic and satirical implications of pieces like 'Lord, We Are Lousy', a parody on that quintessential slice of Victorian sentiment, 'Home, Sweet Home'. Whereas the original song celebrates and supports the cosy images of security, home, comfort and family life, these are inverted in the parody, both through a change in the content from the comfortable pleasures of home to the uncomfortable terrors of lice, and through a change of context to one of death and horror, where 'home' is now an unreachable and, indeed, farcically inconceivable image.[29]

Quite a number of these wartime folksongs operate on this principle of ironic inversion in relation to the sentimental concept of home implicitly contrasted with the grim realities of war — 'My Little Wet Home in the Trench' (parody of 'My Little Grey Home in the West'), 'Down in the Old Frontline' (parody of 'My Home in Tennessee') and 'I Want to go Home', for instance. Closely linked to these are the songs that take popular song originals of a familial nature like 'Hold Your Hand Out, Naughty Boy' and turn them into grimly humorous ditties like 'Hush, Here Comes the Dream-Man', which becomes 'Hush, Here Comes a Whizzbang'.

> Hush, here comes a whizzbang,
> Hush, here comes a whizzbang,
> Now you soldiers get down those stairs,
> Down in your dug-outs and say your prayers.
> Hush, here comes a whizzbang
> And it's making straight for you,
> And you'll see all the wonders of no-man's land
> If a whizzbang (bump) hits you.[30]

Romantic love is another sentiment lampooned by the diggers in song. The popular song 'We're All Waiting for a Girl' is parodied as 'We're All Waiting for a Shell'. Another song, 'I'd Love to Live in Loveland (with a girl like you)' becomes 'I'd Like to Live in Blackboy', the Perth recruiting and training camp at Blackboy Hill. The manner in which the folk parody of the song's chorus significantly alters the meaning can be seen through a comparison of the original lyrics and those of the parody:

I'd like to live in Loveland with a girl like you
And ev'ry day a holiday
With skies of baby blue.
Where roses bloom forever, and sweethearts are always true,
I'd love to live in Loveland with a girl like you.[31]

These saccharine sentiments became:

I'd like to live in Blackboy for a week or two,
And work all day and get no pay
And live on Irish stew.
The potatoes they are rotten and the meat runs after you,
I'd love to live in Blackboy for a week or two.[32]

The popular song original depicts a period of holiday, relaxation, romantic love and eternally benign nature. By contrast, the folk parody transforms these stock images into a depiction of work rather than holiday, of rotting rather than blooming vegetation, of transience rather than permanence. The romantic love of the original becomes a sardonic and sarcastic revulsion of the camp, with the connotations of gloom, death and masculinity contained in the name 'Blackboy'. While the trite imagery of the original song affirms life, sex (covertly) and the vitality of the natural word, the parody inverts these images and is heavy with forebodings of death and the unnatural. Similar parodic transmutations can be seen taking place in other examples mentioned here.

These ironic inversions of the peacetime commonplace set up a façade of 'gallows' or black humour. This translated individual emotions into a form acceptable for public projection in the extreme circumstance of war. Although the songs denote a devil-may-care toughness and bravado appropriate to soldiers on active service, they betray in their parodic origins the individual, human desires for home, family, safety and the mundane. These last are often called 'sentimental', yet they take on a more fundamental pathos and individual significance in circumstances of imminent extinction. The items chosen for parody — including hymn-tunes — are not a random selection but are based upon the particular and fundamental needs of soldiers. The songs parodied allow a public projection of appropriate sardonic machismo while simultaneously eliciting and satisfying the less 'manly' and warlike sentiments beneath the exteriors of most individuals. This point is made by the author of 'Why the Soldiers Sang'.[33]

Other songs that are not direct parodies but simply new words set to old tunes also show the importance of the principles of selection mentioned above. The use of hymn-tunes like 'The Church's One Foundation' ('The Ragtime Army') and 'What a Friend We Have in Jesus' ('When This Wicked War is Over') permits ironic connotation in an age of widespread public and private Christian observance, heightened, of course, by the innumerable personal tragedies of the period.

The role and function of parody and the gallows humour typical of so much digger folklore has been touched upon here. Again, the digger expressions are of the ideologically appropriate mode — complaining, irreverent, tough, sardonic, casual and so on. However, when the original popular songs on which the parodies are built are examined, a different impression of the meaning that such pieces had for the diggers emerges. The black humour and satire of the parodic become a means of invoking or motivating the 'sentimental' meanings of the popular originals themselves. Even though the parodies sing <u>against</u> the originals through their inversions, the originals necessarily sing <u>through</u> the parodies, both because this is the nature of parody and because the melodies are still the inescapable vehicles of the original popular song's meaning or 'sentiment'. Thus, these ostensibly banal ditties resonate with multiple significance and so mediate between the 'hard' orthodoxies of the group ethos and the emotional needs of the individual within the group. Here we begin to understand the enormous significance attached to such expressions by diggers as a group and as individuals. Nor was this significance restricted to the war years but would persist and adapt to the needs of nostalgia, group solidarity and the necessity to perpetuate the digger ethos in the years after the war.

Through similar processes, items of commercial culture were incorporated — in appropriately adapted form — into the folk culture of the digger. Of particular interest is one of the earliest documented examples of AIF singing under fire the song 'This Bit of the World Belongs to Us' (mentioned above). While 'This Bit of the World Belongs to Us' originated as a popular song rather than a folk song, its appropriation by the diggers throws light upon the formally sanctioned attitudes of the time. Consideration of the song reveals that the AIF began their journey from Australia espousing many officially approved attitudes and justifications for war, but from April 1915 ignored, adapted or inverted these within the distinctive culture they developed. The song is quoted in full below:

> Jonathan has visited the lonely Kangaroo,
> Lonely by the old Pacific Sea,
> While his ships went by

We heard a warning cry,
Keep the broad Pacific white and free.
So we've asked the Motherland if she would show us how
Old Britain's ships were sent to steam and fight.
No better guide could be
Than the mistress of the sea,
And we'll help her to maintain the Empire's might.
Nations numerless [sic] swarm the tropic seas,
Where Australia's lonely sentry stands.
Soon our sturdy sons
Must stand beside their guns,
Guns that they have fashioned with their hands.
So our battleships we'll build, to guard our native land,
We'll man them with the bravest at the game;
For what the Yank can do,
The sturdy Kangaroo,
Should give himself a chance to do the same.
Chorus:
And we've got the boys to do it in Australia,
Australia, Australia
The same old blood, the same old speech,
The same old songs are good enough for each.
We'll all stand together, boys, if the foe wants a flutter or a fuss;
And we're hanging out the sign
From the Leeuwin to the line:
'This bit of the world belongs to us'.[34]

Displayed in these lyrics are those emotions and values that initially inspired Australia's — and so the diggers' — enthusiasm for the war. The acceptance of Britain and the Empire as the racial focus of the Australian nation and the concomitant desire to 'help her to maintain the Empire's might' are strongly expressed here. Also of note is the fear of Australia's isolation in the Pacific. While this would be a powerful factor in World War Two, it was well-embedded in the popular mind at this time, along with the disdain for non-white races that would be so typical of the diggers' reactions to the 'Gyppos' and 'wogs' they encountered on their military travels. Australia's 'boys' will protect the Empire's interests 'from the Leeuwin to the line' — there is a hint of the later rivalry that would develop between the Australians and the Americans at the front. The overall message of the song is that Australia will acquit herself very well in the fighting. While these sentiments were prevalent among civilians and the diggers in 1914 and early 1915, they rapidly faded as the full extent of the losses and general disasters of the Dardanelles campaign became apparent. There are no credible accounts of Australian troops going into battle with patriotic songs on their lips after the Gallipoli landings.

In comparing this popular song with the diggers' own expressions, some strong differences are immediately apparent. While 'This Bit of the World Belongs to Us' is based on Empire patriotism, duty and implied sacrifice, the diggers' own songs are concerned with survival, going home, complaints about army life and other such everyday matters. They are never jingoistic. It seems reasonable to suggest from such marked differences of subject and orientation that the diggers generally sang such popular patriotic songs at appropriate, formal moments, much as did the general population. Their own songs and piecemeal appropriations of popular ditties like 'This Bit of the World Belongs to Us' had quite different meanings and functions. These were related directly to the culture of the diggers and the expressions of essential elements of that culture — not, during the war at least, — to the wider world, but to the exclusive group of 'diggers'. The songs reflected the moments that were most central to the diggers' experiences and to the particular view of life and death they developed from those experiences. The digger songs were sung in trenches before attacks, in billets and at other moments and places that typically structured the soldiers' everyday lives. The 'outside' world of popular patriotic ditties, duty, sacrifice and related attributes — integral aspects of the Anzac tradition — impinged rarely and lightly upon this closed world. When such sentiments did gain entry to the diggers' world, it was through the processes of parodisation and selective appropriation by which the formal professions were transmuted into the folkloric attitudes of the diggers. The creation and re-creation of digger song and verse can be seen as metonymic of the larger processes involved in the interactions of the digger and Anzac traditions. One element of this transmutation was the deployment of informal language in digger song, verse and other expressions.

It is clear that most of the printed versions of these songs have been bowdlerised. 'Bloody' becomes 'ruddy', 'bally' or 'blinking'; 'arse' often becomes 'grass' or, like 'shit', 'balls' and other unmentionables, is denoted through dashes. 'Fuck' and 'cunt' are, not surprisingly, without euphemism, and verses that may have contained them are usually either rewritten for print or simply dropped altogether. There is almost no hint, apart from the odd sly aside, of the considerable tradition of army bawdry (none of which has been included here, as much of it pre-dates the war and belongs to the professional army tradition rather than to that of the volunteer civilian).

Many of the writers who reminisce about the diggers' songs some years after 1919 are at pains to point out that very few of the army songs were really crude or obscene and, if they were, the boys did not mean any harm. See 'Why the Soldiers Sang', for instance, and Collins,[35] who begins by telling his readers that 'only a small percentage of soldier songs need expurgation', while on the following page is only able to print the chorus of the army version of the music hall standard, 'She was Poor, but She was Honest'. Another post-war defender of the linguistic probity of the digger rather surprisingly tells his readers that 'bastard' and 'bloody' were the swear-words mostly used by the Australians. It was — perhaps unsurprisingly — the British Tommies whose language was really bad, including the 'lowest' word. By this, the writer presumably meant 'fuck' and its variants, as 'cunt' does not seem to have entered soldier-lore until the 1939–45 conflict.[36] Here we are witnessing the transformation of these authentic contemporary expressions from their original, unofficial and private contexts to a new, public status as time capsules of individual memory and icons of communal nostalgia. In the process of the post-war interactions of the digger and Anzac traditions, sanitisation is a conspicuous element.

The various editions of Brophy and Partridge[37] convey a different impression of the language of soldier songs, as do many of those versions collected from oral tradition. There is no doubt that digger expressions utilised 'swearing' to the full, a confirmation of the status of these items as elements of the digger folk tradition entirely in accordance with their self-image as expert users of bad language. As suggested in relation to a number of the yarns already discussed, swearing was one of the major elements in the diggers' armoury of devices for asserting and maintaining exclusivity, particularly in relation to the Tommies and their officers. As 'bad language' was a commonplace of Australian working-class speech, the use of it as a central indicator of 'diggerness' provides a strong indication of the working-class orientation of that portion of the AIF — mainly the ranks up to Non-Commissioned Officers and those above who were noted by the diggers as deserving of their recognition. As already discussed, this status could be accorded to officers up to and including General Birdwood, due to empathy of attitude. After the war, officers were generally considered to be diggers, a status emphasised by the egalitarian practice of dispensing with marks of rank during Anzac Day marches. Peace also fostered other significant transformations of the digger tradition.

CHAPTER FIVE

Transforming a Tradition

The digger tradition continued through the post-war years as the substantially private ethos of the returned soldiers. However, even while this increasingly nostalgic and ossifying tradition persisted, it strongly influenced the developing public tradition of Anzac through the political and community activities of the RSSILA and through a variety of cultural mediums, including newspapers and ephemeral fiction and non-fiction of various kinds. In addition, there were innumerable articles and related literary forms that, almost imperceptibly but remorselessly, reworked elements of the digger tradition into forms convenient for the Anzac tradition. This process began early in the Great War, particularly through C. J. Dennis's *The Moods of Ginger Mick*, progressed throughout the years of conflict, and continued after the war's end.

Digger into Anzac

The previous chapters have revealed important factors of the folkloric elements integral to the self-image of the digger from around 1915. The culture of the digger is very much a private tradition developed by a highly specialised group of primarily youthful males. While some members of this group had prior military experience or training, mostly in the Boer War, the AIF was predominantly a civilian volunteer infantry organisation. In the forcing ground of mass mobilisation, international travel and unimagined conditions of armed combat, this group fused a cluster of pre-existing cultural traditions and more recent experiences into an ethos appropriate to the time and the circumstances.

Essential facets of this ethos were a degree of exclusivity, often expressed in terms of national pride and involving the largely negative stereotyping of other groups with whom the diggers came in contact. These groups included the 'Gyppos' or 'niggers', as Australian troops constantly referred to the Egyptian people, nearly always in terms of profound disgust and contempt.[1] While the diggers reserved their deepest loathing for the 'Gyppos', they were also disparaging about the physical, mental and military abilities of their British equivalent, the Tommy. Australian troops frequently portrayed themselves in a better light than the British foot soldier and played upon those elements they imagined marked the digger as distinct from the Tommy in some way — attitudes to authority, the use of bad language and the deployment of an 'Australian' language the Tommies could not comprehend. Related to this particular contempt was that felt and expressed towards British officers. Notwithstanding the fact that the diggers' hero, Birdwood, was himself English, Australians mercilessly pilloried the upper-class, monocled British officer of stereotype in their songs, yarns and activities.

Closely related to the diggers' dislike of British officers was the Australians' refusal to take seriously the usual requirements of military command and discipline. Diggers were notorious throughout the allied forces for what was considered by the British to be their slack discipline and propensity for drinking, brawling, whoring and thieving. The exploits of the AIF in Egypt and elsewhere are well-documented, revealing the depths of digger anti-authoritarianism.[2] Allied with this was the obligatory air of nonchalance and an accompanying casual attitude to the rigours of combat. Both the self-image and the projected image of the digger were determinedly informal, even anti-official.

The digger ethos, expressed in song, verse, anecdote and action, contained irreverence and — in the terms of the time — immorality. It included a propensity to complain about most aspects of the military system in which the diggers found themselves, and an increasingly explicit disloyalty towards British and other allies, and so the imperialist enterprise in which they had become, at first enthusiastically, engaged. From the initially jingoistic and emotionally shallow reaction of hatred for 'the Hun' and the Turks, the digger evolved an ambivalent mixture of caution, respect and, in times of extremity, of fellow-feeling.[3] Such characteristics were not all unique to the digger, of course, but the blend and balance that the exigencies of time, place and circumstance produced was an identifiable and useable image.

This particular combination of elements constituted the tradition of the digger. As with all folk traditions, this one had a variety of facets and functions. It provided the esoteric sense of identity and coherence that welded the primarily non-officer members of the AIF into a group with shared customs, speech, values, beliefs and attitudes. As well, the digger tradition had a public persona, which the members of the group habitually projected to the non-digger world. The diggers assumed that this persona defined the way the men were viewed by significant 'others', such as the British public, British army officers, some AIF officers, and the people back home. The diggers generally 'played up' to these stereotypical representations for a number of reasons. Firstly, because they knew it was expected of them; secondly, because it genuinely amused them; and, thirdly, because acting out this communal public persona also reinforced their esoteric view of themselves as larrikin, knockabout blokes facing death with a joke and a song. From this complex intersection of images, beliefs and stereotypes, it was possible to select and transform those elements most appropriate to the invention of a national warrior tradition.

Very few of the constituent elements of the digger tradition were appropriated in unaltered form. Perhaps the least altered was the egalitarian impulse that was such a marked and remarked upon aspect of the AIF. This characteristic Australian shibboleth was inducted directly into the Anzac tradition. However, once appropriated, it was shorn of its most excessive manifestations, such as antipathy towards officers and the resulting problems of indiscipline. In its sanitised peacetime form, digger anti-authoritarianism became the egalitarianism of the broader Australian society, expressed on Anzac Day when officers and men marched as equals, without display of previous or existing military rank or, for that matter, of civilian status. Other elements of the digger tradition underwent varying degrees of transformation.

Cynical, black and often desperate humour motivated much digger folk expression, particularly in the area of song parody and in yarns indicating nonchalant attitudes to imminent extinction. This was adapted in the Anzac tradition to become the stoic acceptance of dying with a joke and a 'fag' in the Anzac tradition, much as 'Ginger Mick' expires:

> ... near the end,
> 'E starts a fag an' grins orl bright an' gay.
> An' when they arsts fer messages to send
> To friends, 'is look goes dreamin' far away.
> 'Look after Rose,' 'e sez, 'when I move on.
> Look after ... Rose ... Mafeesh!' An 'e wus gone.[4]

Such images were allied with notions of duty, courage and sacrifice, which were fundamental to the Anzac tradition but formed no part of the digger folk tradition.

Elements of the digger tradition that were quietly ignored in the official construction of Anzac were the diggers' vehement racism and prejudices against allies. While prejuduce against non-white 'races' was characteristic of the broader Australian society at this time,[5] the expressions of dislike and contempt for British officers and the class they were perceived by many diggers to represent was an embarrassment, as was (if to a lesser degree) the diggers' expressed antagonisms towards the Tommy, the *poilu* and other allied troops.

The diggers' distrust of the efficacy of the formal tenets of religion is absent from the Anzac tradition. While diggers generally had great respect for 'Padres' (so-called whatever the denomination of a cleric) in combat areas, the expression and observance of religious beliefs was discouraged within digger culture.[6] The forms and philosophies of formal religious observance and belief are not, as shown in previous chapters, subjects dealt with in digger song, verse or narrative. Rather, to a significant extent they are subverted through the parody of hymns.

Likewise omitted from the Anzac tradition was, by the public standards of the time, the 'immorality' of much digger behaviour. Popular songs, verse and images of estaminets and sightseeing tours to the Pyramids projected a cosy and morally acceptable impression of AIF leisure activities, a view encouraged by the diggers, of course. But the reality was a high incidence of soldiers going Absent Without Leave (AWL) and of venereal infection.[7] The private tradition of the digger valued and celebrated this behaviour, but such attitudes and activities were not appropriate for public, official commemoration.

Simply ignored by the creators of the Anzac tradition was the sentimental side of digger culture and the related feminine or 'soft' elements of that culture. Such attributes, while integral to the diggers' view of themselves, were not projected outside the digger group, nor were they conducive to the creation of the warrior image required by the Anzac tradition. The sentimental element, while contradicting the warrior masculinity of the digger, nevertheless had its origins and, hence, some degree of acceptability in the nineteenth-century bush codes of mateship, where caring for one's mate both physically and spiritually was considered a primary duty. However, the closely related feminine elements were anathema both to the public projection of the diggers' own persona and to the official warrior elements of Anzac.

Nonetheless, the feminine, or at least those characteristics then associated with it, was not absent from the male digger tradition. A definitely non-masculine 'softness' can be discerned in the private repositories of letters and diaries: 'our boys have hearts as soft as women as well as stout as steel', wrote Charles Sullivan from the Western Front in 1916.[8] In a letter from a digger printed in the *Argus* in August, 1915, the writer described his comrades as men who 'fight like wildcats and yet are as tender as girls'.[9] This 'softness' is also present in trench journals and in some genres of digger verse, particularly those that aspire to 'literary' form and content rather than the more functional and down-to-earth ballad styles.[10] There are also suggestions of, if not distinctly feminine, then certainly non-masculinist and anti-militarist characteristics in digger folksong and the processes of parody applied in their creation. These include the desire to be 'out of it' or 'at home' heard in more than a few songs.

The 'tender as girls' element within digger culture was only ambiguously or indirectly expressed in the lore of the diggers. It was never acknowledged by the digger tradition and could never be acknowledged. The diggers as a warrior group wished to think of themselves as being 'stout as steel', indeed had to think of themselves so in order to take part in armed conflict. Individuals might profess unmanly emotions only in the rarefied and safely contained form of literary verse, or in the privacy of letters and diaries.[11] In such highly compartmentalised and personal forms, these emotions — while totally at odds with the warrior image, yet a logical resolution of the mateship code — could be briefly but safely expressed.[12] Not only did the diggers fail (or refuse) to acknowledge the feminine within themselves, the Anzac tradition also ignored such 'softness'.

The fear of acknowledging 'softness' is also implicated in the diggers' sardonic nonchalance towards death. The possible imminence of extinction was dealt with in digger culture by simply ignoring it, by transforming it into music-hall satire through the song parodies, by incorporating the possibility into the realms of superstition, or by dismissing it to an arena where its expression could do little real harm — in the effusions of poets and authors with literary aspirations. As noted, digger folk expressions rarely engaged with the notion of death. When they did, the subject was generally played for a laugh. This casual, even contemptuous dismissal of death as a serious matter was one facet of the digger tradition that could, with little refinement, be taken directly into the Anzac tradition. There it fitted conveniently and comfortably with the requirements of sacrifice and duty. One important means of accomplishing this process was through the official appropriation of what were, for a little time, the diggers' own 'media', the trench newspapers.

Written in the Trenches

While rumours, songs, beliefs, verse and narratives circulated orally, they also overflowed into the diggers' published expressions, forming an interface between the oral culture of the digger and the more formal, official milieu of the army organisation and power structure. It is at this point of interface between the official and the unofficial that we can best see the ideological and oppositional elements of digger culture interacting. Here is the indefinite,

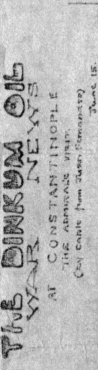

Seal, Graham, 'Dinkum Oil, one of the earliest Australian trench journals produced on Gallipoli in 1915', image from ' "Written in the trenches": Trench newspapers of the first world war', *JAWM*, no. 16, p. 32.

The " Kookaburra "

" Laugh! and the World Laughs with You."

AN AUSTRALIAN CORPS TROOPS AND MOTOR TRANSPORT MAGAZINE.

(Registered at the Field Post Office for transmission by Post as a Hot Air Exhaust).

Vol. 2.   In the Field, France. July, 1917.   Price 25 centimes.

" Dont Croak—Chuckle! "

The Burra looked wise on the grey gum tree, as he gazed on a blaze of blossoms sublime···
Then he laughed and chuckled aloud with glee in the fragrant breeze···it was wattle time.

Near by sat a crow with a downcast look, while faintly the breeze bore the stock-bells' chime;
"Oh! you laugh too much" he cro·ked "old Kook···wi·l you laugh as loud in the winter time?"

The Burra still sat on the grey gum tree (a solid old Kook in a sunny clime,)
"I'll laugh as long as you croak" laughed he "in the spring and summer and winter time."

PIP.

Hell and the Hun,

"Satan's Resignation" in the last issue of *Kookaburra* is evidently apropos of the frame of mind of little Willie, for our senior Blighty contemporary the *Daily Mail*, of a later date, describes Willie's praises of his Berlin boys thusly:—

"With such troops I can fetch the Devil from hell!"

Oh! Willie we'll have missed you,
When troops in hell assist you.

Now let's have a shot at prophecy——we'll project on the screen a futurist pen-picture of big Willie, in the frightful tragedy of a mighty failure,

Man—is it man, this wastrel, naked, shivering, lean?
The one-time earth-lord and sea-lord, forgetful of what has been?
He stands 'mid a wrecked creation, on burnt and blasted lands
With the seed of the ghastly failure still clutched in his trembling hands.

Seal, Graham, ' "*Kookaburra*": *An Australian Corps Troops and Motor Transport Magazine*, typical of the standard of production possible in the settled circumstances behind the front in France, 1917–18', image from ' "Written in the trenches": Trench newspapers of the first world war', *JAWM*, no. 16, p. 33.

blurred dividing line between the informal digger tradition and the related, though autonomous, invention of the Anzac myth.

Australian soldiers of the Great War produced a considerable body of publications on active duty and even in the front line. Within six weeks of the Gallipoli landings, a number of trench newspapers were circulating among the 'dugouts' and 'possies' of Anzac. This tradition of unit publications, established aboard the transports taking the First AIF to Egypt[13] and eventually broadening, continued through the rest of the war, producing some sophisticated magazines and journals, such as *The Digger* and *Aussie*, the latter even continuing into civilian life as the voice of returned servicemen.

The term 'trench newspaper' is a generic one used here to describe a variety of newssheets, magazines and similar periodicals (periodical in intent, at least; some only lasted one issue) produced on active duty. Containing verse, song, rumour, anecdotes and various forms of written and graphic humour, trench newspapers, especially the less-sophisticated, were almost totally written by their readers, the diggers.[14]

Trench newspapers were produced under conditions of active service, in many cases while at or close to the front line.[15] At their most basic level, such publications were extremely crude in terms of technology and production, sometimes being created with a pencil, old pieces of notepaper and some sheets of carbon, such as *Sniper's Shots* and *The Bran Mash*. Those like *The 7th FAB Yandoo* (the title of the FAB [Field Artillery Brigade] paper was often shortened to *Yandoo*) were produced in the relative calm of a headquarters or unit office often using early reprographic equipment such as jelly or spirit duplicators, while some even had access to small printing presses. The most refined, such as *Aussie* and *The Rising Sun*, had the services of professional and semi-professional journalists, and operated with the blessing and support of the AIF itself.

A distinction must be made between trench newspapers and compilations like *The Anzac Book*.[16] Trench newspapers were produced entirely for consumption by soldiers on active service, while *The Anzac Book* was always intended as much, if not more, for home front audiences as for the diggers themselves. Unlike trench papers, *The Anzac Book* had no news-giving function (spurious or otherwise) and is not much concerned with some of the other central genres of the trench newspaper, mainly the furphy and the humorous letter. The officers who first proposed an 'Anzac Annual' to Bean[17] probably got the idea from the trench papers that circulated on Anzac. And although Bean included a little material taken from these publications, the intent of his work on *The Anzac Book* was to present a broader readership of non-diggers with his own particular view of Anzac and its meaning. Here, as elsewhere, Bean was appropriating and reworking for other purposes certain aspects of the diggers' own culture. Bean's experience editing the Gallipoli trench paper *Dinkum Oil* also put him in a position to both appreciate and channel the power of the diggers' authentic articulations, a skill that he refined when editing *The Rising Sun* in France.

Trench newspapers can be conveniently grouped into three rough, overlapping categories. The first category contains those publications produced under the most difficult frontline circumstances, sometimes literally 'in the trenches'. *The Bran Mash*,[18] for instance, was the product of the 4th Light Horse at Gallipoli. It seems only to have lasted for one number and was written in pencil on two leaves of Commonwealth typing paper, apparently duplicated by sheets of carbon. With a dateline of 'Anzac Cove, Gallipoli June 15, 1915' *The Bran Mash* began its first — and last — editorial with 'Whirr-Whiz-z-BANG!' (a reference to the sound of falling shells, soon to be universally known as 'whizz-bangs') and apologised for the 'lack of conveniences necessary for its completely satisfactory production'. As would be the case with most trench newspapers, this one asked for contributions from its readership, provided a selection of rumours or 'furphys', some basic 'art' (a black oblong titled 'Night' by O. Keapit-Darke) and 'Original verse' titled 'The Trooper's Lament', an early example of what was to become a standard genre of digger literature — the complaint in verse. The first stanza of this gives the tone and style, and also nicely highlights the extent to which the earlier tradition of bush versification was in the process of being incorporated into the lore of the digger:

> I come from good old Woop Woop and me monicker's Gus Headers
> An' I joined the 4th Light ..._____... 'orse out at Broad_____... Meadows.
> I brings along me own old prad, and shoves the claim in 'ot.
> But the ..._____... vet 'e crools me pitch, an 'arf was all I got.
> I gathers in the ..._____... cash and gets off on the spree,
> And th' CO ups and passes me a week's C ..._____... B.
> GORSTRUTH!![19]

Much of the literary material in trench newspapers fell somewhere between the popular verse of the day and the folkloric expressions of the digger that existed primarily in oral forms. These rarely appeared in print at the time they were in circulation, though many of them appear in veteran's publications produced after the war, when the sentiments they expressed were no longer subversive or otherwise unacceptable for official promulgation in print. The soldiers' oral culture, of which digger folklore was a substantial element, was a constant underpinning of much of the material contributed to trench papers by the diggers themselves, although published material usually bears the marks of editorial polishing. Oral items were also anonymous and communal. When individual diggers felt the need to express themselves in forms suitable for print, even anonymously or pseudonymously, they almost always adopted a style derived from the popular literature of the period, as in 'The Trooper's Lament' and similar publications in other trench journals.

A longer survivor of the Gallipoli trench press was *The Dinkum Oil*,[20] which began on June 11 and lasted for eight issues into July 1915. *The Dinkum Oil* was the offspring of a paper founded and edited by Sergeant Max Noonan for the 6th Battalion, titled *Sniper's Shots*. The Australian War Memorial's copy of *Sniper's Shots* is written in pencil on a double sheet of lined octavo paper and is almost identical in format and in some of its content to its progeny. *The Dinkum Oil* was apparently conceived because Major Blamey (1st Division intelligence officer), worried about the potential damage to morale of the intense rumour-mongering among the troops, asked Bean in early June of 1915 to 'get out a "furfies [sic] gazette"', with these furfies so exaggerated as to laugh them out of court'.[21] Bean was impressed with the spontaneous *Sniper's Shots* and on June 11 assisted Noonan in compiling the first *Dinkum Oil*. The trench newspaper *Dinkum Oil* therefore originated in response to an official desire to intervene in the unofficial digger oral culture. As such, it was a forerunner of the later, more sophisticated third-category papers that flourished almost entirely under official sanction. The appropriation of the form and manipulation of the contributed content of official and semi-official trench journals is a constant theme in the brief but intense history of these publications.

The concern with attracting and amplifying key aspects of the diggers' oral culture was carried over into the second category of trench papers, typified by productions such as *Yandoo* and *Honk!* Although some of the papers in this category began life as troopship journals, their frontline formats were distinctively 'trench'. Billed as 'The Voice of the Benzine Lancers and Organ of the Gear-Box', *Honk!* originated as the journal of the Australian Ammunition Park on board troopship A40 in January 1915. From issue number eight of August 1915, it was published 'in the field' in France. It was a printed paper, each issue usually running to six pages. In addition to the basic trench paper requirements of verse, furphies and humour, *Honk!* included snippets of 'News from Down Under', AIF sporting competition news and results, and even practical articles such as how to purify water.[22] In common with most other papers in this category, such as the *14th Company Magazine* and *Yandoo*, *Honk!* was a relatively sophisticated product, able to print snippets of news from Australia less than two weeks old, letters from personnel on Anzac and back home, and to reprint patriotic verse from the Sydney *Sun* newspaper. However, *Honk!* also carried literary items of the type common to all trench journals. The aims and fundamental content of these second-category journals were much the same as their less sophisticated forbears.

Generally, the third-category journals were produced in a professional manner, on printing presses, with journalistic expertise and official blessing at high levels of the army hierarchy. They were able to draw upon official resources for their distribution, thereby ensuring a substantial and broad readership. Photographs and a variety of other illustrative and graphic forms were reproduced in these journals, as were items culled from Australian and, occasionally, British newspapers. Such sophistication, while not unknown in the second category publications, was rare and irregular. The best known of the third-category publications are *Aussie* and *The Kia Ora Coo-ee*.[23] Less well known are *The Digger*[24] and the magazine that grew out of *Honk!* — *The Rising Sun*.[25]

Edited by the ubiquitous Bean, assisted by A. Bazley and printed 'Somewhere in France', *The Rising Sun* claimed to be 'A Journal of the AIF in France' and published its first issue on Christmas Day 1916. It included the usual fare of the more sophisticated trench paper — some Australian news, some general and sporting news, anecdotes, humour and parody advertisements. It also carried verse and even printed poems that had not made it into the *Anzac Book*, as Bean was still carrying the rejected manuscripts wherever he went.[26] Bean's diary for December 16, 1916 indicates his ambivalent feelings about the first *Rising Sun*: 'I spent today stringing together the stuff. It is not up to the Anzac Book — and only just eno' to make the issue. However, it won't do badly'.[27]

In February, 1917, *The Rising Sun* published 'Why Mick went to War' from *The Moods of Ginger Mick*. Clearly the resources of this paper were some levels above those of *The Dinkum Oil* and papers of the second category, though the functions of all these publications were the same: the boosting of morale through a carefully selected, edited and presented combination of war- and home-front news and information, together with poetic, humorous and occasional prose fiction items contributed by the diggers themselves. By the time the trench newspaper had reached this level of sophistication, it had long moved from its origins in the oral culture of the digger. This did not affect the popularity of such publications with the diggers. Just as they continued to accept the official trench newspapers as an appropriate forum for the image they wished the outside world to see, so they accepted an outsider's artful depiction of their ethos. Such productions as *The Moods of*

Seal, Graham, 'Cacolet, the journal of the Australian Camel Field Ambulance. Printed by the Nile Mission Press, Cairo, Cacolet is an example
of the most sophisticated trench journals', image from ' "Written in the
trenches": Trench newspapers of the first world war', JAWM, no. 16,
p. 35.

Ginger Mick were acceptable as they allowed the expression of emotions that were not sanctioned within the oral culture of the diggers.

'Ginger Mick' Goes to War

The difficulties occasioned by the 'hearts ... soft as women ... stout as steel' contradiction that underlay digger culture were dealt with in a number of ways. The singing of sentimental popular songs and their parodies was one means of mediating the conflict. For a few, there were the possibilities of literary verse, outlets for which increased with the publication of the second- and third-category trench journals discussed above. However, for most men the only outlets for such emotions were their journals and letters written to loved ones. Private thoughts and communications with home and family were the only permissible modes and moments for the expression of personal sentiment (as opposed to the generalised, mass sentimentality involved in the singing of popular songs). This sentimentality was given a public arena by the timely publication of C.J. Dennis's best-sellers *The Songs of A Sentimental Bloke* (1915) and *The Moods of Ginger Mick* (1916). These works provided the means by which sentimentality was allowed, channelled and defused from any potentially dangerous intersection with its taboo extension — the 'soft' feminine. The literary work that was most influential and effective in acknowledging sentiment while keeping softness at bay was *The Moods of Ginger Mick*. It is, therefore, a pivotal work in the processes of transforming selected elements of the private digger ethos into the public tradition of Anzac.

Angus and Robertson published *The Moods of Ginger Mick* in October, 1916. The book sold over 42,000 copies within 6 months and was followed by a 'Pocket Edition for the Trenches', which also sold very well. By 1920, sales were in excess of 70,000 copies in Australia and overseas.[28] 'Ginger Mick' is the mate of Dennis's earlier best-selling character, 'The Sentimental Bloke', a tough but lovable larrikin who eventually goes 'soft' on Doreen, marrying her, moving to the countryside to raise children and run a farm, a movement concluded in the final poem of *The Sentimental Bloke*, titled 'The Mooch o' Life'. The Bloke's attainment of this Australian idyll is counterpointed in *The Moods of Ginger Mick* by Ginger Mick's apotheosis and martyrdom as a digger hero at Gallipoli. Originally opposed to the war — '*Blarst* the flamin' war!/I ain't got nothin' worth the fightin' for', Mick opines in the poem 'War' — he declares in 'The Call of Stoush' that ' 'e dam well 'ad to go.' The remainder of the book consists of the Bloke's poetic renditions of Mick's letters from the front, which catalogue Mick's transformation from the hard-bitten street-brawler, rabbit-seller and cynic into the heroic and idealistically nationalist digger — 'But the reel, ribuck Australia's 'ere, among the fightin' men', he concludes in 'The Call of Stoush'.

Mick also discovers something at odds with the folk prejudices of the digger: British officers and gentlemen in general, 'toffs', as Mick calls them, could be 'white men'. Here we see a little of the literary processes by which the class conflict and antagonism to aspects of Empire that were integral to the digger ethos were ameliorated and ultimately incorporated into the Anzac tradition. The enormous popularity of 'Ginger Mick' with the diggers themselves highlights the hegemonic effectiveness of Dennis's 'Ginger Mick'. While the expression of such attitudes would not have been tolerated within the digger folk tradition it was accepted in expressive forms such as *The Moods of Ginger Mick*. In most other respects the figure of Mick is replete with the characteristics of the digger's self-image and of their preferred projections of this image to the outside world. As well, of course, the populist nationalism of the work that made it such a favourite with the broader Australian population also considerably aided its acceptance by the diggers on overseas service, aching for news of 'home' and those things that were both dear and familiar.

Mick is wounded and taken to hospital, but returns, as so many did, to the fighting on the Peninsula. In the poem titled 'The Game' (a reflection of the frequent characterisation of the war as a sporting competition)[29] Mick is made a Corporal because 'over 'ere I answers to the call' and 'some shrewd 'ead — took a chance on Ginger Mick, an' I 'ave snared me strip'. Again, this favourable depiction of officers as 'shrewd' is directly at odds with the anti-authoritarian strand of the digger tradition.

Inevitably, Mick 'passes out'. News of his death is communicated to the Bloke in a letter from the English 'toff', Trent. In the poem 'A Gallant Gentleman', Trent portrays Mick in just these terms, much to the Bloke's initial puzzlement. According to the Bloke's rendering of Trent's letter, Mick died in 'some great 'eroic lurk'. They find him dying, and, as quoted more fully above, Mick 'starts a fag an grins orl bright an' gay'. They bury him on the beach, placing mimosa on the mound — 'Twas the nearest thing in reach/To golden wattle uv 'is native land.' The Bloke is impressed by the praise of the English Trent for Mick's heroic end and speculates that 'p'raps gentlemen an' men is much the same'. It is not simply the gallant deeds of Ginger Mick that make him heroic, but the acknowledgment of the heroism of those deeds by an English officer. This resonated strongly with the imperialistic tone and context of Australian nationalism, during and after the war, that provided the dominant ideology of the Anzac tradition.

The unbridled sentimentality of Dennis's work, particularly in the context familiar to the diggers and those who would become such, provided a channel in which the tears of sentiment were allowed to flow. Dennis, through the aptly named 'Sentimental Bloke' and the transformation of his mate Mick into 'an Australian' and a corpse, made it permissible for the digger to be sentimental — at least in certain specified modes and circumstances. These, given the nature of the overseas digger experience, were basically circumstances involving home, family, loved ones and country. Together with the use of colloquial speech and the brilliance of Dennis's poetry and characterisation, this explains the popularity of Dennis's ultimately depressing work with the AIF and the general populace. Through Ginger Mick and, to a lesser though important extent, the Bloke, Dennis provided images of the Australian at war that became those the digger was expected to publicly present after the enormous sales of the work.

Dennis, like Bean, thus acted as midwife both to the birth of the private digger tradition and to the later incorporation of elements of that tradition into the imperial, nationalistic and formal tradition of Anzac. Ginger Mick's stoic acceptance of death, his acceptance of a British officer's recognition of Australian heroism (something Australia was hungry for) and his pride in promotion because an officer had singled him out for doing his duty well are all antagonistic to the digger tradition yet integral to the Anzac tradition. That they could co-exist in their contradictions is a mark of the complexities of cultural interactions involved here, and highlights the intersecting character of the two traditions.

One of the most intriguing complexities of the relationship between the traditions of digger and Anzac involves a significant absence in the expressive traditions of the digger: the lack of articulation of the notion of mateship, at least as a coherent philosophy. While the camaraderie of war is usually an unspoken assumption, it seems peculiar that mateship, usually considered to be the core of the digger ethos and 'the spirit of Anzac', barely appears in the diggers' own expressions at this time. The elaboration of the philosophy of 'mateship', while having its roots in the wartime digger experience, was related more closely to the erection of the Anzac tradition.[30]

Masculinity and Mateship

At the core of digger culture was the assumption and assertion of masculinity. To be 'digger' was to be male. The experiences and expressions of digger were male. The female was a world away — wives, mothers, sisters and, perhaps, the 'tabby' or girlfriend at 'home'. These were unattainable on active service. Some contact with women serving as nurses might have been possible for the wounded. On 'Blighty leave' in England, female companionship was likely for a few days or weeks at most. Otherwise the only possible male-female relationships were the transitory attentions of an Egyptian prostitute or a 'mademoiselle' in a French 'estaminet'.[31]

The masculinist nature of the digger tradition did not spawn a profoundly anti-female ethos like that of some other military groupings, such as the German *Freikorps* documented in Theweleit's massive *Male Fantasies*.[32] But the *Freikorps* and other such bodies were essentially professional soldiers, brutalised by their sadomasochistic military customs and ethos. The diggers were, in their own naïve view and in reality, a mob of blokes going off to do a job of work. The location was far from home, the chores dirty and dangerous, but someone had to roll up their sleeves and get on with the digging. The digger idea of womanhood was the thoroughly conventional, sentimentalised view of the Edwardian family: patronisingly patriarchal, but not especially misogynist. Mothers were treated with a special, detached reverence not unlike that accorded 'the little Irish mother'. It was permissible to let out a few nasty facts about war, but most diggers were reticent in their letters to 'dearest Mother'. Sisters were often the recipients of their brother's anguish and penned by return mail, in neat hands, many words of comfort. The impression left of the diggers' approach to women is of naïveté, even shyness. The 'tabby' back home is treated in jovial but ultimately respectful terms, as a kind of fragile memory that must be carefully dusted for fear of breakage. Despite the high rate of venereal disease and the riots in Cairo's red-light Wazzir district, the reader of today is left with the unprovable but tenacious suspicion that many of those censored letters and army issue postcards describing for the family the delights of rambles with mates through the Cairo Museum, the pyramids, Parisian architecture and the English countryside may just have told the full story for many.

The distinguishing characteristic of Australian masculinity was 'mateship'. Mateship was the unquestioning loyalty of a man for his 'mate' and is a familiar feature of the idealised bushman of the nineteenth century. While the digger would come to be presented in the Anzac tradition as possessing the virtues of courage, resourcefulness, egalitarianism and independence that contribute to his soldierly prowess, it is the notion of undying loyalty to one's mates that both distinguishes the digger's Australian-ness and his ability as a warrior. Thus it is in the concept of mateship that the national-military myth most powerfully incorporates both the imperatives of the warrior and of the nation. The code of mateship is, then, one of the major points of complementarity between the folk tradition of the digger and the invented tradition of Anzac.

In his discussion of mateship and egalitarianism, John Carroll presents oral history evidence that 'the mateship ethic was first and foremost, and the finest memory of [the] war years'.[33] Mateship was frequently cited as the most important memory of wartime experience by returned soldiers interviewed by Carroll's student, Ruth Krake. However, the interviewees also indicated that there was nothing unique about such wartime comradeship and that it was equally prevalent among the British and German troops. For a passionate evocation of the mateship ideal we can turn to Donald Hankey writing of British troops in 1916. Hankey first describes the virtues of inculcating loyalty in regimental recruits, then writes:

> Besides this, he [the recruit] is learning to share with his mates instead of to grab. He is learning to 'play the game' by them to think more of fairness all round than of his own personal benefit. He does his bit and takes his share, and as long as the other fellows do ditto, he is content. It is impressed on his mind that for the honour of the company they must all be tolerant, and pull together. Also he has a 'chum'. As far as his chum is concerned the good soldier obeys the 'golden rule' in its literal sense. He shares with him. He divides with him his parcel from home, he helps him to clean his rifle and equipment, he is a friend in the Baconian sense, who halves sorrows and doubles joys. The recruit is all the better for observing the golden rule even towards one person.[34]

Couched in the moralistic language of the period, this is nevertheless a clear evocation of what would be called 'mateship' in an Australian context. Mateship, it seems, cannot be said to be an exclusive or defining Australian characteristic, although it is presented as such in the Anzac tradition. The absence of mateship as an articulated philosophy or even as a topic in digger folk expressions of song, verse and yarn is significant.

While wartime comradeship was certainly an important part of the digger wartime experience, this is not articulated and comprehended as 'mateship' by the diggers themselves until the post-war years. Then, under the growing influence of the developing Anzac tradition, diggers recollect and express their experiences of comradeship in the language conveniently provided by the Anzac tradition. This accounts for the frequent references to mateship in oral and written recollections of the war,[35] as well as to the omission of the term and the concept from the diggers' own wartime articulations.

It is extremely convenient for a military force to be able to utilise a civilian ethos that promotes *esprit de corps* and mutual support in the mass-mobilisation wars that typified the twentieth century, and of which the Great War was the first and, so far, the worst example. When such an ethos is centrally integrated into powerful and widespread notions of national identity, character and coherence, the potency of that combination may be overwhelming, both for individual psychologies and for many social groups. The hegemonic potential of a warrior comradeship and a popular, nationalistic ideal is considerable. Not only does it assist to displace the true nature of war but makes active participation in such actions a concrete expression of an individual's identity as a member of a national group.[36] The means by which 'mateship' came to form so central a part of the Anzac tradition and such a pervasive influence upon the recollections of diggers in the post-war years were various. Important among them were literary representations of the wartime experiences and attitudes of the digger.

One common literary method was to directly invoke the existing civilian mateship code in the context of war. Ambrose Cull, a celebrator of 'the magnificent brotherhood of battle', provides such an account of the wartime existence of 'mateship' in his 1919 memoir, *At All Costs*. Here, mateship is allied to another prized attribute of the Australian legend and the digger tradition — resourcefulness, often without much consideration of the finer points of ownership. Cull describes the ability of an appropriately named Australian everyman, a pre-war shearer named Private Jones, to procure anything, anywhere, at any time. Cull, an officer, promptly enlists Jones as his batman, writing: 'He [Jones] had the high Australian estimate of Mateship. For sake of it was [sic] prepared to beg, borrow or steal'.[37]

The same memoirist also utilises more sophisticated techniques in delivering an image of the digger appropriate to the Anzac tradition. He describes the strain of waiting in the trenches at dawn for the order to attack, regretting the non-masculine and 'loving softness' that may detract from the warrior's ability to kill:

> ... one saw quiet tears trickling down drawn, trench-stained faces. That is a bad time for the fighting man, a bad time for his mission. Through the mass of humanity that leaven of loving softness spreads far too easily. It is one of the reasons why 'Home, Sweet Home' and other tender melodies are banned as battle songs, why one should never take photographs into the front line, or look at them when he is there.[38]

Cull also refers to the mixture of savagery and sentiment that characterised the diggers. Under the strain of combat:

> The roughest become gentle ... all selfishness disappears. You have an overpowering impulse to put your arm around your next man's neck, to say something decent, human, gentle. It is the love of suffering man for his fellows in suffering ...[39]

Just before this passage, Cull extols the barbaric warrior qualities of the digger: 'The cultivated graces have been shed away, the primitive man is uppermost. Civilisation has lost hold for the moment, Savagery is almost supreme'.[40]

The coexistence of sentiment and savagery within the psychology of the digger is clearly discerned here. The contradictions are ignored, and the 'soft' emotions are portrayed as something that the warrior needs to control rather than the human response to emotional and imminent physical extremity. In his book, Cull also explains and appropriates the egalitarianism, initiative, comradeship and black humour of the digger to the Anzac tradition. He utilises a similar technique to describe the 'reality', ameliorating it by appeal to the exigencies of war, as in his explanation of diggers jokingly placing a tin of bully beef in the shrunken, black hand of a corpse extending from a trench wall: 'It was the big bluff, in normal circumstances it would have been instantly resented as something too gross even for war. But under such a strain men both do and say things which would revolt them in ordinary life ...'[41] His other method is simply to deny the unacceptable. After noting the Australian pride in indiscipline, Cull makes this statement:

> The fact is that in the essentials of discipline, absolute obedience in battle, the end at which all the ridiculed formalities of peacetime aim, the Australian had no superior. He not only possessed discipline, but was proud of possessing it.[42]

There were numerous important ambivalences in the self-image of the digger. Yet the image of the digger projected publicly by the propagandists of Anzac was, as Cull demonstrates, unequivocal. The digger, while jestingly encouraging an air of indiscipline, was a fine and disciplined fighter in battle, a realist, a practical man who got on with the job in hand, a humorist, and a natural leader who also respected the true qualities of leadership in others with little regard for their official rank. These characteristics were derived from the public representation that, as a group, the diggers were generally pleased to promote to the world. This communal *persona* motivated their public actions and those of their publications meant for a non-digger readership, such as *The Anzac Book* and the more sophisticated categories of trench journals. It also conditioned the public presentations of their real experiences, in forums such as newspapers, unit histories, memoirs and anthologies of verse, song and anecdote. The officially sanctioned characteristics were highlighted, in recast form, in the Anzac tradition.

Sitting at the *Round Table* of Empire

Typically, the recasting and incorporation of the digger was accomplished through linguistic and rhetorical transformations, such as those of memoirists like Ambrose Cull and accounts like that which appeared in the elite London-published, Empire-focused journal *Round Table* in March, 1919.[43] The anonymous author[44] of this article provides another example of the techniques by which the diggers' often-problematic characteristics could be made to appear as the positive attributes of the Australian warrior, seen as a representative of the Australian character — 'the best thing that Australia has yet produced'.[45]

The *Round Table* article begins by hailing the digger as 'original' and 'unique'. The diggers' reputation for indiscipline and general riotousness is not denied, as it is by Cull, but is admitted in order that it can be ameliorated and annexed to his fighting abilities — 'Hard to manage in camp, he improved in morale as he neared the firing line'. According to the author of this piece, the digger 'behaved in the Strand as he would have done on a Saturday night on the streets of Wagga Wagga'. Therefore, the diggers' 'defiance of convention' and apparent indiscipline was simply 'a pose', and 'there was no body of men who so triumphantly satisfied the supreme test of discipline — in the field'. Digger courage 'was never buoyed up by sentiment or illusion' and the digger would face reality, 'looking at the worst and defying it'.[46]

The diggers' complaining and reluctance to take orders becomes a virtue. Although 'seldom an optimist' and 'always a critic', the digger had 'a fierce lust to accomplish the job he had been set' and a 'clearness of vision gave him that initiative, that skill under fire, which made up so large a part of his value in the field'. Digger animosity to military control becomes the virtue of leadership — 'Every second man was a potential leader'. Dislike and distrust of officers and unproven, unearned rank, is seen as an expression of the democratic spirit — 'The officer was the subject of scrutiny from above and a never ceasing suffrage from below — The Australian Army was in real fact a democratic army'.[47]

Mateship, while not named as such in the article, is presented as an Australian characteristic — 'few soldiers have had in such measure the supreme soldierly gift of comradeship'. This comradeship, which according to the Anzac tradition, applied as much to carousing as to fighting, becomes here a valued virtue — 'Whenever they were in a fight, breaking King's regulations, or raiding the Hun trenches, they stuck together'.[48]

Digger humour, predominantly bleak and subversive, is presented as the expression of 'his soul, his criticism of life, with its wonderful range of insight and feeling, now grotesque, now gay, now grim and sardonic, feeding on the terrible contrasts of the life around him'. The article ends with what would

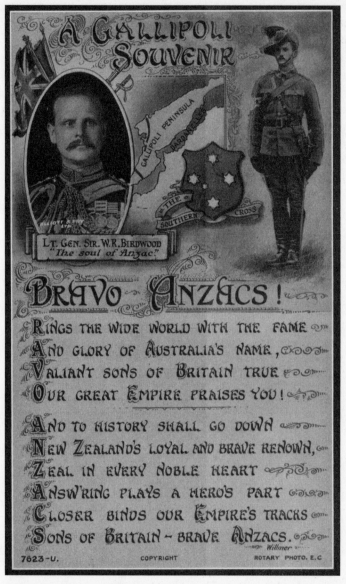

A GALLIPOLI SOUVENIR

GALLIPOLI PENINSULA
DARDANELLES

THE SOUTHERN CROSS

LT. GEN. SIR. W.R. BIRDWOOD
"The soul of Anzac."

BRAVO ANZACS!

RINGS THE WIDE WORLD WITH THE FAME
AND GLORY OF AUSTRALIA'S NAME,
VALIANT SONS OF BRITAIN TRUE
OUR GREAT EMPIRE PRAISES YOU!

AND TO HISTORY SHALL GO DOWN
NEW ZEALAND'S LOYAL AND BRAVE RENOWN,
ZEAL IN EVERY NOBLE HEART
ANSW'RING PLAYS A HERO'S PART
CLOSER BINDS OUR EMPIRE'S TRACKS
SONS OF BRITAIN – BRAVE ANZACS.
Willmer

7623–U.   COPYRIGHT   ROTARY PHOTO. E.C

Cover image *A Gallipoli Souvenir*, 'A patriotic postcard, printed in Britain as a souvenir of Gallipoli. The card was donated to the Memorial by the family to Private Q.J. Hunter, who served with the 9th Battalion on Gallipoli and in France where he was killed in action in 1917 (Printed Records collection, 3DRL 6223)', *JAWM*, no. 16, p. 2.

become a common rhetorical device presented as the view that such skills displayed and honed in the war would provide the basis for a bright development of the country: 'The achievement of these men will play an integrating part in the future of Australia. They will form the basis of a noble national tradition'.[49]

That tradition would be the official, invented tradition of Anzac. The extent to which elements of the digger tradition were incorporated into the Anzac tradition, and the literary means through which this would be accomplished, was already in evidence as the peace began.

CHAPTER SIX

The Echo of an Anzac's Cooee:
Perpetuating a Tradition

The echoes of the war were long and lasting for many diggers, resounding not only in the practices of the 'smoker', the reunion and Anzac Day itself, but also in the pages of the digger press; in the sub-economic publication of 'ephemera' as well as in the everyday discourses of informal written and oral communication. In these modes were continued the oral and literary forms of the digger.[1] The distinctive traditions of the digger were also preserved, becoming ever more potent with nostalgia even while — and partly because — the circumstances that created that culture became more distant in time and memory.

The Digger Yarn Industry

One of the most characteristic and revealing expressive forms of the digger was the yarn. These humorous anecdotes, discussed in the context of their wartime origins earlier, became time capsules of nostalgia for the returned soldiers in the post-war period. Favourite anecdotes were continually recycled in print and, as can be deduced from various sources,[2] in oral form as well.

Immediately after the war ended, the yarn industry gathered pace. At first it persisted in the pages of *Aussie*, the wartime periodical that became a conscious peacetime voice of the digger. It was *Aussie's* practice to reprint large sections of prose, poetry, cartoons and other material from trench journals, from returning troopship publications and from its own wartime pages. Naturally, a good deal of this material consisted of yarns. Other important publications for the recycling of the tried-and-true favourites were the various state League publications and those independent publications, such as *The Listening Post* in Western Australia, that were so closely linked with the RSSILA as to be indistinguishable from its own organs. Also frequently utilising yarns were newspaper columns devoted to the interests of the digger. These tended to come and go throughout the 1920s and '30s in accordance with how individual newspapers perceived public interest in matters pertaining to returned soldiers. Reunion programs and commemorative publications of all kinds also often printed yarns, as did commemorative anthologies, such as the various issues of *The Anzac Memorial* (1916, 1917) and *The WA Digger Book*. The latter was published by the Western Australian branch of the RSSILA in 1929, both as a commemoration of the role of the diggers and of the centenary of the state — another indication of the close links between the digger and, in this particular case, a parochial form of nationalism. A relatively restricted corpus of yarns was continually recycled in one form or another throughout the peacetime years.

The important sub-genre of digger yarns concerning general Birdwood's real or apocryphal actions and verbal reactions have already been mentioned in the context of the development of digger wartime attitudes towards authority. These and other Birdwood yarns also figure frequently in post-war digger publications and oral tradition.[3] The same egalitarian theme permeates many other digger yarns reprinted in the post-war period. For example, the yarn about the two diggers who fool the sentry into believing that they are leaving camp rather than returning to it late by facing the other way appears in *Aussie*[4] and in *Digger Aussiosities*.[5] Often these are inflected with anti-British sentiment, as in the yarn about the digger who, failing to salute a British officer, is remonstrated with by the officer and replies by telling him 'Shut up, you bastard'. The outraged British officer reports this to an Australian officer standing nearby. 'You're not one [a bastard] are you?' asks the Australian officer. 'Certainly not', sputters the British officer. 'Well, run back and tell him he's a bloody liar', advises the Australian.[6]

The nonchalance of the digger under fire was another persistent theme of post-war yarning. Often this was combined with the diggers' love of the gambling game 'two-up', a signifier of digger-ness that not only persisted after the war but became synonymous with the digger's image and with the Anzac myth itself. Two-up, as an authentic element of wartime digger culture, was an ideal peacetime focus for the digger and the Anzac (and their associated traditions) because of its ambivalent status. It was technically illegal to play the game, yet this law was blatantly flouted on Anzac Day and was tolerated by authorities in the carnivalesque atmosphere of the afternoon of April 25. Thus, two-up yarns emphasising the lauded casualness of the digger were particularly appropriate texts for recycling, not only orally, but also in a variety of printed forms. The following yarn first appears in print (probably) in 1919. Similar yarns were published in various publications in the post-war years.

Recently, one of our patrols was overdue, and I was detailed as one of a search party ... Suddenly we saw the shadows of a number of men standing silently in the darkness. 'Fritzes!' said someone, and we all ducked into shell-holes. Fritz's next flare revealed a small party, all stooping and gazing intently on the ground. Then one of them cried softly and exultantly, 'Two heads are right!' picked up the pennies and pocketed the winnings. It was the lost patrol. They were making their bets and tossing the coins in the darkness, and then waiting for the light from a Fritz flare to see the result.[7]

Related to the two-up yarns were numerous other anecdotes that likewise highlight the studied casualness of the digger under fire. These included such situations as a group of diggers continuing their card game even as the enemy advances in great strength, and those like this one, reported in the British *Evening News* of October 16, 1918 and reprinted in the *Australian Corps News Sheet* of November 6 the same year under the title 'Taking the war calmly':

An Australian told me this: — We were advancing, and had been going about an hour, and my platoon numbered about fifteen men. Going over a ridge we saw a pill-box. We poured machine-gun fire at it, and threw grenades too. No reply came, and we congratulated ourselves that we had no casualties.

All the time we could see smoke coming from the aperture; this worried us so we decided to charge it. We had our charge, with whoops and yells. I got to the door-way, and was met with, 'Say, Digger, what the ..._ is all the noise about?'

There stood an Australian, with a frying-pan in his hand, cooking bully beef over a fire which the Huns had left.'[8]

Yarns exhibiting the diggers' notoriety for swearing also appeared in peacetime publications, again reinforcing an important attribute of digger identity. Sometimes these anecdotes were simply evocations of abuse and bad language, as in the example of the 'Who called the cook a bastard' chestnut, and variants, already quoted.[9] Other 'bad language yarns' had the additional appeal of satirising the perceived verbal rectitude of British officers with whom the diggers came into regular contact during the war. In the peace, such yarns became lovingly polished icons of Australian distinctiveness expressed in colloquial language with a consequent (real or imagined, it mattered little) affront to the British officers.[10]

In line with the ostensibly self-deprecating element in the psychology of the digger, there were also yarns that showed the Australian volunteer foot soldier in a less-than-favourable light. The yarn about the enemy bullets that were heard twice by the diggers was a favourite of this genre.[11] While such stories appear to relate to cowardice in the face of the enemy, this negative connotation is always elided through the wittiness and humour inherent in the text. Further, the effect of such yarns is to present a manifestly negative action in a sardonically acceptable manner that effectively bolsters the balance of bravery and realism the diggers tended to project in their cultural expressions.

Of course, there were also many yarns in which digger is shown to outdo or outsmart either — sometimes both — the British and the Americans. Often these are in the form of tall-tale competitions, such as the reworking of an old bush yarn quoted in chapter three of this volume.[12] Such fare was a staple of the post-war digger publishing industry and, along with a range of other expressive forms, contributed to the perpetuation of those attitudes formed by the diggers from 1915 onwards. Yarns, of course, were not the only forms of digger lore and literature to soldier on after the conflict.

The Culture of Nostalgia

Digger verse and song lived on in the mouths of old soldiers as well as in the pages of their journals, reunion publications and associated ephemera. Many of these items were variants of those discussed previously; many were newly composed in the same style as the wartime originals, celebrating the same perceived virtues and now time-worn verities.[13] In 1931 *The Listening Post* in Perth, published yet another 'digger alphabet', that hoary genre of soldier versification exemplified in chapter two. Authored by C.R. Collins (digger, physical education trainer and avid writer on all matters digger),[14] this particular alphabet might well have been composed anytime between 1916 and 1918 but for one or two post-war references. The tone of the piece is in the approved world-weary, sardonic mode of digger versification and manages a few references to perceived post-war injustices. While such a poem might have resonated deeply of recent events and memories in 1918, in 1931 the effect of 'Zeppelins', 'Mademoiselle from Armentieres' and 'Horseferry Road' must have been bathetic. To any other than diggers, it would surely have seemed at least faintly anachronistic. But diggerhood was not something to be sloughed off with the uniform at the ending of hostilities, it was a status that remained with the individual forever. There may have been ex-soldiers or ex-servicemen, but there was no such thing as an ex-digger.[15]

The Digger's Alphabet

A for the Adjutants, dashing young blades,
B for the Batmen who dodged all parades.
C for the Clink, aftermath of the spree,

The home of the birds who go making too free.
D for the Digger, the casual brute,
Who sauntered past 'Birdie' and didn't salute.
E for the 'Eggsers' who turned their hats down,
The married man [sic] have to', we told the whole town.
F for the Furphies, related with zest,
Especially the one of the long-promised rest.
G for the Gunner, a decent old sport,
Except for his habit of dropping 'em short.
H stands for Hindenburg, sturdy and hale,
Till Monash and Co. put a twist in his tail.
I for intelligence, reigning serene,
The reason the blighters were tabbed out in green.
J stands for Jerry, and Jacko the Turk,
Who kept all the diggers in regular work.
K stands for Knighthoods that Generals got,
Except when the profiteers collared the lot.
L for the Legends we told all the flappers,
Of boomerang farms and the jackeroo-trappers.
M stand [sic] for Mademoiselle. It appears
That she lived in the town we pronounced 'Armenteers.'
N for the Nips that were seldom repaid,
Horseferry Road was the nub of this trade.
O for the OBEs dished out in millions,
To actors and women and other civilians.
P for the Padre, the shifter of sin,
When you nipped him for gaspers you'd get the whole tin.
Q for the 'Quack' with his quick Number Nine,
And also the Quarter-bloke, dodging the line.
R for the Ration-state, figured and cinched,
Except for the Rum that the Quarter-bloke pinched.
S for the Sisters, the pride of the show,
But how they endured us, I'm hanged if I know.
T stands for 'Two-up' the national game;
When Princes have played it, are we much to blame?
U for the U-boats that scuttled in flight
Whene'er a destroyer would steam up in sight.
V for the 'vin blong' estaminets sold,
A potent prescription to keep out the cold.
W for War Books, so smutty in places,

'Anzac: — "We're havin' a night out tonight, and we want to deposit the bail" ', Cecil L.
Hartt, *Humorosities* [1917], Australian War Memorial, Canberra, 1985, np.

All written by ladies or blokes from the bases.
X for the marks that they put upon casks,
To empty the same were our happiest tasks.
Y for the Y plus the M and CA,
The one little show that could make the war pay.
Z for the Zeppelins, purveyors of hate,
And also for Zero, the dread hour of fate.[16]

Here are many of the elements of the diggers' self-image: his casual attitude to regulations and military discipline, particularly to saluting officers; gripes against civilians, the YMCA Comforts Fund activities (a common complaint during the war); the near-sanctity of two-up; contempt for 'the Quarter-bloke' and other 'base wallahs', who were believed to do no fighting; escapades in estaminets; drinking, and so on. All this presented in impeccable 'diggerese' as though it were still 1917.

In addition to such new-yet-old material, post-war digger periodicals published copious selections of material dating from the war. A.B. 'Banjo' Paterson's 'Swinging the Lead', composed in Egypt in 1918, was republished in *The Listening Post*,[17] as was his 'To Anzacs, Touching Reinforcements'.[18] Songs also made occasional appearances, including 'The Long, Long Trail'[19] and 'Take Me Back to dear Old Aussie'.[20] *Aussie*, in its peacetime version, devoted at least two pages per issue to reprints from various trench journals and ships' papers throughout 1920s.[21] Other songs were perpetuated at reunions large and small. A typical reunion souvenir program or songster might contain the tried and true favourites — suitably sanitised — such as 'Mademoiselle from Armentieres', 'The Ragtime Army', 'I Want to Go Home', 'Hanging on the Old Barbed Wire', 'Down in the Old Front Line', 'Good Soldiers Never Die', 'Rolling Home', Bread and Tinkler's Jam' and 'When This Wicked/Blessed/_____ War is Over' in one or more of its numerous variants.[22]

These musical expressions contained all the contemporary connotations of wartime diggerhood, yet became increasingly lustred with nostalgia as the glasses were drained and the years passed by. Whereas they had once expressed the hopes and fears of men in armed conflict, they now came to evoke the bittersweet memories of youth, comradeship and the romance of battle rather than the reality of the war that had engendered such expressions in the first place. The specific circumstances of composition and circulation were no longer vital to the meaning of these texts. It was enough — more than enough — that they, like the old diggers, had survived the war. Their essential significance now resided in this fact, a metaphor of the social status and meaning of being a digger. Because of this the songs were extremely important emotional links with the receding past and contributed to the survival of the digger ethos in the post-war years.

The main institutional focus for post-war digger activities and the main-tenance of the digger ethos was to be the RSSILA (later 'Airmen' was added, later still the name of the organisation was changed to Returned Servicemen's League — the RSL). The RSSILA evolved from the numerous battalion and state returned servicemen's organisations that began to appear in numbers from 1915. By the end of the war, the RSSILA had become a national organisation formed from strong state Returned Soldiers' Associations that affiliated with the central body. The League was to be an important political force in both state and federal politics, as detailed by Kristianson and other writers.[23] The social aspects of the League provided opportunities for its members to stay in touch with each other, to receive publications that reflected and reinforced the digger view of the world and, perhaps most importantly for many diggers, the chance to get together with old comrades to drink, yarn and reminisce. These occasions very soon became ritualised in the form of the 'reunion'.

The ex-service association reunion, together with RSSILA meetings, was the vital focus for the perpetuation of digger cultural forms, both old and new. Reunions varied in size and structure. Regular get-togethers of old comrades in their ex-service associations might happen on a monthly basis, as with the 2nd Battalion, AIF, which met on the last Monday of the month at 89 Phillip Street, Sydney. Others met less frequently, though a yearly gathering would seem to have been the favoured duration for these customary gatherings, judging from the 116 Ex-Service Association reunions across the country noted in 1932.[24] Undoubtedly there were many more such meetings that were not published in the returned soldiers' journals. An inkling of the regularity and nature of these events may be gained from the frequent references to reunions and 'smoke nights' (all-male evenings of carousal) in *The Listening Post* and other digger-oriented publications, such as 'A Digger's Diary' in the *Western Mail*. In the latter column, for example, a diggers 'smoker' at Southern Cross was 'a memorable evening of song and story [that] finished just on midnight'.[25] In September of 1929 the South Perth sub-branch of the League recreated the lighter moments of the Western Front with an 'estaminet'.[26] Reunions were so popular in Western Australia that men traveled over a hundred miles in order to attend.[27] By 1929 a regular 'Reunion Week' became established in Perth, conveniently during 'Show Week' (the week of the Royal Perth Agricultural Show), when many rural diggers would be in town.[28] Indeed, there were so many reunions that

'Non-com', the compiler of 'A Digger's Diary' complained that 'the ordinary "smoko" has become stereotyped'.[29] The proliferation of reunions at this period is in accordance with the rise in League membership that Kristianson notes from 1924, though in Western Australia, membership remained firm throughout the decade.[30] By the end of the decade, the spontaneous desire of old soldiers to join together from time to time had become a standard calendar custom, a ritual of nostalgia that could briefly reunite the members of a particular unit, section, or other military grouping.

From time to time, often at ten-yearly intervals, much larger reunions were held. These might be Divisional reunions, such as that of the 4th and 56th Battalions' Reunion in Sydney (probably sometime in the 1920s)[31] or specific to particular specialties within the forces, such as artillery or medical corps. At one such event in Sydney during September of 1929, a digger reunion attracted 3,000 participants, who consumed 1,200 gallons of beer.[32] Another possibility was a general reunion of all who served, such as that in Bunbury, WA, in 1929, which was a highly organised and publicised event, and lasted for several days.[33] While such events were occasions for the display and celebration of digger culture, their size, public nature and the participation of others (including wives, children and other family members) meant that they were more closely related to the formal observances that constituted Anzac Day rather than to the all-digger, all-male, private 'smoker'.

By such communication and semi-ritualistic interaction did diggers continue their informal, mostly private traditions into and through peacetime. The network of old comrades thus established and maintained provided the social basis for the continuation of digger culture. It was a culture that was almost entirely backward-looking, feeding on the past for its modes of expression, values and attitudes. Eventually, of course, such a culture must stultify and reify, failing (as digger culture largely did) to keep pace with the changes in Australian and international society. The signal success of the digger culture was in the establishment of Anzac Day as a national public observance by 1930. As discussed later in this volume, Anzac Day was partly motivated by the diggers' desire to display their private traditions, and so must be considered the most important reunion of them all. The informal networks of unit association and the more formal activities of the League, in concert with Anzac Day, constituted an ongoing matrix of mateship, nostalgia, mutual aid and support that inevitably perpetuated distinctly digger forms of literary and oral expression.

Another facet of this cultural milieu was the frequent publication of reminiscences or anthologies of verse, yarns and other digger expressive forms. Little study of this output has been made, either by literary scholars or by historians. One reason for this is undoubtedly the difficulty of obtaining the material, a considerable proportion of which was self-published or published and distributed in very localised and specialised groups, often by and through local newspapers or ex-service associations. Some of this material consisted of self-penned and self-published anthologies of verse sold in the street by the author/publisher, a digger fallen on hard times. Publications of this sort, not surprisingly, increased during the depression years, but were also quite common during the 1920s.[34] Another reason for the dearth of scholarship in this area is that such material is generally perceived as having little literary value and as being of trivial historical interest. In terms of the present work, however, the continued existence and new composition of such material is a vital indicator of the persistence of the digger tradition in the post-war period.

Post-war anthologies of digger versification were not far removed from the obsolete form of the broadside ballad. Like the earlier broadsides they were often hawked in the streets and from door-to-door by ex-servicemen, sometimes maimed (or apparently so) and often claiming financial hardship as the cause of their efforts at authorship, publishing and distribution. The one-time field editor of the famous trench paper published in Cairo, *The Kia Ora Coo-ee*, 'Frank Reid' or A.V. Vennard, made a living from this line of work in the post-war years.[35] While the material contained in these anthologies could hardly be considered to be 'news', it was usually presented as authentic, true-to-life recollections of the authors' wartime experiences, or as poetry composed 'under fire', 'in the trenches', 'on active service' or some other form of words connoting authority and authenticity of experience. If not self-published it was sometimes published by a local suburban or country newspaper, a further link with the development of popular literature.[36]

The reasons for this sub-economic form of publication and distribution related to the fact that few of the digger versifiers were experienced with the technology of the industrial aspects of publishing, and few would have possessed sufficient capital to fund such enterprises, anyway. Even when these factors were not an impediment, it seems that the attitude of commercial publishers during the immediate post-war years was that there was no market for war books. Alexander Vennard ('Bill Bowyang' — previously 'Frank Reid' of the *Kia Ora Coo-ee*)[37] was told by George Robertson (of Angus and Robertson) that, even with a preface by Henry Lawson, Vennard's manuscript 'Confessions of an Anzac' could not be published as there was no demand for war books. The conventional wisdom in the Australian publishing industry was that it would be about ten years or so before the reading public began to take an interest in the war.[38] By then, the passing of time would have invested the subject with the appropriate aura to justify the investment of publishing capital. The effect of this was to generate a modest but persistent self-publishing movement among diggers, very little of which has been noticed by librarians and literary bibliographers, even as 'ephemera'.

Much of this material was of the autobiographical type that, in more conventionally produced forms, is usually termed the 'memoir'. As well as retailing 'true' experiences, old yarns and jokes were given yet another airing in many of these publications. The verse was predominantly in the ballad form, or variants of it, with 'Ginger Mick'-inspired items and wartime variants of the bush ballad predominating. 'Trench Morals', an item appearing in one of the numerous ephemeral anthologies 'by a returned Soldier' published in Melbourne, probably around the late 1920s, is reproduced here as an example of the mediocre verse that usually appeared in post-war digger ephemera:

> When you're in the trenches, boys, don't cuss,
> If you do the Heads will make a fuss,
> It's got to cease occurring, this awful wanton swearing,
> So boys, just take this good advice from us.
> So when you shoot and miss the wily Turk,
> Don't swear, but pull your bolt back with a jerk,
> And should the cartridge jamb it, don't forget yourself and damn
>   it,
> But go like H___! until you make it work.
> And when a bullet skims just by your head,
> Don't be ignorant and sing out, 'Strike me dead!'
> Never detract from your daring by this wicked, useless swearing,
> But return the compliment with bits of lead.
> They evidently think we'll fight the better,
> By carrying out instructions to the letter,
> But will we fight the worse, 'cause occasionally we curse,
> Because upon our lips they've put a fetter.
> When you're tortured by an elderly, fat louse,
> Of the 'active service' kind that makes one rouse,
> Don't 'carry on' with swearing, look to see how he is faring,
> And if you catch him — do a gentle wowse.
> Then boys, when in the trenches you're reclining,
> And long-forgotten swear words you're repining,
> You'll never gain your wings, if you use cuss words and things,
> or join the Angel throng, so bright and shining.[39]

Such verse could still appeal to readers in the 1920s and 1930s. Like the digger verse and song composed and published during the war, this post-war echo is complete with slang, digger jargon and digger allusions. It is redolent with digger philosophy and the humorous satirisation of military and orthodox civilian morality. Reading this and the reams of similar material published in ephemeral publications, returned soldier periodicals and even occasionally in the mainstream press, it seems that, for many returned men, the war had never ended.

Self-published anthologies of this type were generally greeted with enthusiasm and warmth in the digger and digger-oriented periodicals of the time. The same periodicals, however, could react to any questioning of the sanitised digger and Anzac image with near hysteria. Robert Graves's *Goodbye To All That* (1929), in which the poet and author claimed that Australians mistreated and even murdered prisoners, was savaged as lies and hearsay by a reviewer in *The Listening Post* under the heading 'A Grave Furphy'.[40] Against the background of the 'red scare' a *Listening Post* editorial scathingly castigated the editor of the *Western Congregationalist* for daring to ask 'Why are the State celebrations of Anzac Day controlled by the RSL?' After pointing out that Anzac Day in Perth, 1930, was not restricted to members and ex-members of the military (Scouts, Guides and the Young Australia League, among others, were present) the editor went on to charge the hapless questioner with 'pacifism', cowardice and, penultimately, with communism — 'red-rag propaganda'. This lengthy condemnation — over two pages — provides an indication of the seriousness of those who considered themselves the bearers of the diggers' peacetime image.[41] Such expressions were to become increasingly common and increasingly shrill in the following decade.

The post-war period was characterised by escalating political and social conflict between the right and the left, a conflict exacerbated by the economic hardships of the 1930s and the resultant polarisation of well-defined interest groups, most extremely the New Guard and the Communist party. The RSL was involved in these conflicts, as were most other elements of Australian society — though, as Humphrey McQueen has argued, the League cannot be identified as an organisation of the right or the left. More importantly for the arguments here, the digger tradition (despite its regressive elements) was not a 'pipeline' of recruits and attitudes for extreme right-wing organisations like the New South Wales-centred New Guard and the Victorian White Guard (sometimes referred to as 'Army'). While these conflicts had their origins in the wartime homefront disputes over conscription and the nature of the war itself, the battlelines began to be drawn in 1919. As the AIF returned to the civilian mundanities of work, domesticity and politics, the strain in the social order quickly became apparent. There was anti-Bolshevik rioting by returned men in Brisbane and riots and industrial unrest in Fremantle during 1919. An eighteen-month strike began in Broken Hill in 1920, and there were violent confrontations between loyalists and carriers of red flags at Peace Day marches.[42]

Within this conflict, which, as Gavin Souter points out, increasingly reflected the major class divisions in Australian society created during the war,[43] League members played diverse roles. McQueen provides evidence and an argument to show that, despite implications that the AIF was the major recruiting area for such right-wing organisations as the New Guard, 'a statistical analysis of RSL membership makes it clear that the RSL was far too small to have acted as a conduit from the AIF to the New Guard'. McQueen concludes that the New Guard (and, by implication, other extremist conservative groups such as the Dominion League of Western Australia, among others) was an expression of bourgeois and petit-bourgeois class interests rather than a reflection of the 'multi-class' AIF. Importantly, McQueen also emphasises that he does not argue for the establishment of a 'counter-tradition of militant left-wing diggers'.[44] The post-war diggers must not, therefore, be seen as a monolithic, conservative group, but more accurately as reflecting the various points of view and political positions competing in Australian society during the period. This is a valuable adjustment to the influential argument of Geoffrey Serle, who sees 'the digger legend' being appropriated by the imperialist, racist and Protestant middle class.[45] Only selected elements of what Serle calls the digger 'legend' were appropriated by the middle class and incorporated into the hegemonic Anzac tradition.

The demotic tradition of the digger persisted through the post-war years in publications, reunions and other informal intercourses, as well as in the more formal arena of the mainstream press. Chief among these publications was the periodical that, among other sobriquets, became known as 'the digger's bible' — *Smith's Weekly*, and another influential survivor of wartime trench journals, *Aussie*.

'The Unofficial History of the AIF' — *Smith's Weekly* and *Aussie*

Smith's Weekly, beginning publication on March 1, 1921, was a weekly Sydney broadsheet, the creation of its long-time editor Claude McKay and cabin-boy turned millionaire, Sir James Joynton Smith. From the beginning, the paper was populist, egalitarian, crusading and aggressively nationalistic. In the list of *Smith's* loves and hates provided by *Smith's* journalist George Blaikie in his remembrance of the paper can be discerned the main pillars of *Smith's* ideological position, at least insofar as the paper could be said to have any consistent position given its crusading against sacred cows, pomposity and any other established activity or perquisite that it considered inequitable.[46] The diversity of *Smith's* targets makes it difficult to categorise the publication in terms of any particular political point of view. However, 'the digger's bible' was not, in general, a progressive publication. According to Blaikie, and confirmed by a reading of the newspaper itself, *Smith's* loved, among other things: Australia, the genuine unemployed, white-collar workers, the White Australia Policy, diggers, underdogs, Australian success stories, Billy Hughes and jokes. *Smith's* hated: profiteers, military police, Jehovah's Witnesses, 'Japs' (in the North), black men with white women, bureaucrats, pomposity, 'Dagoes' and Communists. The eccentric but broadly appealing nature of the newspaper is apparent from these lists, though took some time to develop. The first issue sold 35,000 copies (at two pence each). In January 1923 circulation was over 165,000 and by 1927 in excess of 200,000. By 1939 circulation had fallen to 80,000, though World War Two led to a revival in which sales reached 300,000.[47]

From the first issue in 1919, *Smith's Weekly* bristled with fervent declarations of gratitude to the diggers and a bellicose nationalistic pride in their wartime achievements.[48] *Smith's* also took an enthusiastic, even belligerent interest in the affairs of the returned soldier. Blaikie writes that the paper created 'what was generally called "The *Smith's Weekly* Soldier". There was a very curious phenomenon associated with this figure: it looked completely different when viewed from different angles.' One of these angles provided a view of the digger as:

> ... an undisciplined larrikin who would not button his tunic, delighted in insulting his officers and dodging his proper duties, and made a virtue out of going AWL and resisting Military Police.[49]

This was a concise view of the diggers' own self-image, that which was consistently projected to the outside world. *Smith's Weekly* not only promoted this representation of the digger but also supported digger points of view with an almost fanatical devotion. The paper crusaded on behalf of diggers and their families who had a grievance of some kind or whom *Smith's* felt had been poorly treated by authority. As a logical consequence of this stance, *Smith's* encouraged the submission of digger-related 'pars' and 'gags' from its readers. From late 1924 these became a regular feature of the paper titled 'The Unofficial History of the AIF', remaining for many years one of the paper's most popular attributes.

While some of these 'gags' and 'pars' are yarns of the type described above, the predominant genre is the moralising vignette or anecdote. It seems that many of these items were provided partly by *Smith's Weekly* staff journalists, though the majority were contributed by interested readers or freelancers who, like many contributors to the early *Bulletin*, wrote to a formula in order to augment other incomes. Blaikie points out some contributors would send in twenty or thirty items each week and that 'The most successful contributor of ideas bought himself a fine home from his earnings from *Smith's*'.[50]

The 'pars' were carefully constructed pieces designed to appeal to diggers through the use of nostalgia and the invocation of one or more elements of the digger self-image — anti-authoritarianism, comradeship, cool non-chalance under fire, and so on. Such items were of a different and slightly more sophisticated genre to the more humble digger yarn, which described a single event, was specific to a time and place, and was shaped by its primarily oral provenance. Nevertheless, these more consciously 'literary' items have much the same purpose as the tried-and-true, oft-told tales that were trans-mitted orally and which turn up again and again in the post-war anthologies of digger humour discussed above. Just as furphies, yarns, jokes, songs and other items of digger oral culture cohabited happily with short stories and high-flown poetic attempts in the pages of trench journals, so in the post-war period both oral and literary effusions continued to act as vehicles for the perpetuation of the culture of the digger. Such items were also able to survive and perform their functions because they could be seen to be outside of politics. They resonated with all things digger from that (paradoxically) golden era of death and terror. In the vastly more complex world of peace, with its economic and power conflicts, the 'red scare', conflict between unionists and the League, such items were happily non-partisan and could be enjoyed by all diggers, regardless of political persuasion. Thus, these forms of digger culture not only survived but proliferated at a time when formal adherence to the RSSILA fluctuated.[51] While it would be too much to claim that the phenomenal success of *Smith's Weekly* was solely due to its appeal to diggers, this was certainly a significant element in that success.

The introduction of the column titled 'The Unofficial History of the AIF' was part of *Smith's Weekly's* ongoing concern for the interests and rights (and the subscriptions) of the peacetime digger. From its earliest editions the newspaper had a strong interest in the digger and his doings, running a regular column that investigated the inequities and indignities that diggers (or their surviving family) were subjected to by governments and private employers. On May 21, 1921, a column titled 'Secret History' appeared, filled with gossip, scandal and rumour of the usual *Smith's* type. This occasionally ran items of digger interest, such as 'The Facts of Les Darcy's Enlistment'.[52] The following year this column became 'Secret History of the Day' and on September 13, 1924, the column appeared as 'The Unofficial History of the AIF' for the first time.[53] There was a request printed for digger stories, with two pounds and two shillings for the best story published each week. 'Live the old scenes over again. Give us your impressions of camp, troopship, trench and hospital. Mention your old cobbers ...' Couched in such terms, the invitation was clearly aimed at capitalising on the digger nostalgia industry. *Smith's* also wrote in the invitation that 'The truth is not objected to', a signal to the diggers that their traditional expressive forms were welcomed.[54] As Blaikie put it when describing the drawings made for this feature: 'The one essential of a *Smith's* digger joke drawing was that it should demonstrate one of the digger's virtues — his indifference to danger, orders, officers, rank and discomfort; his scorn of the foe, overwhelming odds, military police, and so on'.[55]

'The Unofficial History of the AIF' ran most weeks throughout the decade, carrying a mix of personal anecdotes, reminiscence and yarns. On February 14, 1925, for instance, the column carried the story of twin brothers who received exactly the same wound on the same day. The March 28 edition printed the yarn about the shell that had a digger's regimental number on its base. There were also occasional notices of reunions,[56] and another *Smith's* column, the 'Anthology of Anecdote' often appeared alongside or beneath the 'Unofficial History of the AIF', itself carrying items of digger interest.

Blaikie points out that *Smith's* was the first paper to realise that the Australian soldier of the AIF had gone to the war as a civilian rather than as a 'formal warrior' and that, back at home and a civilian again, he retained 'a nostalgia for his gay soldiering days'. 'The paper catered with enthusiasm for the nostalgia factor'.[57] Simple but carefully constructed anecdotes were the foundational elements of the 'Unofficial History'. Set during the war or just after, written in the past tense and from a first-person, participant-observer perspective and utilising digger slang, these anecdotes were redolent with nostalgia and typically 'digger' events and attitudes. 'Base Wallah' contributed this one:

> After the Armistice the troops were sent to Le Havre in a car-de-luxe of the '*8 chevaux ou 40 hommes*' brand. The weather being cold, the food crook, and the journey taking anything up to four days, the troops arrived at their destination in a somewhat peevish mood.
>
> Our crowd was reported to have busted open some railway trucks at Abbeville and helped themselves to cognac, and the OC No 5 Company at the Australian

delousing camp was deputed to intercept the train at Revelles and search it. He carried out his duties faithfully by telling the O.C. train his orders and saying 'I shall be back in twenty minutes with my staff and I will search thoroughly. If I find any cognac, heaven help anyone found with it.'

When the search was made the honour of the AIF was vindicated. Next morning, the OC No 5 found a bottle of cognac on his bunk.[58]

Again we find the essential digger motifs: putting up with the hardship of being transported in a horse carriage, cold weather and 'crook' food, all causes for complaint. The 'light fingered' nature of the diggers is emphasised here through their burglary of the cognac. Most importantly, the author lauds the diggers' ability to avoid detection and, the point of the story, their disdain for the official strictures of military rank is conveyed.

'The Unofficial History of the AIF' was a miniature *Aussie,* appearing in an otherwise mainstream, mass circulation weekly newspaper. In combination with *Smith's* other digger interests and its crusading ethos, the newspaper soon earned its sobriquet of 'The Digger's Bible'. *Smith's Weekly* thus became an important forum for the public presentation of peacetime digger concerns to a larger public than the more specialised *Aussie* and the essentially internal League or League-related journals, such as *The Listening Post*, *The Bayonet* and *League Post*.

While not having the same inspired feature titles, cartooning and writing talents that the pugnacious racism and yellow journalism of *Smith's Weekly* attracted, the peacetime rebirth of *Aussie* — the diggers' own paper — was even more specifically targeted to the needs and problems of the returned soldier. Under its wartime editor, Phil Harris, *Aussie* was revived in Sydney from April, 1920. In its pages were published much the same type of digger humour, nostalgia and prejudice as appeared in *Smith's* and elsewhere, much of it recycled from *Aussie's* own wartime pages or those of other trench journals, such as the *Kia Ora Coo-ee.* Monthly from April to December 1920, *Aussie* republished pages of cartoons, anecdotes, verse and related items from trench journals and ships' magazines under the heading 'Digger Journalism on Land and Sea'. This material was the staple fare of the trench journal, including items on 'The Compleat Cobber' and poems such as Paterson's 'Moving On', and Vance Palmer's 'Girls', both above the average quality of digger versification. Along with these works was an account of the sinking of the homeward-bound troopship *Ballarat* on Anzac Day, 1919, and a column entitled 'Prickly Pars' featuring such items as: 'A Corporal in 28 Mess whilst eating his dinner, discovered a button in the meat. He was told not to be afraid, as it was only part of the dressing', along with other assorted chestnuts like: 'If you want to make pants last, make the coat first'.[59] The sources for these items indicate an amazing number of outward- and homeward-bound troopship journals complementing the primarily land-based, active service trench journals. These publications[60] filled the long boredom and anticipation of the homeward-bound voyage of every returning digger. It is reasonable to suppose that few diggers would not have been exposed to the now full-blown expressions of digger culture contained in these publications. While these publications may have been avoidable from necessity or even choice on active service, there was little chance of avoiding them in the confines of a troopship. They were given an additional significance by their obvious status as souvenirs; mementos of a past horror survived that could be taken home to waiting loved ones. Homeward-bound troopship journals were therefore a most important mechanism for the process of nostalgia, bridging the hiatus between the active service trench journals and the peacetime continuations of those journals and their contents discussed above. *Aussie* made full use of their contents in constructing a mix of digger nostalgia and peacetime returned men's interests — the economy, advertisements for farming implements and for various male accoutrements, such as smoking pipes and, under the heading 'DIGGERS', an advertisement for 'Gumlypta Training Oil — used by all prominent athletes'. The demand for wartime nostalgia was also satisfied by the reprinting of all the wartime issues of *Aussie* in 1920 — 'on sale at all booksellers and by the Australian War Museum' (as the Australian War Memorial was originally called).[61]

While *Smith's Weekly* was a journal designed to appeal to a broad working- and middle-class readership, and reflected this in its more or less orthodox journalistic activities and interests, the peacetime *Aussie* was of and for diggers. Its interests were those of the digger's past, present and future. Politics, economics, women's views, finance, and so on, unless in some way related to the concerns of the returned soldier, were of little interest to *Aussie*. In this sense, *Aussie* was closer in its orientation to the various publications of state League branches or publications closely associated with the League. These included *The Listening Post* in Western Australia, *The Diggers' Gazette* in South Australia, *The Bayonet* in Victoria, the *Soldier* in New South Wales, and the *National Leader* (later *Leader*) and *Queensland Digger* in Queensland.

As well as these League and League-associated publications, there were also numerous publications from other returned organisations, such as the *Australian*, which was produced by the Returned Soldiers' Association in Perth in 1918. These generally lasted only a few issues, fading away as the organisations that published them became moribund or were absorbed into the RSSILA. Despite their origins and ultimate fate, there was a remarkable similarity of content in all these periodicals, with anecdotes, jokes, verse and

' "What do you think of London, Mate?" "There ain't a blessed verandah-post in it!" ', Cecil L. Hartt, *Humorosities* [1917], Australian War Memorial, Canberra, 1985, np.

other forms of digger culture being published, along with news items and comment upon issues of importance to returned men.

In peacetime, the diggers maintained their core traditions and self-image to a remarkable degree. Not only was the digger ethos celebrated, perpetuated and finally reified in those publications of the diggers' own organisations, but mainstream publications like *Smith's Weekly* also took an active, even pro-active interest in the affairs and sensitivities of the peacetime digger. It was this intersection of public and private, of folk tradition and nationalistic mystique that made possible the invention of the Anzac mythology and its 'Fifty-third Sunday' — Anzac Day.

CHAPTER SEVEN

'The Fifty-third Sunday'

Under the heading AIF — QUIET PASSING AWAY, the souvenir programme of the 1921 Anzac Day Commemoration Concert of the New South Wales RSSIL (it was still an Imperial rather than an Australian Imperial League at this point) carried this message:

> The following resolution was recently carried by the New South Wales Branch of the League:- 'That, in view of the official demobilisation of the AIF, effected as from today, this council places on record its hope that the traditions of the AIF will never be allowed to die, and that all ex-members of the AIF will, as the years roll on, stand together in civilian life as they did in time of war, all imbued with a desire to serve Australia with that spirit of self-sacrifice and loyalty with which, as sailors and soldiers, they served Australia and the Empire, inculcating loyalty and securing patriotic service in the interests of both as is laid down in the constitution of this League.[1]

This statement encapsulated the sentiments of the League and its members, sentiments that would — eventually — be given political and social effect. The desire for the 'traditions', the character, and the meaning of the AIF to carry through into the peace and to be turned to the building of a nation are clearly laid out here. The spirit of the AIF was not to be allowed to fade away but was to be transmuted into civil battle lines for the good of the country. The battle was fought on a number of fronts, though on none more fiercely than the struggle for the day itself.

'ANZAC' and Anzac Day

In his discussion of the development of Anzac Day, John Robertson points out that the first anniversary of the Gallipoli landing in 1916 took governments — federal, state and British — by surprise. A variety of mostly small-scale events had been organised by the states and a march of Australian veterans was scheduled to take place in London, ending symbolically at Westminster Abbey.[2] The federal government did no more than officially name April 25 'Anzac Day'. There were, however, many other unofficial activities spontaneously organised by groups in Britain, Egypt and across Australia. As Robertson notes, 'Little of the activity had been *formally* organized' (original italics).[3]

In its earliest form, then, Anzac Day was very much the product of popular enthusiasm and a widespread desire to mark the events at Gallipoli in some significant way. While it would be some years before the Commonwealth government officially proclaimed 'Anzac Day', it was from the very first observance so-named by organisations such as the Returned Soldiers Association of New South Wales (later to become part of the RSSILA).[4] The succeeding history of Anzac Day is a story of growing formal involvement as governments strove variously to contain and manipulate the potent emotional, nationalistic and militaristic elements that April 25 increasingly focused.

It is difficult to track any clear path of dates, events and personalities in the impetus towards having Anzac Day established as the central national observance. This is mainly because the RSSILA, the main pressure group proponent for such an observance, held national congresses and had a profile in the centres of federal power, but the organisation's main strength was in its state branches. At state meetings and congresses, a range of views about Anzac Day were expressed by various individuals and factions. However, from the early 1920s a consensus emerged, facilitating agitation for 'the 53rd Sunday' at both state and federal levels. The situation was further complicated by the fact that, with the exception of federal public service departments and the territories, each state had control of its own public holidays. This ensured that the type of political issue that Anzac Day became would differ in each state.

The first state to officially declare Anzac Day a public holiday was Western Australia. In 1919 the briefly reigning National Party Premier, Hal Colebatch, declared that returned soldiers in the employ of the state should be given the day off work with full pay. Anzac Day was made a statutory public service and bank holiday later that same year by the James Mitchell National-Country Party coalition government, though exactly which day it was to fall on and how it was to be observed was not stated. Accordingly, there was considerable confusion the following year, when some shops remained open and sporting fixtures, including horse racing, generally proceeded. Elsewhere confusion also reigned and it would be some years before a nationwide agreement would become installed as federal and state government legislation.

In 1921 Prime Minister William 'Billy' Hughes had suggested at the Premiers' Conference for the year that the numerous and various observances of April 25 taking place in venues large and small around the country might be regularised in some way.[5] In this, Hughes was only echoing the thoughts and statements that had been made by numerous state Premiers, League officials and others since 1916. Nevertheless, the significance of this federal suggestion was not lost on the League and its state branches. Over the next two years state congresses habitually discussed the question of Anzac Day in the expectation that the matter was now on the Commonwealth agenda and would be appropriately dealt with in due course. By 1922 the League had adopted a policy of advocating that Anzac Day be observed on April 25, that it be a gazetted and statutory holiday, and that it be regarded as Australia's National Day. The League prescribed that the morning would be appropriately solemn and commemorative, and the afternoon 'designed to inculcate the spirit of national pride and service in the people as a whole, and particularly school children'. Finally, the League wanted race meetings be forbidden and 'any sports to be held to be such as will develop a clean mind in a healthy body'.[6] At the 1923 Premiers' Conference in Melbourne, it was recommended that Anzac Day should be Australia's National Day; that it be celebrated on April 25; that each state would take whatever steps were necessary to implement the day's observance; and that the morning would be religious and commemorative, while the afternoon would be devoted to various appropriate addresses and the inculcation of Anzac into children.[7] These recommendations were in line with the general opinions of the returned soldiers' organisations and most of the digger periodicals. In 1920, for example, *Aussie* had suggested that Anzac Day be called 'Australia Day'.[8]

By 1923, then, the League had succeeded in having the essentials, if not the entirety, of its Anzac Day platform endorsed by the Commonwealth and the states. But implementation of these arrangements was to prove a long and difficult task, given the Commonwealth's lack of power to control holidays outside the territories and federal public service. From 1923 all offices of the Commonwealth government were closed on Anzac Day. Difficulties and delays in passing appropriate legislation at the state level, however, meant that a variety of Anzac Day arrangements were in place until the end of the decade. The processes and the perspectives involved in the attainment of the League's aims can best be appreciated through an examination and comparison of events in Western Australia, Queensland and Victoria.

The Battle for the Fifty-third Sunday

The battle for the fifty-third Sunday was fought in every state and at the national level through the lobbying activities of the League. In Western Australia the major thrust underlying the manoeuvres of the decade involved the resolutions of the RSSILA accepted at annual state conferences and, more importantly, the political machinations involved in having these resolutions translated into legislative reality. These activities mirrored similar moves in other states that were also reflected in the influential RSSILA

Federal Congresses. The 1922 Federal Congress, for instance, debated at length the appropriate manner in which Anzac Day should be 'celebrated', and adopted, among others, the following resolution: 'That Anzac Day be known as Australia's Nation [sic] Day and be observed only on April 25, and that it be gazetted by Commonwealth and State Governments as a statutory Public Holiday'. The conflation of celebration and commemoration that gives Anzac Day its peculiar resonance — and its primary function — was encapsulated in a Tasmanian resolution: 'That the Day be observed in such a manner as to combine the memory of the Fallen with rejoicing at the birth of Australia as a nation'. The Tasmanian delegates also proposed a practical solution to the problem of the conflicting aims of 'the Day'. This resolution simply and clearly reveals the underlying purpose of Anzac Day, the resolution of the tensions between the folklore of the digger and the national-military Anzac myth: 'That the morning be observed in strictly solemn manner and the afternoon be devoted to sports and carnivals of a national character designed to inculcate into the rising generation the highest national ideals'. Other resolutions involved deputations to the Prime Minister and Premiers, and the proper manner in which the Australian flag should be flown.[9]

As the editorial in *The Listening Post* pointed out on October 26, 1923:

> One of the most important decisions arrived at by Congress concerned the mode of celebration of Anzac Day. It was considered high time for this matter to be stabilised, so that the sorry spectacle of seeing the day spent by some in high glee and by others for personal profit, would not be repeated.[10]

By December *The Listening Post* was wailing 'League's Desires Flouted' when, under the Premiership of James Mitchell, the coalition government's *Anzac Day Observance Bill* provided for the closing of hotels and the prevention of race meetings on Anzac Day, but did not have the desired effect of treating the day as a Sunday. Forgetting the date and the status of RSSILA members (and his grammar), *The Listening Post's* editor claimed: 'The soldiers' wishes have been flouted on a subject that they would expect their views to receive tangible consideration'.[11] Things were no better the following year, when Anzac Day again received considerable attention at the State Conference and *The Listening Post* wrote of the need to make representations to the Premier regarding Anzac Day being made a 'sacred day'.[12] In 1925 the ninth annual federal Congress wanted Anzac Day to be treated as a Sunday. The August issue of *The Listening Post*, as well as reporting on the Congress, carried a bizarre anti-Communist advertisement on its back cover and a reprint of an article from *The Anzac Book*. This was a symbolic convergence of past, present and future that would increasingly characterise both the League and its 'organ' as both struggled towards the attainment of 'the fifty-third Sunday'.[13]

These machinations and their accompanying rhetoric became more insistent in every state as the decade progressed. The reason for this is suggested by Marilyn Lake. Writing of the national politics of the League, she says:

> As the conservatives consolidated their control of the RSSILA, so its membership declined. From an Australia-wide membership of 114,700 in October 1919, numbers plummeted to 49,721 in 1920, then 24,482 in 1923 ...Yet significantly, as its social base narrowed, the authority of the League as the representative voice of returned soldiers strengthened. Then, in the late 1920s and 1930s, as the depression deepened, membership slowly rose again.[14]

In 1929 the dawn service had been introduced to the Western Australian observance of Anzac Day — as had the official laying of wreaths on the (unfinished) Monument and the inclusion in the march of the sons (but not the daughters) of fallen comrades.[15] The essentials of the present Anzac Day ceremony were established by 1929. Anzac Day would now begin with the ghostly 'dawn service', consisting of a simple observance, the laying of wreaths, silence and a military salute, the ritual ending with the bugle solo. 'The march', always a feature of Anzac Day, had hovered around various starting times but now settled upon mid-morning, allowing diggers to lunch convivially in the early afternoon and subsequently to pursue the folkloric elements of 'the Day'. An essential aspect of Anzac Day was the targetting of the young for the inculcation of the ideals of Anzac, which, as noted, were heavily imbued with notions of sacrifice, duty and above all, of nationhood. None of these elements was restricted to the west.

Victoria's first observance of the achievements of Anzac extended over a period of two weeks in 1916, beginning with 'Anzac Week'. There were memorial services, public speeches, sports carnivals and fireworks. The *Age* published lengthy accounts of the action at Anzac[16] and patriotic editorials.[17] Melbourne had an enthusiastic second anniversary 'celebrating' the Gallipoli landing in 1917, sandwiched between the debates and campaigns of the first and second conscription referenda. According to the *Anzac Bulletin*, Melbourne Town Hall experienced 'an enthusiastic demonstration' at which a message from Prime Minister Hughes was read. This message was, not surprisingly, full of the diction that had been so conveniently to hand: 'valour', 'sacrifice', 'mantle of glory', 'Australia is united by the cement of their blood and sacrifice', and similar phrases. Some newspapers ran special articles and verse, there were special church services and 'State schools' had 'combined

children's and parents' demonstrations'. There was a march of veterans through
the streets, organised by the returned soldiers themselves, with services at
churches around the state, including one at the Melbourne Cricket Ground
attended by 15,000 people.[18]

The immediate post-war years saw an irregular but generally declining
pattern of observance, with a downward trend in participants. There was one
Anzac Day march organised by the League in 1921, when 24,000 men
paraded along Flinders Street to the Melbourne Cricket Ground. However,
it was not until 1925 that another march was organised and this attracted
only 7,000 participants. This number more than doubled in 1926 and in
1927, 38,000 diggers attended the march. This rise of interest in public
observance — at a time when League membership had been in serious
decline[19] — increased pressure on the Victorian Parliament to legislate for
a public holiday on April 25, in accordance with the undertakings of the
1925 Premiers' Conference.[20]

Despite the support of the RSL and their Anzac Day Commemoration
Council, which was chaired by Sir John Monash, the Country–National
Coalition's introduction of the *Anzac Day Bill* was opposed by commercial
interests when it was debated in the Parliament during 1925. It was argued
that another public holiday would unduly interfere with the organisation
and financial viability of businesses. The Labor Party and unions criticised
the Bill as a threat to workers' pay and charged that the League was not a
truly representative organisation, comprising only ten per cent of returned
soldiers. In an unlikely alliance, both business and labour interests were in
favour of Anzac Day being held on a Sunday, when it would inconvenience
neither workers nor their employers.

As elsewhere, debate also raged around the balance of commemoration
and celebration appropriate to the Day. Would all licensed premises and
racecourses be closed? Should they be closed only in the mornings; in the
morning and afternoon? Should there be sports and games? Was Anzac Day
to become, to all intents and purposes, a 'holy day'? Ultimately, as Wilson
puts it, 'against odds, governmental procedures had laid the essential foundation
for future Anzac commemoration in Melbourne by declaring Anzac Day a
statutory holiday in Victoria'.[21] On November 2, 1925, 'An Act to constitute
Anzac Day a Public and Bank Holiday and for other purposes' passed into
law. The effect on Melbourne's Anzac Day apathy was dramatic. The 1928
Anzac Day march was 25,000-strong, there was a successful and spirited
digger reunion at the Exhibition Building on 'Anzac Eve', and the Shrine
of Remembrance was now a viable project. The reasons Wilson gives for
Melbourne's sudden discovery of Anzac Day during this period are related

to the 'corporate significance' of various events and trends. These included the chance arrival of the Duke and Duchess of York in Melbourne on April 21, 1927, *en route* to Canberra for the official declaration of the national capital; Monash's personal appeal for all diggers to march; the support of the *Age* in publishing details of points of assembly, the march route and related information; and the march of Victoria Cross-holders organised by *Smith's Weekly*. Wilson also adduces a 'last chance' element in the fact that Melbourne was still the capital of Australia and sees this as 'the crucial factor' in ensuring the success of the Melbourne marches.[22] From this time on, Anzac Day was firmly established in the calendar of Melbourne's ritual moments. The 1929 observation warranted major coverage in the *Age* of April 25 and 26, including an editorial stressing the heavy cost of the Dardanelles campaign for Australia. Sir John Monash, who led Anzac Day marches until his death in 1931, told his 'Graphic Story' of the landing,[23] and a photograph of the wreath-covered Cenotaph provided impressive testimony to the public expression of Anzac Day sentiment.[24] There was a Commemorative Service[25] at the Exhibition Building in the morning, from where approximately 25,000 ex-servicemen (and some nurses) marched to the ceremony at the Cenotaph near State Parliament House.[26] Forty-eight bands accompanied the marchers, while the day was a 'strict holiday'.[27]

As in most of the states and territories, there was an early anxiety amongst Queensland returned mens' organisations and the Labor government to observe the anniversary of the Gallipoli landings in an appropriate manner. According to an anonymous historian of the Anzac Day movement in Queensland (probably H. Diddams), the suggestion for a suitable commemoration came from Labor Premier T.A. Ryan late in 1915 or early the following year. The Mayor of Brisbane then called a meeting on January 12, 1916, at which the Premier was present, as was the Governor (Sir Hamilton Goold-Adams), the Inspector-General of the Commonwealth Forces, the Leader of the Opposition, the Minister for Lands, Archbishop Duhig and a number of other religious and clergy. This group constituted itself the official Anzac Day Commemoration Committee of Queensland, holding its first meeting (and all subsequent ones to 1921) in the office of the Premier, on February 3, 1916.[28]

Here can be seen the beginning of the official processes involved in the invention of Anzac Day in one particular state. The representatives of imperial, political, military and religious power were brought together to ensure that Anzac Day would be 'suitably celebrated'.[29] The Committee noted that Anzac Day fell on a Christian Saint's feast day — that of St Mark — and adopted St Mark's winged-lion symbol of superhuman strength as an appropriate emblem. The following year a number of other officials and representatives of formally constituted interest groups expanded the Committee. These included more religious, both civil and military; six more Members of Parliament; Chancellor and Vice-Chancellor of the University; Under-Secretary for Public Instruction; and representatives of the National Societies of St George, the Caledonians, the Irish, the Overseas Club and the Australian Natives' Association, as well as the Military and Naval Commandants. In subsequent years representatives of the Returned Sailors and Soldiers' organisations were added, together with those of the Fathers' Association, the Chamber of Commerce and the Employers' Federation.[30]

Apart from the noticeable absence of any worker representatives, the makeup of the Anzac Day Commemoration Committee of Queensland very quickly came to reflect the main power and interest groups with a stake in the creation and the maintenance of the national-military mythology of Anzac. The failure or disinclination of the Committee, formed and steered by Labor Premiers T.J. Ryan and E.G. 'Red Ted' Theodore, to include union representation was a significant reflection of the cleavages between the official myth of Anzac and the informal traditions of the digger (the temporarily military 'bloke'). Whereas those attributes of the digger deemed useful to the Anzac myth — bravery, toughness and resourcefulness — were continually extolled by politicians of all parties and military commentators, the ordinary diggers themselves were usually excluded from participation in decision-making activities of any consequence throughout the post-war years.[31]

Also worthy of note are the inherent contradictions in the rhetoric and terminology of this group. As noted in Western Australia and elsewhere in the country, the problem of whether Anzac Day would be a 'celebration' or a 'commemoration' was present at the very founding of the Anzac Day 'movement' in Queensland. This problem was initially resolved in Queensland by the Committee's insistence that an appropriate observance of the day would discourage 'an unrestricted holiday' as the day 'should be observed most solemnly' and that amusement and sport should be discouraged.[32] Businesses and licensed premises were closed during the morning services, while returned soldiers were given the day off by both government and private employers. In 1921 the Committee wished to go even further than this and supported: 'a public holiday on the lines recently introduced in New Zealand, where by legislation race meetings and sports gatherings are prohibited, and licensed premises are closed on Anzac Day'.[33]

By 1918 the need for a recurrent structure to the Anzac Day observance had become strong. The Committee's Honorary Secretary, Canon Garland, proposed a set of arrangements that included 'the minute's reverent silence' as well as requiem or memorial services held early in the morning by the Church of England and the Roman Catholic churches, followed later in the day by all other denominations. There were also interdenominational evening meetings 'of an essentially solemn nature', allowing participants to pay 'their tribute to the dead, while renewing their promise to support and show sympathy for the living'. In 1921 the placing of flowers on the graves of soldiers accompanied by short services in the cemeteries was added. Its success guaranteed its inclusion in the standard program for future Anzac Days.[34]

The invention of Anzac Day in Queensland was also accompanied by the usual rhetoric:

> Queensland has taken the lead in the celebration of this day, on which Australia, by the valour of her sons, became entitled through an ordeal of blood, fire, and suffering to take her place among the great nations of the world, and to stand on equal terms with those peoples, both past and present, who have given of their best that humanity might benefit ...[35]

So began the author of the history of Queensland's Anzac Day movement in 1921. In a period notable for what now reads as near-hysterical expressions of imperialistic vainglory, this overlong sentence stands out through its combination of state parochialism, nationalism, militarism, masculinism and incipient racism. The author touches upon each of the crucial elements of the Anzac tradition, entwining them in a metaphor that encapsulates the dominant meanings that Anzac had for the members of the RSSILA and, it is reasonable to assume, for the many diggers who were not affiliated. Anzac — and hence its annual observance — is a 'celebration' of the valour, sacrifice and duty of Australia's fighting men. Those qualities, proven to all the world, or at least those nations of it deemed to be 'great', are those that entitle Australia to nationhood on equal terms with others who have also 'given of their best' for the good of all 'humanity'. Significantly, the past is linked directly to the present with the consequent implication of a continuity of virtues that reside in Australia's 'sons'. As usual with such rhetoric, the role of women as nurses, as family support and on the home front is ignored. Also avoided are the less salubrious activities and characteristics of Australia's valiant sons — their incidence of venereal disease, desertion, mutiny, the murder of prisoners, brawling, irreverence, swearing, drinking, gambling, the refusal to obey orders and general disdain for almost anything that did not fit comfortably within their narrow view of how the world should be.[36] In another formulation, that of the digger tradition, these attributes would be presented as virtues, but they were not characteristics useful to those intent on constructing a national–military mythology. These central themes of the Anzac tradition were echoed throughout the subsequent twenty-five sermons and speeches delivered by clergy and local dignitaries in Queensland on Anzac Day, 1921, and published in *Anzac Commemoration*. Of course, these themes were not unique to the Queensland view of the significance and appropriate observance of Anzac Day, as discussed elsewhere in this volume. Such was the grist of all the official expostulations of the national-military myth. The capturing of Anzac Day by the forces of officialdom in Queensland was replicated throughout the country.

Also replicated throughout the nation was the insistence on equality and comprehensive participation in the observance of Anzac Day. As the historian of the Queensland movement had it: 'The programme of the celebration gives ample opportunity for everyone, irrespective of creed or politics, to take part in the observance'.[37] This concern for as high a participation rate as possible is an essential element of Anzac and is found in all agitations for the declaration of April 25 as a national holiday. In Queensland the impulse for this was also well reflected in the broad — if not totally encompassing — constitution of the Anzac Day Commemoration Committee of Queensland. By the end of the decade, the Queensland proponents of Anzac Day as a national holiday had succeeded in having the day observed as such throughout the state,[38] as it would be in New South Wales, South Australia and Tasmania.

The 1921 observance of Anzac Day demonstrated a broad consensus regarding the perceived significance of the day and the events, historical and mythic, that it represented. All states other than Labor New South Wales declared the day a public holiday, and April 25 was made a public holiday for federal public servants. The national conference of the League in August decided that the structure of Anzac Day should reflect both the commemorative and celebratory impulses, with military and religious observances in the morning and, in the afternoon, 'sports and celebrations as become Australia's National Day'.[39] At the Premiers' Conference in October, agreement was reached that Anzac Day would be observed Australia-wide on April 25, regardless of which day of the week it fell. Although this decision was taken at the conference, it was not consistently implemented in each state. The conflicting interests of employers wishing to decrease the number of public holidays, of workers wanting to increase them, of governments seeking community consensus and of the League's influence on both government and the public debate, ensured that Anzac Day would be inconsistently observed for some years yet. In the process of debating a decrease in public holidays, South Australia's conservative Barwell government lost a parliamentary debate on public holidays. The result was that Anzac Day was declared one of the state's ten statutory holidays in November, 1922.

New South Wales became locked in deep conflict over the issue of the Anzac Day holiday, again involving the same interest groups of business, the labour movement, the League and the political leanings of successive governments. It was not until December, 1925, that the Labor Lang government succeeded in having Anzac Day established as a public holiday, with the proviso that when it fell on a Sunday, the following Monday would be a bank holiday. In the same month, Tasmania legislated for Anzac Day to be a 'close' holiday, following in 1927 with an amendment that dropped the King's Birthday in favour of Anzac Day as one of the state's statutory public holidays.[40]

There would be continued skirmishing between the same interest groups around and about Anzac Day well into the 1930s and later. But by 1929 the battle for Anzac Day as a national, 'close' public holiday, combining commemoration and celebration, had been substantially won. In Sydney it was estimated that approximately 15,000 people participated in the Anzac Day activities. There was a 'united' service in the Domain (though no Roman Catholic clergy were mentioned as being among the speakers), following the march from Government House that began at 9.45 am. Despite a dispute between the League and the Licensed Victuallers' Association over the opening hours of public houses, the *Sydney Morning Herald* was able, the following morning, to regale its readers with an impressive photo-essay of Anzac Day in Sydney.[41]

By the decade's end the RSSILA attained its objective of having Anzac Day gazetted as 'the fifty-third Sunday', not only in the west but in all states and territories of Australia. The states of Victoria, New South Wales and Queensland enacted legislation in accordance with the League's objectives — by 1925 in New South Wales under J.T. Lang's Labor government; by 1927 in Tasmania; by 1928 in Victoria under John Allan's National-Country coalition (though not instituted until 1930); and by 1930 in Queensland under A.E. Moore's Nationalist–Country Party coalition.[42] Although there were some differences of detail between these states, the effect of each one's legislation was to turn April 25 into a uniform or 'close' public holiday comparable to the religious days of Good Friday and Christmas Day. Rural communities continued their regional and communal varieties of observance, though these too gradually became more like the standard ritual that is the formal part of Anzac Day 'commemoration' throughout the country.[43] Anzac Day had, at last, been invented in the image that the diggers, through their organisation and their publications, desired. This invention accorded well

with the existing cultural and political imperatives within Australian society
at this time. As the 'Great' depression loomed and warlike rumblings were
heard from Japan and Germany, an annual ritual, a national calendar custom
emphasising populist nationalism within a framework of Empire loyalty,
military sacrifice and mainstream Christian dogma was not an objectionable
concept. That this formal structure might also have to tolerate some more
objectionable minor forms of social disobedience and excess was to be a
matter of complaint in the newspapers but hardly a serious problem. After
all, the structure of the simultaneously 'commemorative' and 'celebratory'
ritual had been established in such a way as to allow for both the formal
and the informal observance of the Day. These oppositions were perfectly
expressed in the relatively spontaneous innovation of the dawn ceremony
in the late 1920s. Later, the formal and the informal would meld. For now,
they were a metaphor of the oppositions involved in the observance of
Anzac.

The Great Inventor

It was fitting that in 1929, the year of national consolidation of the Anzac
Day observance, the Australian War Memorial would be inaugurated at the
national capital, which had been confirmed as such only two years earlier.
In the context of this monumental structure and national symbolism, the
figure of C.E.W. Bean again becomes of considerable importance.

War correspondent, diarist, editor, official historian, author and man of
troubled conscience, C.E.W. Bean has already featured at pivotal points in
the invention of Anzac. Bean has been shown at work on the trench journals
of Gallipoli, and on *The Anzac Book*. He has been exposed labouring on the
trench journals in France and as a journalist contributing to various official
and semi-official publications. Bean has been revealed as a war correspondent
through his dispatches, and as the mythographer of the bushman in his
pre-war journalism and related writings. Bean's inventiveness and energy
were not restricted to these considerable endeavours but included related
roles as the dreamer of national shrines and midwife at the birth of a central
'legend' within the national-military myth.

In an article published in the *Royal Australian Historical Society Journal* in
1927,[44] Bean provides convincing evidence that his earlier views on the
Australian bushman as a 'natural man' and his transferral of that perception
to the figure of the Australian soldier were still central to his portrayal of
the digger and the Anzac tradition. Bean repeats his view of the bushman
as a heroic battler against the inevitably overwhelming forces of nature and

sees this as the significant element in the Australian character. In wartime, this character manifested itself in what Bean was by 1927 able to describe as 'the old Anzac type', which he contrasted against the soldiery of other allied nations, writing 'that the Australian soldier was probably gayer, less stern and more a child of nature'. Bean depicted the diggers' anti-authoritarianism, particularly as it applied against the military hierarchy and related discipline, as being the self-image of the Australian male who, Bean said, 'called no man master'. The essentially civilian nature of the members of the AIF, their air of nonchalance, described as 'devil may care', and their prodigious feats of arms and bravery were all, according to Bean, essential indicators of 'Australian character'. This clear articulation of his continued lauding of the digger as a typical Australian bushman indicates that Bean's belief in this creed (which he had played a large role in inventing) had not diminished since the war. If anything, it had become more fervent, as his post-war involvement with the *Official History* and the Australian War Memorial both channeled and confirmed Bean's faith.

Although removed by distance and bureaucracy from the more mundane concerns of most diggers and other Australians, the creation of the Australian War Memorial in Canberra was another potent element in the invention of Anzac. The War Memorial was symbolic in its commemorative function as a memorial and tangible in its museological function of preserving and displaying the sacred artefacts of war. Ideologically, the War Memorial also had an overtly nationalistic philosophy and role that accurately reflected the aspirations and the ideals of those with an interest in the construction and perpetuation of the Anzac tradition. It combined the sacrifice commemorated in the memorials of each state capital with the aspirations of nationhood represented in Canberra itself.

Like so much else in the Anzac tradition, the War Memorial had its genesis on Gallipoli and in the passion and the perseverance of C.E.W. Bean. Just as *The Anzac Book* was a sacred memorial to the deeds of the digger,[45] so the Memorial was planned as a far grander monument to the heroism of the diggers, an imposing edifice of gleaming white marble (which proved too expensive, hence the sandstone) located fittingly in the nation's capital. Bean's vision and his agitation, aided by the support of General Brudenell White and other military and civilian persons of influence, sparked an increasing activity in the collection of artefacts and their preservation, together with the improvement of existing records, particularly war diaries. But this did not begin seriously until the British declared their intention to establish a National (susbsequently Imperial) War Museum in early 1917.[46] This decision implied that Australian war trophies might well end up in a British museum. In addition to these motivations, there was high-level interest in securing Australian war artefacts in Australia. By the end of August 1917, Federal Cabinet had approved the establishment of a war trophies committee. This soon metamorphosed into the War Museum Committee from June 1918. By this time, despite the reluctance of Britain to allow Australia, or other colonial participants, the right to transport trophies to their own countries, the collecting, classifying and preserving efforts of the Committee proceeded strongly. By 1918–19 there were almost six hundred Australians in London working on War Memorial activities, headquartered in thirteen rooms in Horseferry Road. At the end of the following year, the Australian team returned to Melbourne where its members were absorbed into the Commonwealth Department of Home and Territories as the nucleus of what would be the Australian War Memorial. Paradoxically, the Memorial was not opened until two years into the next war.

Bean's aspirations for the Memorial, as for so many other things, were written in his diary during 1918. Long before he was appointed Official War Historian, Bean declared the superior importance of Australian museums over those of Britain:

> For us, they are the foundation of our national museums; the beginnings of a series of national institutions, which I hope will equal anything in the world ... We want to encourage in Australian centres [of study and research] the principle that they are centres and not appendages of other greater centres elsewhere. We shall never get the best out of our peoples until this attitude, this enthusiasm and this national spirit is established ...[47]

Here is clearly enunciated the guiding beliefs and attitudes of Bean and, as Anne Millar concludes in her account of the memorial's origins:

> Bean's notion that the relics were 'sacred', that they required a 'final resting place', that the men of the AIF needed to be 'worshipped', and that the names of the fallen should be recorded on the walls of the building imbued the Memorial with the same quasi-religious sentiment. Irrevocably linked with the Anzac mythology, these ideas became firmly embedded not only within the precincts of the Memorial, but within Australia's national consciousness.[48]

While Millar takes the history of the War Memorial only to the end of 1919, and the Memorial would have to wait another twenty-two years before it was opened to those Australians Bean so desperately sought to unify, one important aspect of the invention of Anzac was unveiled in 1929. On the morning of April 25 that year, the Prime Minister, Mr Stanley Bruce, his wife and numerous military, political and civic dignitaries waited near the site of what would one day be the Australian War Memorial for the arrival of Lord Stonehaven, Governor-General. The Governor-General unveiled a white marble tablet that commemorated Australia's war dead, while a Guard of Honour paraded. The guard consisted of members of the armed forces in appropriate ceremonial accoutrements, Boy Scouts, members of the junior Red Cross girls, Girl Guides and schoolchildren. At 11 am this guard, together with the assembled returned soldiers, was inspected by the Governor-General, accompanied by the Chief of the General Staff, Lieutenant-General Sir Harry Chauvel and Rear-Admiral Napier. The official party also included most of the senior Federal ministers of the day.[49]

Bruce spoke of 'the sacred significance of the occasion' and said that the War Memorial was 'destined to stand as a symbol of Australia's nationhood'. Lord Stonehaven spoke of the spirit of sacrifice displayed by 'more than 60,000 Australian soldiers [who] had died to save the institutions and the birthright of all those who inhabited British soil'. 'The Last Post' was sounded at the completion of his Excellency's speech, there was one minute's silence, followed by 'Reveille'. Lord Stonehaven placed a wreath on the Memorial, as did Captain J.C. Dyett, Federal President of the RSL. The Bishop of Ballarat, deputising for the Anglican Chaplain-General, then pronounced the blessing.[50]

It would have to do for the time being. Bean's marble memorial did not yet stand (and never would), yet all that its (conception) stood for was appropriately and formally instituted on that day. The spirit, as yet, had little substance in the nation's capital. The Memorial's Eternal Flame could not yet be lit. But in concert with all those other Anzac Day observances, memorials and cenotaphs, the spirit and the myth of Anzac burned brightly enough.[51]

CHAPTER EIGHT

The Great Spectacle

Anzac Day is the most significant expression of the national–military myth. At the same time, and in the same places, it is the moment in which many elements of the official tradition of Anzac and the folk traditions of the digger are displayed. On this 'one day of the year' the public mythology of Anzac and the private, esoteric folklore of the diggers combine, collude and collide. Anzac Day is the expression, the practice, and the pilgrimage of Anzac. At one level, Anzac Day is symbolic of all that is the national–military myth — 'a central rite of the state', as anthropologist Bruce Kapferer describes the Day.[1] Yet it is also far more than a symbol; in an important sense it *is* the physical manifestation and validation of that myth and its meanings. Unlike most myths and the discourses that perpetuate them, the national–military myth can be observed in concrete form on Anzac Day. It can be observed in particular on Anzac Day 1929, the day on which this festival of nation achieved its familiar form in ceremonies observed around the country.

Anzac Day, 1929

Perth's 1929 Anzac observance shows that the now-familiar shape of Anzac Day ritual, formal and informal, was by this time established. The 1929 observance was the largest that Perth had experienced to that date. It was also the first year in which a 'dawn ceremony' was introduced to the commemorations. The *Western Mail's* reporter described this new element of Anzac Day in reverent prose:

> In the cold, clear air and dim light in the dawn of Anzac Day, many hundreds of returned soldiers and other citizens assembled in King's Park to lay fresh flowers at the foot of the State War Memorial in tender remembrance of the dead. It was a remarkable gathering for that early hour. A great muster of returned soldiers, and the warm response of the public, young and old, to the invitation of the Returned Soldiers' League to assemble there, must surely lead to this innovation becoming an established custom.[2]

This new custom, apparently emanating from a League suggestion,[3] began at 6 am, with a bugle call summoning participants to the Queen Victoria Memorial in King's Park, from where they walked to the still unfinished

War Memorial nearby.[4] Representatives of the interested parties laid wreaths on the Memorial. These included tributes from various military units, disabled veterans, the RSL, the Perth Legacy Club, Lieutenant-General Sir Talbot Hobbs, as well as the many private tokens from soldiers' friends, relatives and sympathisers. The dawn ceremony ended with 'Reveille', followed by a single shot and 'The Last Post'.

The marchers assembled well before the starting time and, according to the *Western Mail* reporter, in the unstructured moments before the procession: 'a merry time ensued, the men moving about meeting old comrades and telling old jokes. They made light of the tragedy that had marked them, but to the outsider, their excited jollity conveyed an indelible impression of pathos'. A bugle called the men to the march — it was usually referred to as a 'parade' — at 10 am where 'those who had prospered rubbed shoulders with those who, too plainly, had not'. The march was headed by thirty automobiles bearing the returned maimed, followed by the sons of fallen soldiers wearing their fathers' medals. Then came some of Western Australia's VC winners, including Captain Hugo Throssell. The VC heroes were followed by the commander of the parade and the staff and executive of the RSL. Then came the various military units, flanked by the Young Australia League, Boy Scouts and Girl Guides. Various bands, including those of the Salvation Army, Perth City and the Young Australia League, accompanied the marchers. In all, it was estimated that over 3,500 joined the march, more than 2,000 of them being returned soldiers. In the previous year only 2,326 had marched. The procession traversed the route from St George's Terrace through Barrack Street, Hay Street, William Street and on to the Esplanade, where the official service was to be held at 10.45 am.

Here at Perth's waterfront Esplanade 11,000 more than had attended the previous year's service turned out — an estimated total of 35,000. The official party consisted of Sir Robert McMillan, representing the King, attended by an Aide-de-Camp and accompanied by Lady McMillan and Lady Campion. The Governor-General was represented by Colonel H. Pope; the military by Lieutenant-General Sir J. Talbot Hobbs and Brigadier-General C.H. Jess, the District Commandant; the returned men by State president of the RSL, Colonel H.B. Collett; the state government by the members of the State Executive, the Minister for Railways, Mr Willcock; and the City of Perth by the Mayor, Mr J.T. Franklin. Not on the dais but in the enclosure nearby 'was a contingent of gowned students, representing the University Guild of Undergraduates'. These added, perhaps, a touch of colonial medieval ceremonial to this still-developing tradition.

The service began with six bars of the National Anthem, followed by the hymn 'Lest We Forget'. There was then a two-minute silence, followed by 'The Last Post'. Prayers were said, the hymn 'For All the Saints' was sung, followed by the Lesson and the hymn 'O, Praise the Lord'. The Anglican Archbishop of Perth, C.O.L. Riley, was Chaplain-General. Due to ill health, his address was read by Padre Riley, the Archbishop's son. The Archbishop extolled the moral virtues and the value of Gallipoli and the wartime struggle in general, appropriately alluding to the pioneering past: 'It showed to the world that though we were all far away from the homeland we were not far away from the old qualities which have made the race a name for itself and enabled us to subdue nature in many a new land'. The Archbishop regretted that the State War Memorial in King's Park could not have been completed as planned and supported the efforts of the RSL in regard to the welfare of returned soldiers, observing rather tartly that: 'The promise was "The last man and the last shilling". The last shilling is sometimes hard to extract'.

Various awards for merit were given to members of the armed forces, followed by the hymn 'Lead Kindly Light', then 'Reveille', the Benediction and the National Anthem once again. The March Past concluded the occasion. So ended the formal commemoration of Anzac Day in Perth, 1929.

The Meanings of the Moment

The competing and conflicting themes of commemoration and celebration noted in the very earliest Anzac Day observances are clearly visible in Perth in 1929. The official observance of the day is supposed to be solemn and reverential, as the headlines of the newspaper accounts are at pains to reinforce. However, at various points the informal and the demotic breaks into the formal and the official, communitas[5] threatens to swamp structure by filling with informality those spaces and moments left void by the official apparatus. The innovation of the dawn ceremony, an essentially spontaneous prelude to the day, was quickly appropriated by the Christian religious elements of the observance through the use of the term 'service'[6] — something it was not originally though has since become. Later that day, in the moments before being summoned to the march, old comrades appropriated the time and the public space outside the Soldiers' Institute building in St George's Terrace. Their mood and activity was hardly reverential, at least in the solemn sense required by the official mode of the morning. Attempting to reconcile these apparent ambiguities and oppositions, the *Western Mail's* reporter interpreted them as 'pathos'. The effect of such rhetoric was the incorporation of the demotic spirit of the digger, so obviously at odds with the 'sacred memories' and 'solemn observance' that headlined this article, into the official mood of mourning. Rhetorical devices such as this assisted the incorporation of select aspects of the digger tradition into the invented tradition of Anzac.

There is a strong hint of the egalitarian orthodoxy of the digger in the reporter's observation that the successful and the less so 'rubbed shoulders together'. The extension of this essential digger characteristic to the general community is seen in the involvement of schoolchildren, youth groups such as the Scouts and Guides and the Young Australia League. This was, as already observed, a consistent element of Anzac Day formalities — the attempt to involve as many members of the community and representatives of social groups as possible, particularly the young.

The emphasis on Empire and the British 'race' was still strong, though this was linked closely to Australian nationhood, and the loyalty and sacrifice demonstrated by the soldiers to ensure continued freedom. It seems likely that the emphasis given to these themes may have been a reflection of the fact that 1929 was the year of Western Australia's Centenary celebrations. However, matters related to 'the crimson thread of kinship',[7] as Sir Henry Parkes had memorably encapsulated the familial, social and cultural links with Britain, remained important across the country in relation to the promulgation of the Anzac tradition and its great annual spectacle.

The official segment of Anzac Day in Perth in 1929 was redolent with the symbols and signifiers of sacrifice, militarism, formal Christian belief and expression, loyalty to Empire, Australian nationhood and community participation. Nevertheless, as noted above, at crucial points in this carefully constructed ceremonial artifice, the festival articulations and activities of the digger threatened to subvert the formal framework. While these were relatively easily contained and/or incorporated into the formal ideology of commemoration, after the official morning ended, these folkloric elements needed to be given relatively free reign. The official ends to be succeeded — and balanced by — the folkloric. These informalities are discussed later. For now, it is appropriate to analyse the underlying structure and function of this Anzac Day observance.

The Ritual Structure of Anzac Day

The approach to 'festival' developed by Alessandro Falassi is particularly useful for illuminating the structure and meaning of Anzac Day. In his *Time Out of Time: Essays on the Festival*,[8] Falassi comprehensively surveys the historical, anthropological and folkloric approaches to festival, its meanings, functions and structure. From this study Falassi derives a definition of festival as:

... a periodically recurrent, social occasion in which, through a multiplicity of forms and a series of co-ordinated events, participate directly or indirectly and to various degrees, all members of a whole community, united by ethnic, linguistic, religious, historical bonds, and sharing a worldview.[9]

Anzac Day can be seen as a festival in these terms, particularly when the event was so assiduously promoted by its various sponsors as a day in which all Australians could — and should — participate. Falassi might well have added bonds of nation to this formulation, though he no doubt had in mind that this would be adequately catered for by his several unifying factors.

Falassi is able to construct a morphology, or archetypal structure, of festival that incorporates the various discrete but interacting elements. These elements, or 'building blocks', are ritualistic 'since they happen within an exceptional frame of time and space, and their meaning is considered to go beyond their literal and explicit aspects'.[10] There are ten elements in Falassi's festival morphology:

1. *Valorisation* — the framing ritual that begins the festival and which modifies the usual meanings of time and space. An area is claimed in some way for festival use, by blessing, adorning, delimitation or other means. If the framing ritual is religious in character, the term 'sacralisation' may be applied. As well as the claiming or reclaiming of a particular site, time is also marked in some special way. When festival is underway, daily time ceases and festival time, measured by the movement of the phases of the festival structure, takes over. This is 'time out of time'; a space of time within which the spectacle of the exceptional may be unfolded.

2. *Rites of purification* — formalities that cleanse, exorcise, safeguard and otherwise protect the community against internal and/or external negative forces.

3. *Rites of passage* — rituals marking the transition from one life phase to another. These may include initiation, even execution, and frequently involve younger members of the community.

4. *Rites of reversal* — the symbolic inversion of gender, status, class or other roles. The sacred may become profane, and *vice versa*.

5. *Rites of conspicuous display* — such performances allow the most valued symbolic objects of the community to be displayed, paraded, touched or otherwise honoured. Shrines, holy objects, sites and so forth are prominently displayed, paraded, and/or made the object of pilgrimage. 'In such perambulatory events, along with the community icons, the ruling groups typically display themselves as their guardians and keepers, and as depositories of religious or secular power, authority and military might'.[11]

6. *Rites of conspicuous consumption* — the abundance, even excess, of food

and drink, consumed in solemnity at feasts, banquets or other commemorative meals.

7. *Ritual dramas* — these may be staged in festivals, usually having creation, foundation or other fundamental, mythic significance. They present the sacred story of the community; and where it is not staged directly it is often hinted at in other elements of the festival.

8. *Rites of exchange* — These may involve the exchange of goods, money or symbolic exchanges such as pacification or thanksgiving. The purpose of such rites is 'to express the abstract equality of the community members, their theoretical status as equally relevant members of a *'communitas'*, a community of equals under certain shared laws of reciprocity'.[12]

9. *Rites of competition* — these include games, contests, and competitions of all kinds, including sports, which Falassi likens to ritual combats, the outcomes of which 'may be seen as a metaphor for the emergence and establishment of power ...'[13]

10. *Rite of devalorisation* — this balances the opening ritual of the festival, marking a return to everyday time and space.

Falassi does not argue that all festivals display all of these elements, only that these are the constituents from which all festivals seem to draw their structures and purposes. As he points out, 'a complete, or even an extensive morphology of festivals will correspond to very few — if any — actual events'.[14] The value of such a morphology is that it can be used to dissect a particular festive event in order to determine not only its structure, but the motives *for* that particular structure, and from there some indication of the purposes such a festival serves for its participants, its *communitas*. Anzac Day in Perth, 1929, was an event whose ritual structure can be usefully discerned through Falassi's festival morphology.

Firstly, the 'rites of valorisation' (sacralisation) identified by Falassi can clearly be identified in the sequence of events beginning with the dawn ceremony — the 6 am bugle call summoning participants to King's Park, the laying of wreaths and the ending of the dawn ceremony with 'Reveille', a gunshot and 'The Last Post'. It is important to note here that the term 'dawn service' was rarely used in 1929. The relative spontaneity of the dawn ceremony meant that it was a secular and military observance (a single shot, bugle calls); no religious elements were present, other than the generalised commemoration for those who had died. This facet of Anzac Day was not at this time a 'service'. It was not until some time later that a religious dimension was added to the dawn ceremony — an excellent example of the incorporation of the spontaneous 'communitas' by ideological 'structure'.

The march itself is an example of the 'rites of conspicuous display', in which the War Memorial is the principal shrine. The flags, banners and medals of the marching diggers are also icons of particular significance, as, of course, are the diggers themselves. On this Anzac Day, as on others, many marchers, their friends and families had made a special journey to Perth to participate in the ceremonies. These small pilgrimages are also significant in the light of Falassi's (and others'[15]) observations. Particularly important is the attendance and/or participation of representatives of the various power groups in Australian society. On this day in 1929, these included a representative of the Crown; a substitute for the Governor–General; representatives of the military; the RSL; and the state government, all of whom played prominent roles in the proceedings. Thus the main wielders of power in Empire, Australian and West Australian society displayed themselves as guardians of duly constituted secular authority. Religious authority was represented by the son of Archbishop Riley, Chaplain-General. It is quite clear from the tone and content of the newspaper accounts of Anzac Day in Perth, 1929, that these figures were also understood to possess such ritual status in the formal ceremonies.

The 'rites of reversal' identified by Falassi can be seen in the egalitarian traditions of the march, commented upon in the *Western Mail* report quoted above. This observation reflects the tradition that marchers do not wear insignia of rank. For the period of the march, the streets of the city are transformed from their everyday mundanity into a stage for the sacralised ritual of the procession. The egalitarian ethos already noted above clearly relates to this facet of festival structure.

The presence of the sons of the fallen wearing their fathers' medals[16] as well as the Young Australia League, Boy Scouts, Girl Guides, the junior Red Cross girls and the mandatory attendance of children organised in school groups — is an excellent example of the 'rites of passage' element identified by Falassi, following van Gennep.[17] There is a definite sense in which the participation of youth in the Anzac Day observance is an initiation, partly into 'adulthood', but also into prospective diggers for any future conflict.[18] Additionally, the concern for the inculcation of appropriate knowledge and values in the young is a continual theme of the Anzac mythologising process and is commented upon elsewhere.

Members of the armed forces were given merit awards at one point in the proceedings, a hint perhaps of the competitive elements noted by Falassi. Also, sports were played (despite the strong disapproval of the League) in the afternoon.

The speeches, cloaked in the language of Empire jingoism and racism, were part of a rhetorical approach that was already being called 'the Anzac tradition' in 1921, when the Mayor of Perth, Sir William Lathlain, delivered a speech titled 'The Traditions of Anzac', which was reported in the *Daily News*:

> When they mixed the blood of the Irishman and the Scotchman [sic] in this land of theirs, was it any wonder that they were hot-blooded and were able to fight? Then when they added the blood of the Welshman was it any wonder that they were impulsive? Then when on top of that they added the blood of the Englishmen, with their strong courage and resourcefulness, was it any wonder that they were able to acquit themselves as they had done?[19]

Sir William concluded by exhorting those present to 'live up to the traditions of Anzac'.

The often strident emphasis on the British character of the diggers and the 'spirit' of Anzac was a feature of much Anzac Day rhetoric. Lathlain was doing no more than echoing the sentiments expressed elsewhere around the country, such as those of Queenslander H.J. Diddams, for whom the Australian soldiers of the war were 'British to the core'.[20] Anzac Day speakers also often emphasised the sacrifice of the soldiers for King and country. In this respect, the 1929 Anzac Day observance differed not at all from those held previously. As the *Western Mail* rendered the dominant tone under the sub-heading 'The Message of the Hour', referring to the service on the Esplanade:

> Remembrance of the unreturning dead and sympathy for those who loved them and lost them; thanksgiving for the victory which was the result and the reward of a sense of sacrifice unparalleled in the whole history of the world — these were the emotions predominant in men's hearts at a great combined Anzac Day service ...[21]

This official form of recognition for deeds done fits well with the notion of 'exchange' given by Falassi, though 'recognition' might be a better term for this category of festal structure, at least as it applies to Anzac Day.

Finally, came the ritual at the Esplanade. At this penultimate moment, representatives of the major guardians of authority made their speeches and a clergyman pronounced the blessing. Representatives of the King and the Governor-General were present on the official dais, as were representatives of the armed forces, the RSL and the state government. In accordance with Falassi's morphology, the festival is therefore concluded with a 'rite of de-valorisation' (desacralisation, in this case) that mirrors and balances the opening ritual. In terms of the nationalistic and imperialistic imperatives of Anzac Day, we might also note the function of the 'March Past' as an appropriate conclusion to the appropriation of everyday time and space that occurs during the morning of Anzac Day. The marchers march away from the site of the festival, figuratively carrying with them its meaning.

One other important element identified by Falassi can be recognised here — the ritual drama of Anzac Day. The formal structure of Anzac Day was — and is — designed to ritually replay the events of April 25, 1915. The dawn ceremony was instituted by popular desire (an anonymous suggestion from within or to the League, it seems)[22] to commemorate the moments leading up to the dawn landing. As they did on the fateful morning, the diggers assembled before the march, using the moment for jollity, as had the first Anzacs awaiting the boats to take them to shore at Anzac Cove. The march is the great spectacle of the day and can be interpreted as representing the movement of the troops from the boats to the beaches and, for many, far beyond. In the context of the march itself, this moment has the effect of a 'standing down', symbolic of the laying down of arms and the imminent return of the digger to civilian life, as the marchers do after the final service, marking the sacrifice of those who died — absent comrades.

After the service is completed, the marchers, like the first Anzacs, have completed their 'duty' and are, effectively, 'on leave'. At this point, although the final rites have been carried out, the festival is far from over. Now it is the time for the rites of conspicuous consumption to have their place as the essential, informal obverse of the morning's formalities. The imbibing of alcohol, often to excess, and the numerous Anzac lunches and dinners that complete the day are also part of the festival structure of Anzac Day. These are accompanied by the inversion of the everyday in the playing of the gambling game 'two-up'. Legally proscribed, on Anzac Day the playing of this game is tolerated (usually) by the authorities, as are, up to a point, other antisocial actions that may be carried out under the influence of alcohol.

This discussion of Anzac Day in Perth, 1929, provides a template against which it is possible to compare Anzac Day from place to place. While the details and finer points of local observance vary from community to community, the pool of elements upon which Anzac Day ceremonies can draw remains constant.

Anzac Day in 1929 in other capital cities showed a variety of festival elements drawn from those identified by Falassi. Melbourne, in a year of record attendance at the march and service (approximately 25,000), had no dawn ceremony. There was a morning service, a march and a wreath-laying ceremony at the Cenotaph near State Parliament House.[23] Similar, if smaller, observances were held throughout the state, and there were numerous private and public services and ceremonies at churches, private schools, RSL sub-branches and elsewhere.[24] Adelaide had no dawn ceremony, but the march ended at a 'cross of sacrifice',[25] and sports were played in the afternoon. Brisbane had no dawn ceremony but held a cross of sacrifice before morning church services. Hobart had no dawn ceremony (and most of the event was rained off),[26] while Sydney had a march and service.[27] The Governor, Sir Dudley de Chair, was present at the Domain service, where the Police Band played Chopin's 'Funeral March' and 'Reveille' and 'The Last Post' was sounded.[28] As well, there was a 'service at dawn' at the Cenotaph in Martin Place. This was organised by the Australian Legion of Ex-Servicemen's Clubs of NSW. The hour of the service and wreath-laying was that of the Gallipoli landing, 4.30am.[29] In Canberra there was no dawn service or procession through the city, and the event centred on the standard memorial service on the site of the Australian War Memorial.[30]

The structural elements and, thus, the ostensible meanings of Anzac Day were unchanged across the nation. Likewise its functions and meanings, at least those nearest the ideological imperatives involved in the observance, remained the same. Using the detailed study of Anzac Day in Perth, 1929, in combination with the more general investigation of Anzac Day already undertaken, it is possible to draw some conclusions about the meanings and the purposes of Anzac Day in relation to the two traditions of Anzac and the digger.

Anzac Day provided a moment in which the official promulgation of the national-military myth, and the folkloric formulation of the same myth, was held up for display and participation. Both were present and both collaborated in one another's meaning: the diggers consented to the militaristic and religious authority of the march and service; the forces of authority represented by those institutions colluded in the afternoon of excess and the lifting of certain social and legal proscriptions regarding the diggers' celebration of their private ethos. The two were displayed as different, yet complementary.

This collusion on Anzac Day in Perth, 1929, as elsewhere, generated a spectacle in which numerous semantic pairs or binary oppositions familiar from Western traditions of dualism were invoked and mediated. These included life/death, youth/age, sacred/profane, and body/soul. These pairs are clearly present in the rhetoric and in the structure of the Anzac Day formalities and can be seen in terms of the overall purpose of festival identified by Falassi.

There are also other oppositions that fall into the oppositional categories of structure and anti-structure, or communitas, as identified and interpreted through the symbolic anthropology of Victor Turner:

Structure	**Communitas**
public	private
military	civil
formal	informal
complex	simple
hierarchic	egalitarian

Anzac Day's ability to conflate these oppositions, and so mediate them within its ritual framework, is a process that is usefully seen in terms of Turner's approaches. If Turner is correct about the fundamental need of social and cultural orders for a continual mediation of communitas and structure, the machinations of Anzac Day provide a glimpse of the ongoing processes involved. These processes are generally invisible and unremarked during the rest of the year (though no less potent in their function for this) and are revealed and manipulated in various ways on Anzac Day, where their true symbolic and cultural power is demonstrated and made available for those who wish to partake.

In order that such powerful forces do not break out and threaten, perhaps even fracture, the social order, it is necessary to have some sort of control mechanism. This is provided by the festival structure of Anzac Day's bounded twenty-four hour period of festival in which the forces involved are given expression. Nevertheless, they are well defined and delimited, for such powerful social and cultural forces are extremely dangerous and must be hemmed about by various symbolic forms of control. Even as they are displayed, they must be contained. Hence the elaboration of establishment or mainstream religious ritual, of military ceremony, the well organised 'march' through city streets along the official course. The other formal elements of festival identified by Falassi are all instituted to permit, but also to control.

The body of un-uniformed ex-soldiers constituting the core of the Anzac Day 'march' is symbolic of potent and dangerous powers within society. They represent the inchoate, the anarchic, the savage potential that all societies must hold in reserve for the ultimate barbarity of war. Now they are civilians, but once they were trained bearers of arms, takers of lives and committers of unknown savageries in battle. They were heroes in the right time and place. However, when they returned, particularly at a time of increasing unemployment and in large numbers, they were perceived by many as a potential threat to social order. The mutiny of 15,000 AIF troops at Liverpool and Casula (NSW) on February 14, 1916, had not been forgotten.[31] Nor had the anti-social activities of large numbers of bored returned soldiers during the war. Demobilised soldiers, from early 1919 to June 1920, when

the last of the 270,000 troops posted overseas returned, were restless, troublesome, often unemployed, and sometimes unemployable. What was the
country to do with them?[32] Not only were such men symbolic of the
essential savagery in society and hence apart from other Australians in
significant if unnameable ways, they also represented a very real political
threat to the status quo in the immediate, unstable aftermath of return. They
were, therefore, doubly dangerous.

The immediate post-war period in Australia was one of particular disruption and difficulty. Almost immediately upon the end of hostilities arose
the fear of 'Bolshevism', occasioned by the Russian revolution of 1917 and
the subsequent attaining of power by the Communists. In Australia, this
success emboldened the local socialist and militant industrial groups such as
the Industrial Workers of the World (IWW) and led to public demonstrations
of support for 'Bolshevik' political and social philosophies, or at least such
philosophies sufficiently radical to be considered Bolshevistic by government
and large segments of the press. There were serious anti-Bolshevik riots in
Brisbane in March, 1919, inflamed by a demonstration of former IWW
members in other militant industrial groups such as the Industrial Union
Propaganda League. The demonstrators (some of whom were returned soldiers) displayed red banners in defiance of the *War Precautions Act*,[33] and the
police force promptly stopped the march. Such was the fear of Bolshevism
that a crowd of 8,000 loyalists, consisting mainly of returned soldiers, attacked
the headquarters of the Russian Workers Association. Police met them with
bayonets, there were shots fired, and nineteen rioters and police were wounded.
The following evening, March 25, loyalists (again including large numbers
of uniformed returned men) passed a resolution against the Queensland
Labor government that demanded the gaoling or deportation of Bolsheviks.
This meeting turned into a riot in which revolvers were discharged and a
number of persons injured. Three days later another anti-Bolshevik demonstration was addressed by the president of the Queensland branch of the
League, Pearce Douglas, a Gallipoli veteran. On March 30 almost 2,000
returned soldiers demonstrated against Bolsheviks and anarchists outside
Queensland's Parliament House.[34]

Elsewhere in the country there were similar confrontations between
opposing political and industrial points of view. In May, 1919, returned
soldiers joined Fremantle waterside workers in a series of riots and demonstrations against the conservative Colebatch government's attempt to introduce
non-union labour to the docks. Revolvers and bayonets were deployed against
the strikers by police in a series of bloody confrontations. There were extensive
strikes and confrontations between meat-workers and police in Townsville

during 1919. These involved returned soldiers being employed as 'scab' labour. The national Peace Day procession of Saturday, July 19, was another occasion for the display of political views. In Melbourne the procession proceeded with only minor disruption, but the next evening there was an unsuccessful attack on Victoria Barracks by about sixty uniformed soldiers and sailors. This was followed the next afternoon by a large crowd of mainly serving and discharged soldiers (according to some estimates up to 10,000) marching beneath a Union Jack to a Cabinet meeting in Treasury Gardens. A few hundred entered the Government Offices and presented a set of demands to the Premier. These involved the grievances of the soldiers against police brutality and harassment, and the release of those imprisoned and fined during the disturbances of the previous weekend. The Premier's response was not to the crowd's liking and he was pursued, attacked and effectively held prisoner for an hour or so until over three hundred police managed to restore order. Another crowd of 6,000 attacked the Russell Street police station that night, demanding the release of those arrested during the previous riots.

1919 was also notable for a further outbreak of the pneumonic influenza virus that had killed almost a thousand Australians in 1918. In 1919 the dead numbered over 11,000, mostly young and middle-aged Australians. The epidemic did not end until February, 1920. Unemployment, poverty and general hardship were commonly experienced throughout the country, exacerbated by the great numbers of returned servicemen seeking employment and some way of returning to the 'normality' they remembered of the pre-war years. But Australia, stunned by the impacts of war and divided by the bitterness of the conscription issue, had changed and would continue to change throughout the 1920s. There was to be a further polarisation of conflicting political views. The Australian Communist Party was formed in September, 1920, with branches in Melbourne, Sydney and Perth. The ALP conference of 1921, in Brisbane, adopted the socialisation of the means of production, distribution and exchange as Labor Party policy. Various organisations were formed to combat this threat from the left, such as the murky Melbourne 'White Guard' established in 1923 and a number of other bodies, not formed until the early 1930s, but drawing their philosophies and their members from the political and industrial struggles of the 1920s. The League itself came to officially espouse extremely conservative views, particularly in relation to 'the crimson thread of kinship', and Australia's general relations with Britain and the Empire.

In his study of incipient Australian nationalism, *Lion and Kangaroo* (1976),

Gavin Souter observes of the impact of war upon the previously almost totally Anglo–Celtic and complacently 'British' population of Australia:

> The war had tempered the loyalty of Australians to Britain in two senses of that word: in some cases it had hardened the imperial consciousness; in others it had moderated that consciousness, even replaced it with a new awareness of nationalism.[35]

As Souter notes, the process of slackening the links with Britain undoubtedly stems from the Australian experiences of the Great War. While there clearly remained a great reservoir of popular sentiment towards the Empire connection, as demonstrated by loyalist displays and the need for Anzac Day rhetoric to rehearse the verities of empire loyalty, Prime Minister Hughes's attitudes and activities at the Versailles Peace Conference regarding reparations clearly set the tone for the gradual but definite development of Australia as an autonomous nation-state. In the period under consideration, this development was highlighted by the Balfour Declaration of 1926, which gave all members of the British Commonwealth of Nations equality (at least on paper). An imperial conference of 1929 began work on the document that would, in 1931, become the Statute of Westminster. Although this Statute, which effectively gave Australia total control of its legislation, was not adopted until the fear of Japanese invasion impelled Prime Minister John Curtin's famous speech, realigning Australia away from Britain and toward the USA, it marked the effective end of Australia's political subservience to Britain.

Despite these matters of high policy gradually weakening the political ties, many Australians felt strong emotional links with Britain, its culture and its monarch. The Honour Avenue in King's Park, Perth, was originally planted with oaks.[36] While South Australia abandoned the holidays of the Prince of Wales's Birthday and the King's Accession Day in favour of Anzac Day in 1922,[37] and Empire Day (May 24) degenerated from pomp and ceremony to popular festival,[38] it was still necessary for Anzac Day speakers to emphasise the traditions and 'spirit' of the British 'race', fusing these with Australian nationhood and with the imagery of blood and sacrifice, as did H. Diddams describing the Anzacs in 1921:

> Red with their blood is our new charter of national life and of liberty, the expression of sacrifice which alone can make us a nation worthy of the noblest Commonwealth of Nations. British to the core, they lived and fought and died.[39]

As far as the League and its supporters was concerned, these sentiments were as appropriate in 1929 as they were when first uttered in 1921. The sense of national birth and hence distinct identity believed to have occurred at Gallipoli was given expression on Australia's 'nation day' in terms of the genetic and cultural inheritance of Britain. Australia could not exist as a nation, it seemed, unless enveloped within the traditions of British kinship, a shared monarch and membership of an Empire, even if this last was increasingly termed 'the Commonwealth'. Thus the official expressions of nationhood that filled the air and the newspapers each Anzac Day, while incorporating the distinctive qualities of the digger and his tradition, ignored the awkwardly xenophobic attitude of the AIF, including at least some of its officers,[40] towards the 'Tommy', his superiors, his government, his class system and, after the novelty of 'Blighty' paled, even his weather. Here was yet another point at which the official tradition of Anzac incorporated an ameliorated element of the digger tradition into itself.

These difficulties and conflicts were to be especially troublesome for government and business interests as well as citizens, coming after four years of war during which Australia had lost a significant portion of its young men. The year 1919 was also less than twenty years from Federation, and while it was possible and desirable to celebrate Gallipoli and its successors as the great moment of national birth, it was a very different thing to deal with the practical, day-to-day problems of making such a nation grow to maturity. Glorious deeds of arms were wonderfully symbolic, and essentially so, but their negotiation and incorporation into the ideological necessities of nationalism was a thorny problem. The invention of Anzac was at once a traditional response to the need to commemorate the dead and to celebrate the living, in the anthropological terms outlined by Falassi, but it was also a particularly and cleverly Australian response to immediate and ongoing day-to-day problems of social control. Not only was it culturally appropriate and necessary, it was also of great value politically. Anzac at once helped to defuse the potentially powerful disruptive forces of communism and industrial militancy in general, and also provided a convenient vehicle for manipulating the symbolism of national cohesion and the inculcation of desirable values and attitudes. While those espousing the Anzac ideology were always a minority of politicians, officers and businessmen, Anzac's conflation of elements of the digger tradition with Australian nationalism and empire loyalty gave it an immensely broad appeal in the 1920s. The hegemony of Anzac could also be extended to the young, through refining the story of Simpson and his donkey and through the dragooning of schoolchildren and the sons (later, also the daughters) of the dead heroes into the great spectacle itself.

Anzac Day occurred in a place as much as in a period of time. It was the same event happening at the same time throughout the land. Simultaneously, it symbolically replicated yet another time and place, and an event that occurred there and then. Another time, another place were transported each year to Australian soil to ensure the perpetuation of the most significant moment of the past in the present. The value of that moment lay in its meaning as the birth of an Australian nation, not only in symbolic terms, but in the notions of blood and sacrifice with which Anzac was imbued. It was that specificity of time and place that Anzac Day attempted to recreate as well as to commemorate and celebrate.

Related to the replication of the experience of Gallipoli, particularly of the landing, was the simultaneous observance of the day throughout the country. The great spectacle of Anzac Day was not, in the period under consideration or since, restricted to capital cities. In small cities, country towns, halls and memorial parks across Australia, the same elements of ritual and riotousness were combined in ways appropriate to each community and its resources. The full panoply of dawn service, march, religious service, cross of sacrifice and related ceremony may not have been achievable everywhere. But it was from these common elements that each local community selected those facets of observance appropriate to its needs and possibilities. Often, as in the case of Toowoomba, there were — and continued to be[41] — local embellishments within the overall ritual framework,[42] but always the aim and purpose of the observance remained the same. This national, chronological simultaneity (or as close to it as differing time zones would allow) was central to the nationalist imperative of Anzac Day. The great spectacle was therefore a commemoration of military sacrifice, a celebration of the demotic elements of the digger tradition and an affirmation of nationhood.

But there is a problem here for a nationalistic mythology: the defining event of nationhood did not take place on the nation's own land but in an unknown land on the other side of the world. This rarely acknowledged fact imparts a certain hollowness to the very core of Anzac. To some extent, this explains the increasing fervour with which Anzac Day has been observed. As Richard White, writing of war memorials, points out: 'they are memorials to a trauma that would not go away'.[43] It seems likely, even at these early stages of the invention of Anzac that this was an unacknowledged but tacitly recognised ambivalence that needed to be repressed and smoothed over in the construction of an appropriate mode of observance.

To some extent, imperial rhetoric and its inflated universalisation of the Anglo-Celtic were convenient in disguising this difficulty, but even in the 1920s many were beginning to lose faith in that particular ideology and its ceremonial formalities. There was a need for an element of Anzac Day that avoided the formalities, the imperial and religious rhetoric, the pomp and ceremony; an element that, in no matter how small a way, allowed Australians to stake a claim to their national war heroes in a manner that would affirm the simple but powerful communitas of the dead and the living, the community of the nation rather than the pomp of official nationalism. This grassroots or folk need is, as noted, expressed often in League and other popular publications. It found its ritual expression in the dawn ceremony, that simple, quiet but extremely symbolically charged moment of spontaneous affirmation. The enormous popularity of the dawn ceremonies took Anzac Day proponents and organisers by surprise.[44] It was not long before this event was incorporated into the formal observance of Anzac Day, and it remains one of the most popular modes of commemoration, still thought of by many as the core of Anzac Day.

The dawn ceremony provides another example of the ongoing interaction between the formal and the informal. The contest between these opposing but interrelated imperatives for time and space within the liminal moment of festival reflects the deeper cultural forces involved in Anzac Day. The dawn ceremony was communitas breaking in on structure so as to assert an uncomplicated, even un-hegemonic folk-national meaning[45] for Anzac.[46] The wreaths placed at dawn are mostly woven from Australian flowers. War memorials are frequently made of local materials. Most importantly, they stand on Australian soil. This is one fundamental reason for the amazing number,[47] size and cost of World War One memorials, plaques, honour rolls and similar icons that dot Australia. It is not simply the appalling death rate and its effect on local communities but a related need to connect those faraway tragedies with the land, with the community and so with the nation. While this may be an unsophisticated understanding and articulation of nationhood, it is nevertheless a most profound understanding and a healing of the hollowness at the heart of Australia's 'National Day'.

The 'Old Diggers' Day'

The folkloric imperatives within Anzac Day are various and stem from the distinctive culture of the digger created during the war and perpetuated through peacetime. These imperatives include the desire to keep the observance of the day simple and informal. Related to this are the aspects of carnival and excess that typify the conclusion of the observance — these are the ingestion of food and drink, the playing of sports or games and the symbolic recreation of the experiences of war through the telling of tales and jokes, and the swapping of songs and verse. These demotic elements combined with the formal commemoration of Anzac to provide the great central spectacle of twentieth-century Australia.

The cohabitation of the formal and the informal was present from the very first. John Monash's description of the first Anzac Day in Egypt, 1916, provides excellent evidence for the early blending and inversion of the sacred and profane. This inaugural observance began with a solemn religious commemoration ('short, but very dignified'), climaxed with 'The Last Post' and was followed by 'a skit on the memorable landing by a freak destroyer manned by a lot of corked blackfellows hauling ashore a number of tiny tin boats full of tiny tin soldiers. It was screamingly funny'.[48]

The parodic nature of this Anzac Day commemoration is a clear indication of its folkloricity, particularly as it draws on well-documented British folk ritual traditions involving blackened faces, inversion and pointed humour. An attempt is being made here to find appropriate modes of commemoration for the awesome event that took place twelve months before. The official apparatus responded according to its ceremonial traditions with a Christian service and militaristic bugle music. The diggers — those who were quite possibly about to die — made light of the situation in accordance with the venerable tradition of the carnivalesque, which included sports and amusements in the morning and 'a great aquatic carnival' in the Suez Canal involving, according to Monash,[49] 15,000 diggers swimming and frolicking naked. It was, thought Monash, 'a sight worth seeing'. Monash concluded his account by describing the event as 'this famous day — OUR DAY'.[50] Ever since then, Anzac Day has consisted of this dual character of commemoration and celebration, of the solemn and the silly. In describing this event and commenting that such a response 'in peacetime, would have seemed like blasphemy',[51] Inglis here seems uncharacteristically insensitive to the nature and structure of the Day, and its accompanying rites of the sacred and the profane. The central point and purpose of Anzac Day is to meld the intersecting, if not always complementary, traditions of the digger and of Anzac.

Another element of the Anzac Day observance that emerged very early was the desire of the diggers to keep things simple — a mirroring of their own uncomplicated worldview. While the RSSILA agitated for a public, formal observance of Anzac Day, the peacetime *Aussie* articulated the more demotic viewpoint. Lamenting the 'jazz' appearance of the 1920 march (presumably in Sydney, where *Aussie* was published) the editorial opined: 'The Aussie has not developed the Procession habit. Processions bore him stiff — especially taking part in them'. The editorial went on to suggest a naval and military parade in preference to 'rough processions composed of undrilled ex-soldiers in shabby uniforms and civvie dress'. Then, expressing a view quite common outside the RSSILA, the writer opts for an almost totally informal Anzac Day observance:

It would be advisable to make the day one of memorial services and unit reunions and cut out the military feature as far as the Aussie Army is concerned. The digger is now a civvie. Why make him into an imitation soldier once a year?[52]

This rather more realistic and, given the decline of League membership numbers, probably more widespread appreciation of the status of the digger as an ex-soldier was another indication of the ambivalent and sometimes antagonistic elements requiring accommodation in the invention of Anzac Day. *Aussie* lauded the splendour of the 1919 procession of 5,000 uniformed — and so still-serving — Anzacs through the streets of London. But back home, and out of uniform, *Aussie* put the popular view that a moment of simple observation followed by sanctioned alcoholic excess was appropriate for Anzac Day.

The informal elements integral to the celebration of Anzac Day were the taking of food and drink in specifically commemorative and convivial contexts and manners; the playing of games, whether of a competitive sporting nature or for gambling; and the festive interaction of 'old diggers', involving the previously-mentioned elements and the nostalgic exchange of anecdotes, song, verse and related memorabilia originating in the Great War. While the last of these continued throughout the year at unit reunions, sub-branch 'smoke-nights' and the like, the practice was particularly marked during Anzac Day, where and when it functioned to bring the past into the present within an emotional and symbolically charged ritual moment. It was this convivial interaction, saturated with excess and the carnivalesque, that provided the essential informal obverse of the formal Anzac Day activities and which continually re-vivified the folklore and, hence, the values and attitudes central to 'diggerhood'.

Anthropologists and folklorists have demonstrated the significance and centrality of food preparation and consumption customs, particularly in relation to 'festival' or other ritualised situations. The nature and form of such practices obviously varies with time and place, but certain essential continuities persist. These include the preparation of 'special' or otherwise different foods (including alcoholic or other beverages) to be consumed immediately before, during or after the ritual moment, and the consumption of these foods in circumstances of heightened solemnity or unusual indulgence. Surveying accounts and studies of Anzac Day between 1916 and 1929 shows that food and drink have always been an essential of the informal observance of the Day.

Kitley's study of Anzac Day in Toowoomba (Qld) in 1916 (and, comparatively, 1977) provides evidence of a free dinner for all returned men, the purposes of which were '(1) to honour these men who have done so much for Australia, and (2) to start a reunion dinner, when year after year Anzac men shall meet each other, and with thrilling reminiscences tell of the brave old days when Australia's sons fought for freedom and honour'.[53] As well, various toasts were drunk. Kitley might also have mentioned, according to Sackett's 1985 response to and refinement of Kitley's argument, 'people gathering for drinks prior to their attending dawn services, of the sharing of a morning meal, or what happens in the wake of the afternoon tipple session'.[54] These were, and are, widespread elements of Anzac Day observance, mentioned in many accounts. Worth quoting at length for the light it throws on the importance of food and an unusually detailed ethnographic account of an early Anzac Day observance, is the following on Anzac Day, 1923, at Gutha (WA):

> Much has been said, and much has been written, as to the most appropriate manner in which Anzac Day should be commemorated, but the solution of the problem has been attained by the RSL in the outlying district of Gutha, where the happy medium between wowserism and purely secular celebration was struck.[55]

The observance took place at the home of League President, Mr Frank Kendall:

> Soon after midday all sat down to a sumptuous cold collation, and after the usual loyal toast had been drunk, the President made a short, appropriate speech, and in conclusion asked for a two-minute silence, in memory of fallen comrades, which was observed by all standing to attention. Subsequently, a short toast list was duly honoured. After dinner, until 5.30 pm, was most enjoyably spent by all in gossiping, singing and card-playing, but the most pleasant feature of the afternoon consisted in the remembrance of the children by the returned men. A suitable and expensive present was given to every child in the district, and fruit, lollies, soft drinks, and all the various delights of childhood were present in abundance ...
>
> As the sun was sinking, all were once again summoned to the festive board, which was loaded with all the good things imaginable, surmounted by a huge birthday cake, some two feet high, gaily decorated, symbolical of the birth of Australia as a nation. After tea a euchre tournament [sic] took place, songs were sung, and all went merrily until well towards midnight, when, amidst a salvo of farewells, appreciations of the day's celebrations was expressed on every side ...[56]

The article concluded by thanking those who provide the decorations, the catering and 'a number of songs'.[57]

How representative of other Anzac day observances in smaller communities was this one at Gutha is difficult to know. Detailed accounts such as this are unusual. In its combination of the requirements of Anzac Day observance with an Australia Day celebration, a birthday party, a harvest supper and a village social, Anzac Day at Gutha, 1923, was probably not unrepresentative of such events across the country at this time. Neither the formal nor the informal activities associated with Anzac Day had then settled down into a routine or standard form. People were improvising and, in their improvisation, revealed their ambivalences and their aspirations for the significance of the day.

Accounts of early Anzac Day observance frequently refer to the playing of games and sports, particularly those that took place among serving troops in France. Bean's account of Anzac Day on the Western Front in 1917 is well worth quoting in full, not only for the information it contains but to indicate that Bean was not above purveying the folkloric himself:

> Many of the Australian units marked the day by holding athletic and military sports meetings. The spectacle of five teams of enormous Victorians in a tug-of-war, on a corner of the Somme battlefield where old shell-holes had been filled in, and the whole brigade seated round as in an amphitheatre, was worth travelling leagues to see. Another brigade had a Hindenburg race, confined to men who lately reached and for some hours occupied the Hindenburg line — By a strange coincidence, this was won by a Western Australian who is reputed to have been the first man to reach the line in the fight.[58]

After the war, sporting events of various kinds, such as tennis or lawn bowls, sometimes featured in Anzac Day observances, particularly in country areas. But this practice was increasingly frowned upon, as was made clear in *The Listening Post*:

> That there are still narrow-minded people who cannot grasp the solemnity of Australia's sacred day is proved by the necessity for Archbishop Riley's reproof to the 'flannelled fool' tennis players at Fremantle.[59]

Since 1922 it had been official League policy to advocate that race meetings be forbidden on Anzac Day and that only those sports 'as will develop a clean mind in a healthy body' be allowed. While the Commonwealth government had immediately accepted this policy, it had no power to control holidays in individual states, and this meant that a wide variety of official Anzac Day observances existed. However, while wishing to have gambling on horses banned, the League made no mention of the famous diggers' gambling game 'two-up', an illegal form of gambling that nevertheless persisted in many parts of the country.

'Two-up' or 'swy' is an old gambling game of European origin (it is known primarily in Scots and German forms) that was popularly played by Australian troops during the war. In recounting his experiences aboard an outward-bound transport in 1917, a New Zealander serving with the AIF observed that gambling was a crime, but nevertheless very popular, and that two–up was 'the most favoured game'. He also describes the game being played at the front.[60] A very young Frank Clune wrote home on August 20, 1915, saying that two–up was being played at Gallipoli that day, until shrapnel forced an adjournment.[61] Bean provides a description of the game and further evidence of its popularity:

> 'Two-up' is the universal pastime of the men. This is not the case of a few sharpers, a close set who start a 'school'. A few devotees, as soon as time hangs, get together in the yard or the side street and ask if anyone wants to 'give it a go'.' Someone flings three pennies once or twice — a ringkeeper is chosen; and then 'Two-up' starts.[62]

This account also gives an indication of the ambivalent 'legal' status of the game, which is an important facet of its Anzac Day significance:

> The game is nominally illegal, I think; but at any rate in this company they wink at it. The OC told me that he lets the men get all the drinks they want on a period like this out of the line; and I daresay he looks on 'Two-up' the same way.[63]

The wartime popularity of this game, unlike that of other widely played gambling games, such as 'Nap', 'Poker', 'House', 'Banker' and 'Crown and Anchor',[64] persisted into the peace, quickly establishing itself as an important facet of the diggers' Anzac Day revels.

The playing of two-up on Anzac Day is a practice that signifies far more than the playing of a street or pub gambling game. Two-up is a concretisation of central digger values and attitudes. It is, firstly, a group activity that, through the physical method of playing — a ring or circle of men — compels a physical closeness and focus usually absent in Australian male relations except in a rugby scrum, which a two-up 'school' in many ways resembles. The game therefore mirrors the digger ethic of masculine camaraderie, reinforced by the gambling aspect, which can be seen as a metaphorical transformation of the folkloric belief that life is a lottery. Two-up was therefore particularly well suited to its wartime role, given that it was equally possible to lose one's life as it was to lose one's money. The reverse was also true, of course, and so the game had the function of balancing such ultimate imponderables and of mediating the fundamental tensions involved in them. When the danger of possible extinction was removed, two-up retained its place as an honoured icon of the diggers with the threat of death being replaced by the lesser, but still real, threat of prosecution for participating in an illegal activity. This prohibition was, unofficially at least, removed on Anzac Day itself, a fact that only served to reinforce the anti-authoritarian appeal of two-up. As well as involving illegal and often disapproved behaviour, two-up was played in an atmosphere of drinking and associated rituals of masculinity, such as swearing, competitiveness and occasional violence. It was also (inaccurately), perceived as a uniquely Australian pastime, a factor that increased its appeal to the aggressively nationalistic digger ethos.[65]

It is important to note in relation to this argument that two-up, while played before the war, did not attain its central popularity until after the first experience of battle at Gallipoli, where it attracted an ineffectual 'official taboo', which probably enhanced the game's attractiveness:

> In the hollows and gullies groups of men were often noticed, and the observer would see the faces momentarily turned towards the sky and then towards the earth again — actions denoting interested eyes following the flight of the spinning coins.[66]

All these attributes of the game are implied in the various yarns involving two-up schools mentioned elsewhere. These yarns, as previously noted, frequently show the casual bravery of the digger under stress and under fire, playing during a bombardment by the light of a German flare, or on the beach at Gallipoli despite a fatal hail of Turkish fire.[67] The celebration of such a game in peacetime on each Anzac Day is a continued affirmation of all things digger, a fact that explains the ambivalent, interstitial status of the practice, betwixt and between the legal and the extra-legal.

The toleration of this gambling game, together with its associated and complementary activities of food and drink consumption, and the reproduction of yarns, songs, verse and other oral memorabilia of the Great War, is an indication of the significance that Anzac Day holds. Whatever the religious, civic and military demands that shaped the formal commemoration of Anzac Day, the popular tendency towards celebration was at least as strong. The toleration of the informal by the institutionalised, and *vice versa*, was matched by the participation of the private in the formal. This interaction, this interdependence, produced a potent national spectacle that focused the grassroots and the regional in the national.

Within this interface is the convivial interaction of old comrades reliving their youthful adventures and their moments of glory and inglory. Yarning, singing, reciting, jesting, eating and drinking in festive manner — and, should they wish, risking a few bob on the two-up — the diggers perform the essential obverse of the official Anzac rites. As they did in war, so they have done their duty in peace by attending the various ceremonies, services and parades. They have put up with the brass hats, the politicians, the padres and the cheering, unknowing crowds lining the parade route. After the public spectacle has been performed, it is time for the private confirmation of the diggers' in-group ethos. Each is necessary, each is complete within itself; each validates the other. For these reasons, Anzac Day remained in the form it achieved in 1929, even after the very different military and social experiences of World War Two and after.

CHAPTER NINE

Community and Nation

The Good War

Once again in 1939, this time as a consequence of Britain declaring war on Germany, Australians went to fight on foreign shores. After Prime Minister Menzies announced the sombre news by radio on September 3, it seemed as though what was to become known as 'World War Two' would follow much the same course as the Great War. Although there was not such a great upsurge of Empire and national patriotism, many believed that the war would be over before it began. The conflict was far away; the ties of Empire and motherland were not as strong as they had been; the government was hoping to avoid panic by pushing the slogan 'business as usual'; and, most of all, there did not seem to be any fighting. This new kind of war soon became known as 'the phony war', far away from the sunny outpost of Empire down at the bottom of the globe.

Nevertheless, the country went onto a war footing. HMAS *Hobart* and five destroyers sailed in October. The Empire Air Training Scheme was established in late November and Cabinet decided to raise and send an expeditionary force across the seas. In conscious affirmation of the Great War tradition, this force was named the 2nd AIF and elements of its 6th Division embarked for the Middle East on January 10, 1940. There would be 7th, 8th and 9th Divisions as the war years passed, but the first infantry engagements were in January, 1941, when the 6th Division fought at Bardia and captured Benghazi the next month. Tobruk, held by the 9th Division, was besieged in April and relieved from August that year. Elsewhere, 2nd AIF troops fought in Crete and in Syria. In December the Japanese, already aggressors in Manchuria and Indo-China, attacked Pearl Harbour and Malaya, following up with a rapid advance towards Australia. John Curtin, Labor Prime Minister from October 1940, made the speech in which he stated unequivocally that 'Australia looks to America' in late December, 1941. A few months later Singapore Island surrendered and Japanese bombs fell on Darwin, soon to be followed by raids on Derby, Wyndham and other Western Australian northerly settlements. World War Two had reached Australia's sleeping shores.

In March, the very wide-awake General Douglas Macarthur arrived with the first of what would be by June, 1942, 250,000 American troops scattered, sometimes crammed, into accommodation around the country. While the war in Europe and the Middle East ground on, a new Pacific war was being fought from and around Australia. On these fronts a number of battles and events were seen to resonate strongly with the established ideals of the digger and Anzac. 'Tobruk' was one of these, stimulated by films and books during and after the war referring to the defenders of that city, including the AIF, as 'the Rats of Tobruk'. The dogged jungle fighting over New Guinea's Owen Stanley Ranges from August 1942 to early 1943 added another digger victory to the mythology, as did subsequent operations in the Pacific islands.

In addition to the official naming of World War Two diggers as the 2nd AIF, popular sentiment rapidly linked the warriors of 1939–45 to those who had returned from their battles only twenty years before. *The Bulletin* published a cartoon in October 1940 showing an Australian and New Zealand digger of the time being urged on by an older man in Great War digger uniform, the upturned brim of his traditional digger hat bearing the date '1914'. Nor was it unusual for World War One diggers to enlist in this second round, which may account for the revival and reworking of Great War digger songs, yarns and slang. The World War One 'Horseferry Road', a song with strong anti-authoritarian lyrics, grew a chorus and became one of the most widely-known soldier songs of the war — 'Dinky-Di, Dinky-Di; I am a digger and I won't tell a lie'.

While a few such ditties were used again, the different circumstances of the 1929–45 conflict required new material. This was speedily forthcoming and conformed to the established genre of digger ditties. In the Middle East, the diggers reacted to the Charles Chauvel film *Rats of Tobruk*, in verse:

> They showed a flaming picture 'ere
> So we thought we'd have a look.
> It was supposed to be about
> The blokes who held Tobruk.
>
> Well spare me days, I've knocked around
> And seen a thing or two,
> Was even right there in Tobruk
> For six months of the blue.
>
> That picture was a flaming farce,
> You ask the old brigade.

They only showed the Stukas once,
While on their bombing raids.

The blokes were all clean-shaven
By the barber in the town.
They never showed a dust storm
With its pall of murky brown ...

The poem continues, detailing the considerable shortcomings of the film from the point-of-view of the 'Rats of Tobruk' themselves. The last two stanzas of the fifteen-stanza poem give the final verdict:

Now if you sit this picture out
I'll shout for all the bar;
You can have my boots and webbing
Plus my Western Desert Star.

Oh, we tell you mates, it's awful,
Don't fall for such a show.
If they want to make a picture
LET THE DIGGERS HAVE A GO.[1]

That important element of the digger persona, anti-authoritarianism, often combined with the age-old soldiers' privilege of complaining, was continued and even amplified throughout the Second World War. In New Guinea they expressed their frustrations to the tune of 'Bye, Bye Blackbird':

Pack up all your bags and kit,
This flaming place is up to shit:
Bye, Bye Buna.
Beans for breakfast
Beans for tea
No more flaming beans for me
Bye Bye Buna.

The CO does not love or understand us,
He only loves the bullshit that he hands us.

To the Orderly Room, grab your pass,

> Stick this place right up your arse ...
> Buna, bye bye.[2]

Digger yarning of the Second World War continued the tradition of skiting, big-noting, humorous self-deprecation and, wherever possible, the humiliation of the British and the Americans. There was the one about the the old first war veteran colonel and the young American major who bump into the stock rabble of Australians in Tel-Aviv. The American officer complains to the colonel that the diggers failed to salute. The English colonel's reply is to say that at least the Australians walked around them; 'their World War One fathers would have walked right over us'.[3] This was a re-working of a World War One story, as were a number of others expressing the digger's traditional disdain for rank and ceremony.

The 'bad language' badge continued to be worn with pride and given frequent reinforcement in new versions of old anecdotes like that about the Captain returning late to barracks one night and being unable to recall the password. A dispute ensues between the Captain and the sentry until a hoarse voice calls from a nearby tent 'Don't stand there argufying all night, Dig, shoot the bastard'.[4]

These adaptations and extensions of digger lore drew from the well-established stereotype of the digger. There was no need to invent a new group persona for the Australian foot soldier at the front — it was ready and waiting, already full-blown, polished and resplendent with over two decades of sacred polish applied around the land each Anzac Day. On the other 364 days of the year there had been issues of papers like *Aussie* and *Smith's Weekly*, and the various publications of returned soldiers' organisations. There had been the smokos, the reunions and the funerals as time and wounds took their toll. In the families of diggers around the nation there had been the telling of tales, the singing of the old songs, the recitation of verse and the remembering of good mates gone. That which was digger permeated the cultural being of the nation. Even on the first Anzac Day in 1916, commentators had been describing marching troops as 'a bronzed, hard, wiry lot of men';[5] by the 1930s this language and the stereotypes embedded within it had become the accepted rhetoric of the digger. The next generation, exposed to all this as well as the deeds of valour learned in their school lessons, were already diggers long before they followed their fathers' footsteps across the battlefields of this new distant conflict.

War came to the Australian people at the end of one of the hardest economic decades in the country's history. Large segments of the workforce had been unemployed, sometimes for years, with consequent familial and social disruption. Economic circumstances sharpened existing political and industrial tensions during the 1930s. There was a polarisation of left- and right-wing politics, and a monotonous toll of strikes, lockouts, protests and food marches as the queues at dole-offices and soup kitchens lengthened. In Western Australia over 16,000 people were being paid sustenance relief. The Mitchell National–Country Party government put these to work on public projects of various kinds, including public buildings, roads, sewage and drainage works and reconditioning the goldfields pipeline. In April 1933 these projects accounted for sixty per cent of men receiving government assistance, a figure that had risen to ninety-five per cent by 1935.[6]

Unemployment peaked in the early years of the decade, but joblessness, homelessness and bitter poverty were to be the lot of many through most of the 1930s. Suddenly, as those who experienced it still recall, there was a shortage of labour. The demands of a wartime economy and the raising of large forces of civilian soldiers almost immediately ended unemployment. Women became essential components of the war effort, being employed in manufacturing, munitions, farming and in the armed services in capacities additional to the traditional roles of nurses and entertainers.

Then there were 'the Yanks'. The American use of Australia as a staging base for the re-conquest of the Pacific brought thousands of Americans to a previously insular society. Their dress, speech, habits and, especially, their comparative wealth were an eye-opener to Australians. There were inevitable conflicts between American and Australian troops, with riots and fights, some very serious, becoming almost commonplace. More than a few diggers feared losing the affections of Australian women to the desirable and exotic 'Yanks', as a number of contemporary parodies testify. The 'Digger's Hymn' uses the tune of 'The Marine Hymn' or 'The Halls of Montezuma':

> From the streets of Melbourne city to St Kilda by the sea,
> The Aussie girls are showing us how silly they can be.
> In the good old days before the war the Aussie girls were gay,
> But now they've gone completely mad on the twerps from the
>   USA.
>
> With their dashing Yankee accents and their money flowing free,
> They have stolen all the hearts but those who have got eyes to
>   see.
> And when this war is over and the Yanks are no more seen,
> They'll prefer an Aussie dustman to the glorious marine.

> So, here's to the girls who have been true to the boys of the
>   Southern Cross;
> They have helped the brave to see it through, it will never cost a
>   loss.
> But the girls who skinned the digger for the glamour and the
>   swank,
> When this war is finished it's the Aussies they'll have to thank.[7]

The American threat on the vulnerable homefront was something that the diggers of the first war had not needed to face. There were many relieved Australians — not only men — when the Yanks finally went home in 1945. To the tune of 'When They Sound the Last All-Clear' was sung the words 'When they send the last Yank home, how lonely some women will be'.[8]

Over 33,000 Australian soldiers died during or as a result of the six years of fighting. More than 180,000 were wounded. After the celebrations over victory in Europe and the more significant Victory over Japan Day of August 15, 1945 it was time, for those who could, to get back to their everyday lives as soon as possible. Significant social and political changes had taken place during the war. Australians had to get used to censorship and war effort propaganda on an unprecedented scale. The internment of foreign nationals became a major preoccupation of the authorities throughout the war years.[9] Women had become valued members of the wartime workforce. Demobilisation and post-war reconstruction were certain to be difficult tasks for all governments. Even more difficult for some was the readjustment to civilian life. There was restlessness, discontent and unhappiness, but as the country was still surfing a wave of relative prosperity, the industrial problems that troubled Australia after the first war were not as severe in the late 1940s and 1950s.

RSL membership swelled as troops returned, boosting the still-considerable political influence of the organisation. In 1946 the League boasted almost 374,000 financial members, a historic peak.[10] The experiences of the 2nd AIF had created a whole new generation of diggers. 'Anzac' and 'Gallipoli' were still hallowed terms, but they now reverberated alongside 'Tobruk' and the 'Kokoda Trail', among the many places where the digger tradition had been continued, refined and enriched.

One of the few studies of the popular memories of World War Two soldiers is John Barrett's *We Were There*. This survey of 3,700 diggers questioned, among other things, the subject of 'mateship'. Sixty per cent said that 'mateship' was either their first or highly favoured choice of things they liked about life in the AIF. However, as the author himself notes: 'What did the favoured "mateship" mean? Almost anything could be implied by the many short answers'.[11] There seems little doubt that these men considered mateship to be an essential component of their wartime experience, but as there is relatively little mention of the subject in their songs, yarns or verse, perhaps this is an element that has been reinforced by retrospectivity and four decades of nostalgic reminiscence, polished by reunions, Anzac Day festivities and the inevitable softening of time? This is not to say that mateship was not present, simply that, as in World War One, it was not articulated at the time.[12] Dale Blair's study of the wartime and post-war experiences of the 1st Battalion also suggest that much of the construction of the stereotypical digger, especially in relation to egalitarianism, resourcefulness and initiative, was a retrospective process.[13]

In his study of front line Australian soldiers during World War Two, *At the Front Line*, Mark Johnston reaches a similar conclusion, noting that misery — composed of hardship, grief, separation from home and family and a general disenchantment with the structures of army life — took 'primacy' over the traditions of mateship. The digger of the 1939–45 conflict was a much more critical and individualistic soldier than his father's generation had been in the Great War.[14] There was also serious conflict between the voluntary 2nd AIF and the Civilian Military Force, a standing militia.[15] Nevertheless, the ideal of mateship persisted among frontline soldiers, giving their lives purpose and meaning, and extending the tradition established during 1914–1918. The official mythology of Anzac continued to reinforce the notion of mateship, duty and sacrifice, both throughout and after the war.

The processes that had kept alive the myth of Anzac and of the digger after the First World War continued after the Second. As their fathers had done after the first war, large numbers of men joined returned organisations. Just as they had done for their fathers, these organisations continued to provide a focus for socialising, for welfare and for the ongoing re-creation of wartime experience. 'The Digger's Bible', *Smith's Weekly*, had crept down to a circulation low of 80,000 per week in 1939. During the war it had an enormous revival with circulation, rising to over 300, 000 as peace returned in 1945.[16]

However, by 1950 *Smith's* was out of business, a victim of financial problems and the declining public interest in things 'digger'. The RSL had lost 100,000 members, a decline that would continue until the early 1960s.[17] Australia was in the upward spiral of an economic boom and the beginnings of a mass migration program that would eventually remake the society and its culture. Through the following years the smokos, prawn nights, euchre parties and reunions continued at the many returned soldiers' clubs and other convenient premises around the nation. Yarns were swapped and the old songs were sung in the smoky atmosphere of beery companionship. In New South Wales and in some other states, 'the clubs' became a multi-million dollar industry. This comfortable affluence was insidiously undermined by the increasing Australian involvement with the war in Vietnam.

The Last Anzacs

Australian troops first went to Vietnam as advisers (Australian Army Training Team Vietnam — AATTV) to the South Vietnamese government and its army, which were struggling to hold back a powerful Communist insurgency from the north. That was in 1962. Already there were almost 11,000 American advisers and other military personnel there. The Cold War warmed and the West, the United States in particular, began to perceive a deepening Communist threat in Southeast Asia, so the American presence escalated. As an ally, Australia was expected to, symbolically at least, signify its support and agreement for American action in the region. As the war worsened through the 1960s, America committed ever-greater resources. Australia, under a compliant Liberal-Country Party government, was dragged further into the conflict as well. By 1965 the AATTV numbered one hundred personnel stationed throughout South Vietnam, particularly in the north of the country. In May that year, the first Australian regular army troops left for Vietnam. Still the war escalated as the North Vietnamese Army and Viet Cong guerillas conducted an effective campaign against the South and its protectors. In mid-1966 the government committed another 4,500 regular and national service troops. By 1968 there were over 8,000 Australian military personnel stationed there, mainly in Phuoc Tuy province. Australians ground forces, in alliance with American and South Vietnamese troops, fought a bitter jungle war of counter-insurgency now familiar as the first 'TV war'.

In conjunction with the members of the regular army, already imbued with generations of the digger and Anzac myth, these men[18] would continue the digger tradition, spinning new-yet-old yarns, songs and verse about their situation. The traditional 'alphabet' format reappeared, as did songs, sayings and verse in the traditional mould established by the diggers of the First World War. The yarns about humorous exchanges between soldiers and army doctors continued in stories like the one about the young bloke who is told he has 'Vietnam Rose', a virulent strain of venereal disease. 'You'll have to go to Saigon for a month or so', the doctor tells him. 'Why Saigon, Sir? That's where I got it'.[19] The hard-bitten Aussie image was maintained, especially in the face of the Americans. At a US hospital a medic is collecting urine samples from marines thought to be infected with malaria. By the end of the day he has amassed dozens of specimen bottles. He asks the pathologist-in-charge what he should do with them. 'Send them to the Australians', came the reply, 'they'll drink anything'.[20]

Versifying and songmaking continued, as it had in previous wars. The language and subject matter of Vietnam digger songs is stronger and rather more bitter than that of previous generations, but the tone and intent remain the same, and the soldiers are still 'boys' who, to the tune of 'Jingle Bells', sang 'Christmas in Vietnam':

> Driving through the mud in a Jeep that should be junk,
> Over roads we go, half of us are drunk.
> Wheels on dirt roads bounce, making arses sore,
> Lord, I'd sooner go to hell than finish out this war.
>
> Chorus:
> Jingle bells, mortar shells, VC in the grass,
> We'll get no merry Christmas cheer until this year has passed.
> Jingle bells, mortar shells, VC in the grass,
> Take your merry Christmas cheer and shove it up your arse.
>
> Christmas time is here as everybody knows,
> People think it's dear, Aussies think it blows.
> All at home are gay, children are at play,
> While then boys are stuck out here so bloody far away.
>
> The moral of our song, it's plain as it can be,
> Please, no more midnight carol sings and screw your Christmas
>   tree.
> There's one more thing to say before we have to leave:
> Vietnam is not the place to be on Christmas Eve.[21]

The World War Two digger ditty, 'Bye, Bye Buna', quoted earlier was updated to refer to the main training camp in Victoria:

> Pick up all you bags and kit
> Puckapunyal's up to shit
> Bye, bye Pucka
> Stew for breakfast, stew for tea

no more bloody stew for me
Bye, Bye Pucka.
No more climbing over bloody mountains,
We'll soon be drinking Fosters out of fountains.
No more blanco, no more brass
You can stick them up your arse
Pucka — bye bye.[22]

The classic digger song of World War One and World War Two, 'Dinky Di' or 'Horseferry Road', lived on in the mouths of a new generation of diggers.[23]

As the war in Vietnam escalated, so did the demand for greater Australian participation. By mid-1964 the regular army was being stretched for personnel and resources. Once again the federal government had to contemplate the introduction of compulsory national service — 'conscription', as it was unpopularly known. This time there were no referenda. Conscription, the calling of a set proportion of twenty-year-old males for two years, was introduced by the Commonwealth in 1964–5. Eligibility for call-up was determined by the public relations disaster of a birthday ballot in which those whose birthdays came up in a Lotto-like, random selection of numbered marbles were liable for 'National Service'. A third of the Australian troops who served in Vietnam were 'nashos'.[24]

Although there was no opportunity to canvass public opinion about conscription, as there had been in 1917, the nation was just as effectively split. The conscription issue and the war itself quickly generated an increasingly effective popular opposition that specialised in 'moratoriums', mass public demonstrations and various forms of passive resistance, including 'draft dodging' and conscientious objections of all kinds. 'COs' and 'conchies' were the folk names for conscientious objectors; men of conscriptable age who went underground, often for years, avoiding the authorities dedicated to tracking them down.

The nation had not been as publicly and seriously divided since the conscription referenda of the First World War. Popular sentiment against the war, while never as extreme as it was in America, nevertheless resulted in army personnel being advised not to wear uniforms in public for fear of insult and attack. Even though the withdrawal of Australian troops had been announced by the government in 1971 and was effected in 1972, the electoral success of the Whitlam Labor government that December was, in part, due to the strength of feeling that Australia's participation in the war was wrong or, at least, unwise. Shortly after taking office, Whitlam's government abolished conscription and proclaimed an amnesty for conscientious objectors who were still on the run.

For Australia, the Vietnam War was suddenly over, but its continuing legacy is one of division, bitterness and misunderstanding. The vehemence of public antipathy towards the war and those who went to fight it had never been felt before. Previous generations of diggers had enjoyed the general support of the nation and on their return were often, though not always,[25] duly honoured and compensated for their service and their wounds.

This is not to say that there was no opposition to the First or Second World Wars, only that it was generally muted and, even in the case of the Catholic-Labor axis opposed to conscription spearheaded by Archbishop Mannix was not fought out in the public and electronic arenas, like the debates over Vietnam which involved large-scale protest 'demos' around the country and stage-managed mass media events, such as the burning of conscription notices. Nor was every returned soldier of the First and Second World Wars given large-scale 'welcome home' parades and celebrations. Australian participation in the Korean War of 1950–52 and the later Malaya 'police action' does not receive significant attention. The veterans of those conflicts were, and remain, largely invisible, almost forgotten.

The veterans of the war in Vietnam were also in danger of being forgotten by a nation eager to put the bitterness of the conflict behind them and pursue what promised, at the time, to be a bright cultural and economic future. Even today many Australians are surprised by the raw statistics of the war: 50,000 Australian troops did duty in Vietnam; 501 of them died there.[26] Almost 2,500 were wounded. Four Victoria Crosses were awarded, and a number of new foreign names were added to the annals of military glory, notably Long Tan. Many of those who returned from this surreal wartime experience believed, and still believe, as a result of the political sensitivity of the war and protest against it, that they have been unfairly denied proper recognition or adequate compensation by way of repatriation benefits. The main organised voice of this group is the Vietnam Veterans Association of Australia (VVAA).

Formed in 1980, the VVAA has branches in each state dedicated to the welfare of its members and their families. The organisation has strenuously and often effectively argued its point of view on issues such as the genetic effects of Agent Orange, the neuro-psychological damage to some veterans and, especially, the symbolism of a national homecoming parade or 'welcome home march'. While debate continues on many other matters of concern to the VVA, in 1987 it achieved its aim of a highly visible return ceremony and parade in Sydney, attended by then-Prime Minister, R.J. Hawke. The

'Vietnam Vets', as they are universally known, had, at last, come home. They too would take their place, if less comfortably than their predecessors, in the pantheon of Anzac and in the folklore of the digger. The means through which this uneasy accommodation was accomplished in one particular situation highlights the persistent potency of Anzac and the digger and the ongoing ability of the myth to link the grassroots and the national, the past, the present and the future.

CHAPTER TEN

The Lost Memorial

By the end of 1915, the deeds of the Anzacs on the Gallipoli Peninsula were inscribed on the collective consciousness of the nation. The mad glory of the initial landings; the tennis-court sized killing ground of 'The Nek'; the grim tenacity of 'Quinn's Post' and the implacable savagery of Lone Pine were only the foremost names of honour and sacrifice in a litany of bravery, suffering and death. The Anzacs provided the raw material for war correspondents like Charles Bean, who selected and transmitted their dispatches to Australian newspapers, where they were often given a further gloss of glorification.[1]

Received breathlessly by a country desperate to discover proof of its nationhood just fourteen years after Federation, the events at Gallipoli — the reported events, at least — were immediately accepted. They quickly received their first embellishments from poets, artists, politicians and even local progress associations anxious to commemorate, celebrate and honour the event in whatever way they could.[2] Across the nation, Australians were partaking in the creation of a new mythology, an intermingling of legends, deeds and national aspirations that turned over 416,000 other members of the AIF into 'diggers'. However, it would be some years before the rank-and-file members of the AIF were to be widely known by this folk name; at first they were known only as 'Anzacs'.

Fabricated from the telegraphic address of 'Australian New Zealand Army Corps', the acronym 'ANZAC' rapidly became the neologism 'Anzac'. This 'magic little word', as a journalist described the term in 1916,[3] was quickly enshrined in Federal government legislation. In the first *Anzac Bulletin* of July, 1916, a London-produced news-sheet issued three times each week by authority of the High Commissioner for Australia, the beginning of the institutionalised Anzac tradition was heralded. Under the *War Precautions Act*, a regulation was proposed to ensure that the term 'ANZAC' could not be used for any trade, professional or commercial purpose. The acting Attorney-General of the time, Mr Mahon, stated in Parliament that 'the government would not recognise the right of any person to monopolise a word which, on account of the valiant deeds of the Australian and New Zealand Forces, had become a word full of meaning to Australians'.[4]

Just what that meaning might be was to become clearer as the years passed. Nonetheless, it was certain that the meaning was central to notions of Australian nationhood. From July 1, 1916, a regulation was enacted that forbade the use of the term 'Anzac', or anything resembling it, 'in connection with any trade, business, calling or profession'.[5] The July 28 edition of the *Anzac Bulletin* noted that a Senator Lynch had recently proposed changing the name of the nation's proposed capital to 'Anzac'.[6] On October 20, 1916, the *War Precautions Act* was proclaimed. Part of the Act forbade the use of ANZAC, or any words resembling ANZAC, as the name, or part-name, of any private residence, boat, vehicle, or charitable or other institution. The penalty for so doing was a fine of one hundred pounds or six months' imprisonment.

Anzac quickly became the focal point of a growing and elaborate mythology of national duty, sacrifice and loyalty. It would be counterpointed by an equally evocative word that did not come into general use until 1917. By then 'digger' meant the typical Australian private infantryman. The intertwining of these two words, and the overlaps and tensions between them, generated the durable national mythology of Australia. That mythology continues to be expressed in many forms and in many places around the nation. One of its first manifestations in the everyday lives and beliefs of Australians began in a Perth suburb even while the Anzacs were still at Gallipoli. The people of Mt Hawthorn erected a practical memorial to commemorate the sacrifice of Australian soldiers. They called it 'Anzac Cottage'. The local, state and national intricacies in the building of the memorial and its subsequent history are resonant with the continuing meanings of Anzac.

The Campaign

The campaign to build Anzac Cottage was set in motion in the last months of 1915. 'The Mount is going to erect a monument to the heroes of Gallipoli', 'Advance' trumpeted in the Mt Hawthorn Notes column of the weekly *Westralian Worker,* official organ of the Western Australian branch of the Australian Labor Party. When 'Advance' wrote 'the Mount', he meant the Mt Hawthorn Progress Association, which typical of similar groups formed at the time and since throughout Australia to advance the development of towns, suburbs and local shires.

Like many such groups, the Mt Hawthorn Association was run by those with a strong interest in the locality, often small business people with a firm vision for the future of the area they aimed to 'progress'. The Association had been formed just as the suburb was beginning to attract upper working-class and lower middle-class residents to its leafy sub-divisions, not too far from the city and on the way to the beaches.[7] Many of these people had benefited from the gold rushes of the 1890s and continued to have strong links with localities like Kalgoorlie and Meekatharra, and also with the Labor movement. They were good, solid citizens imbued with the spirit of progress that characterised the turn of that century.

The building of Anzac was announced portentously in the December 17 edition of *The Westralian Worker:*

> Mount Hawthorn is going to do something big — it is going to erect a monument — a monument to the honor [sic] and glorious memory of those gallant and fearless representatives of Australia who brought imperishable renown to this young nation 'neath the Southern Cross on the morning of the 25th of April, in the year nineteen hundred and fifteen ...[8]

The article went on to name the fortunate recipient of this honour and the exact nature of the 'monument'.

> One of those who took his place in the attack on April 25 and who has returned to us disabled for life is private John Porter, and it is intended that the monument to be erected should take the form of a house for Mr Porter and his wife and child ...[9]

A 'working bee' towards the building fund was announced, with a target of 100 pounds. Did anyone have a block of land for sale at Mt Hawthorn?

Quite a few did. Numerous people offered blocks in and around 'the Mount'. While the committee was inspecting and, it seems, accepting these, fund-raising activities swung into full gear. Firstly, three members of the Progress Association[10] chipped in five pounds each. Perth architect, Alfred Levido donated his services. City of Perth Councillor Gibson ran concert-dances at his home on the corner of Kalgoorlie Street and the thoroughfare then called Government Road, but soon to be re-christened 'Anzac Road'.[11] These went on late into the night, with hundreds of people being entertained by 'The Pleezers' and other artists. The band played, the dancers swayed and the lights glittered.

Fundraising continued. By mid-January, 1916 the Anzac Cottage Committee had met and began its work in earnest. Many donations were promised and a number of concerts were advertised. The Junior Cricket Club donated the balance of its end-of-season funds — one pound, ten shillings — to the Cottage. At month's-end the Ladies Patriotic Guild reported that it was to split its funds — fourteen pounds, fifteen shillings and sixpence — in accordance with the advice of the War Council: thirty per cent for materials to the soldiers at the front; fifty per cent to Anzac Cottage, and the remaining twenty per cent to the sandbag fund. The campaign for the cottage was now called a 'movement' and Councillor Gibson was said to hope that it would be widely emulated and would also encourage more married men to enlist. Married or unmarried, men were beginning to disappear from the community, answering the war's need for further sacrifice.[12]

The Attack

In the spirit of the pioneer settlers of the Swan River there was to be a working bee to clear the block of timber. It would start before dawn on Saturday January 29. 'The workers, who are giving their labour freely, will make their 'attack' on 'Anzac Cottage' at the same hour as the men they desire to honour made their wonderful attack on Anzac Beach — 4am'.[13] About thirty men turned up for the block clearing, armed with shovels, saws and axes. 'At 4 o' clock the Ladies Patriotic Guild regaled the workers with afternoon tea' and there was 'a special decoction for the drones'. After this the last standing tree — they called it 'Lone Pine' — was felled and by nightfall had become a stack of firewood[14] — also to be used for fundraising. Some people attended the carpenter's bee, including the architect Alfred Levido, whose wife and daughter helped serve the refreshments. During the following week 'a despicable thief' stole some of the neatly stacked firewood from the block. 'Advance', not entirely facetiously, suggested that the death penalty would be appropriate for a person who would stoop to such depths.[15]

The following Saturday, February 5, seventy drays loaded with donated building materials, formed a half-mile procession through James Street, Perth, accompanied by about one hundred and fifty men, all on their way to the Mt Hawthorn building site. At the head of the procession, seated in 'her motor-car', was the 'Soldiers' Queen'. The car also carried a Metters' stove and a copper. Mostly the drays carried bricks and stone, tiles, timber and other building necessities. There was one dray of 'refreshments'. The procession was viewed by thousands as it proceeded to Mt Hawthorn and, and on arrival at 'Anzac', was greeted by hundreds of enthusiastic men, women and children. The goods were unloaded in readiness for the following Saturday.

On Saturday the twelfth of February, the 'busy bee' construction of the house commenced at 3.30 am when local veteran Tom Savell, closely followed by Jack Coonan singing the hit song of the war, 'It's a Long Way to Tipperary', turned up for work. By 1 pm the number of workmen on the site had reached two hundred, including the 'Mount's' first and oldest resident, Mrs Bramley. 'Like a swarm of bees', the volunteers laid turf, plastered walls and laid 'row after row of red Marseilles tiles'.[16] Hot dinners (in February — a

'The First Trench at Anzac — Mrs C. Roberts, the Soldiers' Queen, starting the first trench for foundations', Anzac Cottage Souvenir of the Monument Erected at Mount Hawthorn 1916, V.K. Jones & Co. Perth, np.

sign of Perth's enduring Anglo-Centricity) were provided for the tradesmen by 'a score of ladies' who served up well over four hundred meals before the day ended.

The Police Band provided the music and a local rifle club fielded the Honour Guard for the Governor, and for his wife, Lady Barron, who laid the inscribed foundation tablet with a specially inscribed trowel: 'This dwelling was erected to commemorate the landing of the Australian Forces at Anzac, April 25, 1915. This tablet was laid by Lady Barron, February 12, 1916'.[17] For her trouble she received a bunch of roses and the trowel. According to the *Western Mail* reporter the trowel was 'inscribed in commemoration of the event', but according to the *Westralian Worker* it was just a 'brickies' trowel' — the latter seems more likely.[18]

Lady members of the St John Ambulance gave a display. Six hundred children from local schools marched through the proceedings and were rewarded with bags of lollies and fruit, while the Girl Guides helped out generally. There were speeches by the Governor, the Mayor, the local MLA, J. Veryard and five others including, of course, Councillor Gibson. To cheers, at 5 pm, Mrs Roberts, the Soldiers' Queen hoisted the Australian flag, 'into which the letters A.N.Z.A.C. had been neatly woven'. A turf lawn was laid under the supervision of the City Gardener and the front cyclone wire fence went up as the outside walls of the house were being raised. It was claimed that four thousand people attended the event.[19]

The *Western Mail* reporter hit on the spirit of the day: 'Instead of the anniversary of some person of renown it was the birth of a new and sacred sentiment of patriotism'. In his speech, the Governor reinforced the need for charitable repatriation work and opined that a soldier returning with only one arm 'was a very much better man than one who had not done his country similar service'. He also hoped that Australia would see the war through to the end, and that the end would not be far off.[20]

In Sunday-best, the thousands in the crowd would all have agreed with the Governor, though they could not know they would have to suffer almost three more years of sacrifice. When it was over, those who were still alive may not have agreed with his sentiments about the patriotic glory of war. But, for now, the spirit of Anzac burned bright and fierce. Those hands that could not, or would not, help out at the front were ready to do their bit at home.

'Building Anzac Cottage — Progress made by the "Busy Bees" up to 2pm', Anzac Cottage Souvenir of the Monument Erected at Mount Hawthorn 1916, V.K. Jones & Co. Perth, np.

The house was built by 'bed time', according to the official souvenir booklet — though, like some other elements of the story, this is not true, as a careful reading of the souvenir booklet and the *Westralian Worker*[21] reveals.[22] The tenacity of this 'furphy' can perhaps be explained by the biblical associations of raising a house in one day, a practice still adhered to by a number of Christian groups. Still, most of the memorial was up by day's end, certainly enough of it to satisfy the dreams and aspirations of its builders. It stood 'in a clearing, which a fortnight ago was the border of fairly heavily timbered country'.[23]

Work continued on the cottage after this grand beginning, with tuckpointers, painters and fencers plying their skills and granolithic pathways being laid. Furniture, bedding and curtains were donated by Perth businesses, including pots and pans from the young ladies of Boans department store. By March 3 'Advance' could report that the cottage was 'practically completed, with the front garden being planted with "ANZAC" flowers by the Perth City Gardener. Only a few hours of finishing-off work remained'.[24] This would be carried out at yet another working bee the following Saturday.

The substantial house erected for Private Porter and his family — 'the prettiest house of its size in the district' — was valued at six hundred pounds. Its design was based on the then-popular[25] English 'bungalow' layout of four rooms with a central hallway. There was the Australian addition of a generous front verandah and the rear of the house, like many others in the suburb, had a substantial annex in which were located the bathroom and laundry facilities. There were two matching gables at the front, the roof being orange clay tiles from Marseilles, a reasonably common building product at the time. The roof-tiles gave a 'pleasant contrasting color [sic] to the surrounding forest greenery'.

Leaded glass side-panels of crossed sabres graced the front door, surmounted by a fanlight with 'ANZAC' spelled in coloured glass. The hall and sitting room had fibrous plaster ceilings and the kitchen/eating room and bedroom at the back of the house, together with the other large front room boasted pressed tin ceilings. There was 'a pretty tiled grate and hearth, patriotic rug, linoleum and electric light chandelier' in the sitting room which had a mantel decorated with 'appropriate pictures' — presumably Gallipoli/Anzac motifs. A feature noted at the time was that every room had electric light. The buffalo-grass front lawn also featured the letters A.N.Z.A.C. laid out centrally in ornamental flowers. A flagpole would be erected in the front garden upon which the Australian flag — bearing the motto 'Anzac' — was to be hoisted at each Anzac Day at 4.30 am.

The Ceremony

Festivities were repeated when the great day came. The cottage was officially opened on April 15. Rain threatened and some fell at 9 am, but by 'noon Old Sol smiled upon us broadly, and a bright blue sky assured a perfect afternoon' for the three thousand who turned up. The Scotch and Irish Pipe band skirled its way through Perth's main streets, then caught the tram to Mt Hawthorn to provide the music for the event, playing as they went. This was sweet success for the Progress Association's tramline campaign. Late in March a deputation from the Progress Association and the local members visited the Premier. Beveridge pointed out one reason for extending the line was that women and children had to wait for the tram outside the pub (the Oxford Hotel) and 'sometimes heard filthy language'.[26] They had finally convinced the Premier to visit the suburb and see for himself the stupidity of not continuing the tramline. He had decreed that the terminus would be extended. 'Advance' was pleased to inform all guests that the tram terminus was 'close to Anzac Cottage'.[27] In a sign of changing times and the development of private transport that was to come, the Police Band came by motor car.

The Premier and Mrs Scaddan headed a long list of distinguished guests. The Premier spoke, addressing an issue that had been raised with him. As reported by the *Westralian Worker*, Premier Scaddan said that he had been asked why Private Porter had been given the cottage and not some other Gallipoli hero. Scaddan was able to reveal that Private Porter had approached the War Council to intervene in the proceedings, saying that he did not wish to have anything that his mates could not have. With difficulty, the Council had 'persuaded him to accept Anzac Cottage. That fact alone stamped Private Porter doubly a hero, worthy of the monument which had been erected to the heroes of Anzac (Applause)'.[28]

The Premier also revealed 'another hero in connection with the movement, and that was the man who had donated the block of land on which the house was erected. He was a man with a small wage yet he had handed the land over to the committee for less than half the amount it had cost him. (Applause)'.[29] This anonymous donor occasioned no curiosity at the time, though as subsequent events would reveal, all was not as it was being presented. The official souvenir booklet of the opening, while generally effusive about donors of materials, equipment and so on, is conspicuously silent on the donation of the land. In referring to the ownership of the property it says only that 'the deeds of the cottage are vested in the Trustees of the Mt Hawthorn Progress Association'.[30]

After the speeches and congratulations, those attending were allowed to walk through the cottage — at sixpence per time. Two thousand were happy to pay their money. As the souvenir booklet put it, 'Mount Hawthorn was *en fete*' all that day. Always alert to a fund-raising opportunity, the Committee raffled off two dozen ducklings, a bag of apples[31] and two extra blocks of land donated to the Anzac Cottage cause. One, adjoining Anzac Cottage, went to a returned soldier for twenty-eight pounds while another, also in Kalgoorlie St, was sold for twenty-six pounds and ten shillings[32]. Together with the two thousand sixpences taken the day before, this would more than clear the Committee's remaining debt of fifty pounds.

The completed and generously furnished house was given to the Porter family the following day — a Sunday. There was even more festivity then, including bands, cadets and Girl Guides 'to witness the handing over of the cottage to Private Porter'. Frank Kelsall read out the conditions of the title 'which give Private Porter and his descendants full ownership rights on condition that they reside there permanently. The place would never be sold as the deeds were invested in trustees as a guarantee that the cottage would remain for all time a monument to the great landing'.[33] Councillor Gibson

' "Anzac Cottage" — Mount Hawthorn's Monument to Australian Valor', Anzac Cottage Souvenir of the Monument Erected at Mount Hawthorn 1916, V.K. Jones & Co. Perth, np.

accepted and responded on behalf of Private Porter, who was still suffering from 'shattered nerves'. The Soldiers' Queen officially handed the building over and hoped the Porters 'would long enjoy their beautiful home'. There were piano solos and the Perth City and YMCA bands played 'Rule Britannia', 'The Song for Me' and 'Home, Sweet Home'. There were many soldiers in the crowd, the authorities having made special provision for them to attend[34] and the proceeding finished with 'cheers for the Anzac Heroes and those associated with Anzac Cottage'. 'Everyone went home well pleased that they had taken part in building the Anzac monument'.

The grassroots activity surrounding the erection and occupation of 'Anzac Cottage' was practical and symbolic. It was not simply an appropriate gesture but an act that expressed local gratitude and sympathy. Additionally, it demonstrated the desire to perpetuate in physical structures and in symbolic forms the Anzac experience and its significance of solemnity and excess, of commemoration and celebration. That impulse would glow brightly through the remaining years of conflict and loss as Australians came to hear of new places and the deeds done in them by their fighting heroes.[35] Pozieres, Polygon Wood and Fromelles were some of those heard in the roll calls of death and glory, taking their place in the lexicon of legend that would become Anzac.

Finding the Lost Memorial

The war ended and the years passed. Children were born and educated at the local primary school. World War Two came and went, and the Porter girls married digger veterans of that war. Each Anzac Day the flag was dutifully raised in the front garden of the cottage. John Porter died in 1964 and his widow continued the Anzac day flag-raising as much as she was able due to advancing years and increasing infirmity. She died in 1968, by which time thousands of Australian troops were serving in Vietnam. A grandson occupied the cottage for a few years, then it was let until 1989. After that, the cottage was unoccupied and fell into disrepair and, finally, to decay. Members of Private Porter's unit group attempted to keep up the cottage and the Anzac Day flag-raising, though the years took their toll. The RSL was briefly involved for some years and, after a number of legal cases about ownership of the property, it fell into the hands of the state government of the day. The government at first offered the cottage to the RSL, who declined. It was then decided to offer it to the Vietnam Veterans. At a ceremony in the front garden of Anzac Cottage, early in 1992, then-Premier Carmen Lawrence officially passed the property into the ownership and safekeeping of the Vietnam Veterans' Association, Western Australian branch, Inc (VVAAWA), the survivors of Australia's longest war.

The house that Premier Lawrence bestowed upon the last Anzacs was a sad sight. Patched up and renovated time and again with each passing generation, the cottage sank into dilapidation hastened by the lashing of Perth's fierce winter storms. The wooden front verandah sagged; the eaves rotted out and the flagpole in the garden capitulated one day to the army of white ants beneath its base. The fence fell down and the garden was overgrown with weeds. Years of neglect, vandalism and scavenging left a leaking roof, smashed windows and the front and back yards full of tipped rubbish. The only sign of the building's significance was in the surviving 'ANZAC' fanlight over the front door and an incongruously new, white-painted flagpole in the front garden.

Uncertain of the property's ownership, local residents wondered and worried at the rapid decay of the building. Using their own time and money they effected extensive, if temporary, repairs to the roof and other parts of the building. They doggedly searched for and located the distinctive Marseilles tiles used for the roof, purchasing these and transporting them from another suburb to Mt Hawthorn. The one remaining original 'Anzac' feature, the front-door fanlight, together with stained glass side-panels, was removed, repaired and stored without charge by a local artisan. A member of the group produced measured drawings of the building as a guide to future renovation; others cleared the rubbish and weeds from the garden, mowed the grass and generally 'kept an eye' on the place, as did one or two of the older neighbours. Unfortunately, there was no money available for restoration. A number of attempts were made to raise funds, including a Remembrance (Armistice) Day wreath-laying ceremony in 1993. But these efforts came to little.

On November 11, Remembrance Day, 1994, representatives of the VVAWA met with members of the Mt Hawthorn Heritage Group, an organisation of residents with an interest in local history.[36] Research by this group had revealed the forgotten importance of Anzac Cottage as Australia's first Great War memorial. A joint Anzac Cottage Restoration Committee was formed to raise funds and generally oversee the restoration and future of the building. On Anzac Day, 1995, a dawn service was held at the Cottage, attracting considerable television and press coverage. As a result, numerous corporations, businesses and individuals offered to donate goods and services to the restoration project, but it was not until funds were granted by the WA Lotteries Commission in December, 1995 that serious restoration work could begin in early 1996.[37]

Eighty Anzac Days after the first observance of April 25 at Anzac Cottage, another tradition was invented. Because the VVAWA had many responsibilities on Anzac Day, 1996, including the Kings Park dawn service, the March and the special Vietnam War observances, members were busy from very early in the morning until mid-afternoon. It was suggested that a 'sunset service' could be held, an event that would allow VVAWA members, local residents and anyone else who wished to attend. The event was organised by the Cottage Restoration Committee, together with the Community Heritage Group and took place in and around Anzac Cottage from 5.00 pm. Kalgoorlie Street was closed to traffic, and the neighbours, community and local authorities were informed and invited, as were the descendants of John and Annie Porter.

They all came. Hundreds of others came too — neighbours, local politicians, veterans of Australia's wars, and lots of children from Mt Hawthorn's large number of young families. A band played. The sacred words were spoken, the Australian flag, raised to the traditional half-mast earlier that day, was

A. Levido, cover image. Anzac Cottage Souvenir of the Monument Erected at Mount Hawthorn 1916, V.K. Jones & Co. Perth,

flown. Hymns were sung, speeches made, wreaths laid. 'A Soldier's Prayer' was recited. The medals of a New Zealand Anzac were generously donated to the house, as were some seedlings from Lone Pine on the Gallipoli Peninsula.[38] A bugler played 'The Last Post' as the sun set on Australia's western edge, illuminating the nation's last possible moment of the Anzac Day observance. There was, it seemed, a very long minute of silence. Anzac Cottage was a memorial once more. The eighty-year-old tradition of Anzac and the digger, together with its surrounding context of war, nation and community, was given substance in this small but significant commemoration and celebration.

The origins and history of Anzac Cottage reveal the grassroots power of Anzac and afford a glimpse of the connections between those local, personal emotions and the larger machinations of the state apparatus. The establishment of the 'sunset service' at Anzac Cottage in suburban Perth consciously balances and echoes the dawn service. It is very much an invented tradition, not of a high political nature but of the everyday community type that has considerable significance for those involved. Although trivial in relation to the scale of the national story, Anzac Cottage highlights the essential interactions of the two traditions. Without the other, each tradition is no more than itself: Anzac, an institutional tradition; the digger, a folk tradition. Together these traditions are more than the sum of their parts. If they were not, Anzac Cottage would never have been built in an obscure Perth suburb, it would never have come into the keeping of the last Anzacs, and a new component, the sunset service, would not have been added to the panoply of Anzac Day events. Myths of any kind can only live when they produce meaning. The invented tradition of Anzac and the folk tradition of the digger continue to mean a great deal to the Australian peoples.

CHAPTER ELEVEN

True Inventions

In a study of the construction of national traditions between 1870 and the start of World War One, the historian Eric Hobsbawm noted, 'Invented traditions have significant social and political functions, and would neither come into existence nor establish themselves if they could not acquire them'.[1] Hobsbawm goes on to discuss the extent to which such invented traditions are vulnerable to, even intended for, political manipulation. His interest is in the nexus between the high political and the nationalistic, but the invention and deployment of grassroots traditions and state traditions, as in the cases surveyed in this volume, are also important to understand. While national and nationalistic traditions, such as Anzac, may be created for political ends, they must possess dimensions or elements that can motivate popular sympathy and participation. It is impossible to establish or maintain for long a public tradition that does not attract popular participation and support. The continuing success of Anzac is due to its ability to simultaneously motivate the higher political (and, on occasion, militaristic) purposes of government and the demotic tradition of 'the digger'.[2]

The need to invent traditions is not restricted to the formal frameworks of the official and the state-sponsored but extends to small-scale, informal acts of observance and belief in obscure suburban streets. As this book has argued, it is in the sometimes complementary, sometimes conflicting intersections of the Anzac and digger traditions that we can discern the motivating power of the dominant national mythology. But understanding better the complexities of the process through which this occurs does not in itself explain the staying power of Anzac. For that we need to acknowledge the relationship between the enduring Australian romanticisation of the bush and its heroes, and the transferral of elements of this romance to the idealised image of the digger.[3] While this topic has long been out of favour with intellectuals, it has enormous popular appeal and significance, as attested by the endless production of 'Australiana' by publishers and other media producers. Even though academics, serious journalists and others who fancy their cosmopolitanism denounce or simply ignore such gum leaf ideology, it remains the standard by which many Australians see the world and their place in it. The mingled traditions of the bush and Anzac are, in many ways, all we have as usable materials for fashioning national identity.

Understanding the cultural processes through which that identity was established and by which it is maintained is inseparable from discerning the forces through which a powerful state ideology was originated and sustained. Central to that task is to appreciate something of the nature of the demotic and the official, together with their interactions. In this book, 'tradition' has been seen as a descriptor for the cultural processes by which human beings — in this case, Australians — link their perceptions of the past and the present, and the implicit transmission of the sum of past and present, into the future. 'Legend' is a useful shorthand for the various articulations of those perceptions, including song, story and verse, a very small sample of which has been noted in the preceding pages. The interaction of the formal imperatives of Anzac and the informal elements of digger lore provide the motivating force for the operation of tradition over time and space. Finally, the sum consequence of all these factors is the powerful 'myth' to which large numbers of Australians continue to cleave in their underlying attitudes and values.

Each April 25 this powerful complex of perception, sentiment and national identity is again displayed, further strengthening the myth and its many meanings. Anzac is an invention, and it is one that is amenable to a host of different, even conflicting, interpretations and uses. It is not simply a militaristic celebration of war and duty, nor is it merely a religious commemoration of death, or a state acknowledgement of sacrifice. It is not just an excuse for old soldiers to retell risqué jokes, recycle old yarns and overindulge. It is all of these things, and more. In its articulation and preservation of these meanings Anzac resonates of those things that most Australians have continued to hold dear about their communal sense of self. Rightly or wrongly, desirably or not, we have invented Anzac in our own image and continue to define our nation by its projections.

The persistent power of these projections to motivate Australians is evidenced in many ways; some of the more significant have been investigated in the previous pages. Others include the great numbers who take part in Anzac Day, either in person at events large and small, public and private across the country, or who participate through the extensive mainstream media coverage. The popularity of the Gallipoli 'pilgrimage' with young — and not-so-young — Australian backpackers is another, as is the appeal of similar visits to the Western Front, whether undertaken as an independent traveler or with any of the various commercial tours now available. The death rate of the First AIF, and the burial of their bodies on or near the site of battles that are charged with myth and emotion, has meant that many Australians have forebears lying in these locations. The development of genealogy and family history as popular pastimes have also contributed to the growth of such experiences which have the ability to transmute what is mythical at home into a lived experience, a kind of displaced reality abroad. While interest in and enthusiasm for such activities waxes and wanes, Anzac and the digger persist as powerful icons of Australian identity.

One explanatory fact of this power is its ability to fill a profound hollowness at the centre of the Australian experience. All of Australia's military under-takings have been conducted in faraway places. Some of our most sacred sites are on the shores of Turkey, France and Vietnam. Some lie far away beneath tonnes of concrete, as in the case of the Changi POW camp in Singapore. Other names and places resonant with myth, emotion and military glory include Papua New Guinea's Kokoda Trail and Tobruk in North Africa. Unlike most countries, even the islands of Britain, no large-scale external military activity or attack has yet taken place on Australian soil.[4] The traditions of Anzac and the digger connect us with highly significant places and events that are not part of the geographical reality of Australians. They allow us to celebrate and commemorate at home deeds done elsewhere by soldiers lying forever in foreign fields. While pilgrimages to Gallipoli and other sites of conflict have been undertaken ever since 1919, the availability of cheap air travel since the late twentieth century has increased the numbers able to visit such places, and they are rapidly becoming part of an Australian diaspora that effectively, if temporarily, extends the national experience across the globe.

Other relevant activities take place continually at home, in the activities of the Australian War Memorial, the teaching of schoolchildren about Anzac, the regular renovations of the myth through film (Peter Weir's *Gallipoli* being the most recent, but far from the first and certainly not the last), through television mini-series and documentaries, through books and so forth. As there has been ever since the first Anzac Day, there is a continual calendar of reunions, returns and social events, a network of convivial and often charitable communication involving returned service associations such as the RSL and the Vietnam Veterans' Association of Australia, and the innumerable unit associations that focus the memories and values of old comrades. These networks of activity and significance are mostly invisible, but nonetheless powerfully permeate the lives of many Australians. The hidden structures of meaning that underlie Anzac reinforce the filaments that bind the official and the unofficial, the formal and the informal tightly together. Meanings of this kind are difficult to discern unless one is a member of their hidden networks, and are also not easily susceptible to documentation as their interactions and expressions are largely oral or carried in obscure publications and ephemeral records of the type dealt with extensively throughout this book.

Within these ever-shifting yet persistent, if unseen, interactions of emotion and identity are almost infinite possibilities for mutation within and between the two traditions. The ability of these interactions to adapt to new circumstances — such as the incorporation of women and old enemies into the march and other activities — is the secret of successful mythologising. The ability of the day itself to generate new ritual and ceremonial forms, from the dawn service to the Fields of Remembrance,[5] as well as less public events like the breakfast and tot of grog at dawn, and the sunset service at Anzac Cottage,[6] are all testimony to Anzac's continuing power to reinvent itself in ways that continue to move many Australians.

Whatever the future of the myth, it is now — and has been for a long time — omnipresent in the Australian experience. Although it receives an annual display and reinfusion of power, the true strength of Anzac lies in the less visible, less remarked upon and taken-for-granted networks connecting everyday experience with national icons, institutions and imperatives. The past, present and possibly future events surrounding Anzac Cottage have their echoes in thousands of Australian communities, wherever memorials stand — from the humblest Honour Board hanging in a dusty bush hall to the small stone obelisk in the village centre, the memorial gardens in the town park and the imposing state memorials in capital cities, all the way to the monumentalism of the Australian War Memorial.[7] Anzac and the digger are always and ever present in the Australian milieu, even if we are only directly aware of this each April 25. While these may take very different, often conflicting forms, each nevertheless complements and confirms the other at every level of Australian life, making Anzac and the digger the central mythology of the Australian people. In these ongoing intersections between the official and the unofficial, the formal and the folkloric can be found the essential motivating force of the myth. From the Australian War Memorial and its many echoes throughout the land, in the institutional legend of Simpson and the donkey learned at school, at the great annual spectacle of Anzac Day fusing the secular and the sacred, through the fictions and factions of the mass media and into the seething underculture of belief, story, verse and song, there is no escape from Anzac. The myth and its many meanings permeate all levels and facets of Australian culture and society. In its omnipresence and in its invented but nevertheless resonant aura of always-everness, in its fusion of the sacred and the secular, of the everyday and the official, Anzac is the modern Australian dreaming.

APPENDIX

Social Statistics of the First AIF

As the arguments advanced in this book partly concern the culture of the digger and the relationship of that culture to national identity, the following figures are provided as a guide to the social composition of the First AIF.

Lloyd Robson has demonstrated the occupational origins of the AIF: 22 per cent were labourers, 20 per cent industrial workers, 17 per cent primary industry workers, 12 per cent worked in commerce, 9 per cent in transport, 5 per cent were clerks and 5 per cent professionals. The remaining 10 per cent were in a variety of other occupations, or their livelihoods are unknown.[1]

A consideration in the social makeup of the First AIF, given the debates regarding the 'Australian' characteristics of the diggers, is the proportion of recruits born outside Australia. Robson's statistical analysis of around 0.5 per cent (2,291) of the more than 417,000 attestation papers available delivers a figure of 18 per cent British-born,[2] which closely reflects the British-born segment of the Australian population during the first years of the century.[3] While this is a statistically significant result, its relevance for the arguments of this book is negligible. As Robson points out, 'it is not possible from the official documents to determine in most cases how long they [the British-born] had been in Australia'.[4] It is therefore not possible to determine to what extent this British-born proportion of the First AIF was or was not influenced by the popular values and attitudes existing in Australia prior to 1914.[5] In any case, place of birth and even long residence there does not necessarily militate against the influence of the cultural mores of one's adopted country, particularly given the ethnic and linguistic connections between Britain and its antipodean colony/Commonwealth. Despite the undoubtedly 'British' nature and orientation of government and official sentiment in Australia, there was a strong tradition of popular 'Australianism', as discussed elsewhere.

Not surprisingly, given the diverse backgrounds suggested in the above figures, recruitment into the AIF was variable. In his *Anzac and Empire: The Tragedy and the Glory of Gallipoli*, John Robertson presents evidence of the different opinions regarding the quality of recruits. In Victoria the recruits were said to be 'good raw material' who soon became good soldiers during training. In New South Wales the commander of the 1st Brigade, Colonel

H.N. MacLaurin, was concerned that the rush to enlist resulted in too many criminals and wastrels, and not enough men from the country.[6] New South Wales Premier Holman and his government were likewise unhappy with the poor results of the August 1915 recruitment campaign,[7] and the problems associated with recruitment after the first patriotic influx of 1914 continued to worry state and federal governments throughout the war, particularly with regard to the attempt to introduce conscription.[8]

Whatever the thoughts of recruiting officers, 116,986 Australian soldiers were encamped in Egypt by the end of 1914. This became the 'First' AIF, a group destined for extraordinary service and extraordinary mythologisation. Their title of 'Australian Imperial Force' was indeed an apt one, with only 72 per cent being Australian born, and the remainder from elsewhere in the Empire, the majority from Britain. They came from all Australian states, and only around 10 per cent were married. Most of the ranks (42 per cent) were aged 26 to 40 years old, 36 per cent were under 25, and 21 per cent under 21 years of age. Officers tended to be older, with 53 per cent in the 25 to 40 range. Unlike later divisions, the members of the First AIF frequently had some form of military training, mostly in the home force and the militia. Some (16 per cent) had previous war service.[9] New South Wales provided 37 per cent of the enlistees in Robson's sample, while Victoria, Queensland, South Australia, Western Australia and Tasmania provided 29, 12, 9, 9 and 4 per cent respectively.[10]

As far as it is possible to tell, approximately 86 per cent of the 1st Division AIF were Protestant, and 15 per cent Roman Catholic. Amongst officers, only 6 per cent were Catholics, a fact that reflects, according to Robertson, who calculated these figures, the 'concentration at that time of this religious group [Roman Catholics] in less well-to-do levels of society'.[11] Robson, sampling the entirety of the AIF rather than Robertson's First Division cohort, also points out that 'significantly few officers were Roman Catholic'[12] and, bearing in mind statistical inadequacies, states 'it may fairly confidently be concluded that the officers of the AIF were overwhelmingly Protestants although no less than 20 per cent of the army was Roman Catholic'.[13] It has been left to Humphrey McQueen to make the consequent assertion 'that 50 per cent of the First AIF came from the working class'.[14]

These social statistics for the First AIF may be compared with those presented by Gammage[15] for the occupations of males aged 15–64 at the 1911 Census. According to Gammage's figures, 4.87 per cent of this group worked in the professions, 2.56 per cent in domestic service, 14.86 per cent in commercial occupations, 8.84 per cent in transport/communication industries, 28.90 per cent were industrial workers, 35 per cent primary producers, and 13 per cent were independents (presumably self- or non-employed). While the categories used to assemble occupational statistics from the 1911 Census, and those used to classify occupations within the AIF were different and so not directly comparable, it is possible to determine that the social makeup of the AIF closely mirrored that of the male segment of Australian society at that time.

In terms of comparing religious affiliations within Australian society and those affiliations given by the members of the AIF, there is generally a close correlation between stated affiliations at the 1911 Census and those of the diggers. Based on the Census figures and those of Butler in *The Official Medical History*, Gammage provides the following figures:

	Males 15 and over in Australia at 1911 Census	AIF embarked
Church of England	39.40	49.22
Roman Catholic	22.30	19.26
Presbyterian	13.29	15.01
Methodist	11.36	10.19
Other denomination	10.92	___

With the exception of the almost 10 per cent disparity in numbers of Church of England affiliations given, there is a close correlation between the general population and the members of the AIF. The larger number of Church of England affiliations given for the AIF may be due to enlistees feeling obliged to enter some religious affiliation on the enlistment form, 'Church of England' being the most generally professed nominal adherence.

Enlistment and casualty figures for the AIF, as for all World War One forces, vary considerably.[16] Gammage calculates that 13.43 per cent of the white male population of Australia, a total of 416,809 enlisted in the AIF. This was probably about half of those eligible. Somewhere between 330,777 and 333,814 went abroad and around 295,000 of these served in France (and, presumably, Belgium, though Gammage does not say so). Between 58,132 and 63,163 died on active service, and between 152,422 and 156,128 were wounded (some later dying). This was a total of approximately 215,585 or almost 65 per cent of total AIF embarkations. On Gallipoli there were 27,594 casualties and 179,537 in France or Belgium. After the war approximately 2,000 were permanantly hospitalised and by 1926 there were over 22,000 veterans in hospital. By 1939, this figure had more than doubled.

As far as such figures are able to indicate, it is reasonable to conclude that the social composition of the AIF was a representative cross-section of the

adult (mostly) male population of Australia. There were no significant im-
balances of age, location, religion or occupation, with the exception of those
few already mentioned. The AIF was a close reflection of Australian manhood
in the period 1911 to 1918 — as Robson puts it 'Approximately 40 per
cent of all Australian men aged between eighteen and forty-five had enlisted
in the AIF'.[17] In the post-war years to 1929, despite the high death rate of
AIF members (and in some ways because of this), a very large segment of
the Australian population — at 1919 around 270,000 living adult males —
had been exposed to the experiences and the attitudes that constituted the
distinctive and distinguishing culture of the digger. This number declined as
age, illness and war wounds took their toll. Humphrey McQueen has calculated
that by the end of 1931, there were approximately 230,000 returned servicemen still alive in Australia.[18] While membership of the RSSILA stood at
150,000 in 1919, by the end of 1920 it was down to 50,000, and by 1923
bottomed at 24,000.[19] Even if some soldiers did not become or remain
members of the League, it is reasonable to assume that many returned men
still considered themselves 'diggers'. Just as importantly, these men continued
to be regarded as such by Australians in general.

Notes

1. Tradition, Myth and Legend

1. *Argus*, April 25, 1916, quoted in L. Robson, *Australia and the Great War*, Melbourne, 1969, pp. 59–60.
2. K. Inglis, 'The Anzac Tradition', *Meanjin*, vol 24, no 1, 1965; K. Inglis, 'The Australians at Gallipoli' Part 1, *Historical Studies*, vol 14, no 54, 1970 — Part 2, vol 14, no 55, 1970. Relevant here, too, is K. Inglis, 'Remembering Australians on the Somme, Anzac Day 1988', *Overland*, no 115, August 1989. Also important are G. Serle, 'The Digger Tradition and Australian Nationalism', *Meanjin*, vol 24, no 2, 1965; N. McLachlan, 'Nationalism and the Divisive Digger', *Meanjin*, vol 27, no 3, 1968; N. McLachlan, *Waiting for the Revolution*, Ringwood, 1988; A.G.L. Shaw, 'Bush Religion: A Discussion of Mateship', *Meanjin Quarterly*, vol 12, no 3, 1953; T. Inglis Moore, 'The Meanings of Mateship', *Meanjin*, vol 24, vol 1, 1965; and S. Alomes, *A Nation at Last? The Changing Character of Australian Nationalism*, Sydney, 1988.
3. J. Ross, *The Myth of the Digger. Australian Soldiers in Two World Wars*, Sydney, 1985; R. Ward, *The Australian Legend*, Melbourne, 1958; Palmer, V., *The Legend of the Nineties*, Melbourne, 1954; and throughout the extensive literature on this topic.
4. Robertson, cited in B. Gammage, 'The Crucible: The Establishment of the Anzac Tradition, 1899–1918', in M. McKernan, and M. Browne (eds), *Australia: Two Centuries of War and Peace*, Canberra, 1988, p. 3.
5. P. Cochrane, *Simpson and the Donkey: The Making of a Legend*, Melbourne, 1992, pp. 8–9.
6. See G. Mosse, *Fallen Soldiers: Reshaping the Memory of the World Wars*, New York, 1990.
7. R. Ely, 'The First Anzac Day: Invented or Discovered?', *Journal of Australian Studies*, no 17, 1985; K. Fewster, 'Ellis Ashmead Bartlett and the Making of the Anzac Legend', *Journal of Australian Studies*, no 10, 1982. Also relevant are W. Gammage, 'Anzac', in J. Carroll (ed), *Intruders in the Bush: The Australian Quest for Identity*, Melbourne, 1982; R. White, *Inventing Australia*, Sydney, 1981; C. Flaherty and M. Roberts, 'The Reproduction of Anzac Symbolism', *Journal of Australian Studies*, no 24, 1989, amongst numerous others.
8. See A. Thomson, *Anzac Memories: Living with the Legend*, Melbourne, 1994, chapter 2 and p. 142 for details of Bean's mythologising. Also D. Kent, 'The Anzac Book and the Anzac Legend: C.E.W. Bean as Editor and Image-Maker', *Australian Historical Studies*, vol 21, no 84, 1985; K. Fewster (ed), *Gallipoli*

Correspondent: The Frontline Diary of C.E.W.Bean, Sydney, 1983. See J.Robertson, *Anzac and Empire*, Port Melbourne, 1990 for a dissenting view and D. Winter '*The Anzac Book*: A Re-appraisal' in *Journal of the Australian War Memorial*, no 16, 1990, which takes issue with Kent's depiction of Bean's editorial work on the *Anzac Book*. The information on Bean's editing of *The Rising Sun*, presented in chapter 5 also bears on this debate.

9. Kent, *op. cit.*; J. Barrett, 'No Straw Man: C.E.W. Bean and Some Critics', *Australian Historical Studies*, no 23, 1988; A. Thomson, 'Steadfast Until Death? C.E.W. Bean and the Representation of Australian Military Manhood', *Australian Historical Studies*, vol 23, no 93, 1989; D. Kent, 'From the Sudan to Saigon: A Critical View of Historical Works', *Australian Literary Studies*, no 12, 1985.

2. The Digger Tradition, 1914–1919

1. See Appendix.

2. In 1914, 24 members of the Australian Army Nursing Service (AANS) embarked with the First AIF from Albany, WA. By the end of 1916, 1,340 AANS nurses were on active service overseas, and a total of 2,139 nurses served in most theatres of the Great War. Of these, 21 died on active service and 385 were decorated. Figures from M. Barker, *Nightingales in the Mud: The Digger Sisters of the Great War, 1914–1918*, Sydney, 1989, pp. 4, 11–12.

3. See *Historical Studies*, October 1978, for a series of articles and arguments devoted to 'the Australian Legend', particularly J.B. Hirst, 'The Pioneer Legend'. See also M. Roe, 'The Australian Legend' in G. Davey and G. Seal (eds), *The Oxford Companion to Australian Folklore*, Melbourne, 1993. Also important is H. McQueen, *A New Britannia,* Ringwood, 1970, for an insistence upon aspects of the radical nationalist tradition underemphasised by Ward and others, including racism, sexism and imperialism.

4. L. Robson, 'The Australian Soldier: Formation of a Stereotype', first published in M. McKernan and M. Browne (eds), *Australia: Two Centuries of War and Peace*, Canberra, 1988; B. Gammage, 'The Crucible', op. cit.

5. Robson, 'The Australian Solder', *op. cit.*, p. 317.

6. ibid., p. 322.

7. ibid., pp.322–3.

8. ibid. p. 323.

9. Gammage, 'The Crucible', *op. cit.*

10. 'Anzac', *On the Anzac Trail: Being Extracts from the Diary of a New Zealand Sapper*, London, 1916, pp. 74–7.

11. ibid.

12. ibid., pp. 121–124.

13. ibid.

14. ibid.

15. Evidence to support the extent and depth of the diggers' prejudices against

almost everyone else is multitudinous, displayed in the majority of primary sources examined and in secondary sources, such as R. White, 'Sun, Sand and Syphilis: Australian Soldiers and the Orient Egypt 1914', in *Australian Cultural History*, no 9, 1990; and Robertson, *Anzac and Empire, op. cit.*, pp. 37, 15, 260.

16. *Anzac Bulletin* 26, July 4 1917, p. . 9.

17. G. Souter, *Lion and Kangaroo: The Initiation of Australia 1901–1919*, Sydney, 1976, p. 242. Unlike the British soldier, only an incapacitating wound would get a digger back home, and not always then.

18. H. Nicholls, 'The Anzac's Forebears', in A.G. Stephens (ed), *The Anzac Memorial*, 2nd edition, Sydney, 1917, pp. 280–84. Also Hirst, *op. cit.*

19. This work is reproduced in black and white and is discussed briefly in N. McLachlan, *Waiting for the Revolution: A History of Australian Nationalism*, Ringwood, 1989, pp. 198–9. An unidentified West Australian at Gallipoli is quoted as follows: 'I'm dying but by God I'll die game', in S. Welborn, *Lords of Death: A people, a place a legend*, Fremantle, 1982, p. 77.

20. J. Hughes (ed), *Australian Words and Their Origins*, Melbourne, 1989, p. 162.

21. ibid. pp. 162–3.

22. *The Rising Sun*, January 22, 1917.

23. ibid.

24. W.F. Adcock, *Genuine War Letters*, Melbourne, nd [c1919], p. 62.

25. *Rising Sun*, February 12, 1917, p. 2.

26. E. Partridge, writing as 'Frank Honeywood', *Frank Honeywood, Private: A Personal Record of the 1914–18 War*, [c1929] Melbourne University Press edition, 1987, with Introduction and annotations by G. Serle, p. 71. This is confirmed by 'Hen', writing to the *Bulletin* in early 1917, quoted in *Anzac Bulletin*, no 14 (new series), April 11 1917, p. 11.

27. *Anzac Bulletin*, no 64, March 29, 1918, p. 11.

28. C.E.W Bean(ed), *The Official History of Australia in the War of 1914–18*, Sydney, 1921–37, vol 4, p. 144.

29. The term does not appear in G.C. Prescott, 'Anzac Vocabulary', in Stephens, *Anzac Memorial, op. cit.*, pp. 300ff, published on Anzac Day and presumably prepared early in 1917.

30. *Aussie*, vol 1, no 2, 1 December 1919, p. 65 [September–October on Gallipoli] and vol 1, no 4, 1 January 1920, p. 21 [3 letters: 2 for WA gold rushes, 1 for Victorian rushes]. See also *The Digger* (being the unofficial record of the early days of the 41st Rft. at sea), nd [c1918], p. 2: 'the word "digger" has lately come to be a term of common use among our New Zealand soldiers ... The New Zealander is the "digger" as the Australian is the "Ossie"'. Clearly, the New Zealanders were not prepared to relinquish their claim to the name.

31. *The Digger*, vol 1, no 24; vol 1, no 25; and vol 1, no 26.

32. *Western Mail,* January 9, 1930. Welborn, op. cit., p. 125 also claims (without evidence) a Western Australian origin for the term at Bullecourt, April–May, 1917.

33. See, for instance, Bill Wannan, *The Australian*, Sydney, 1954, pp. 138–9.

34. A correspondent in *Aussie*, no 8, October 1918, p. 2 complained that 'Billjim' was never used by the troops. In the following Christmas issue, p. 2, another correspondent pointed out that 'Billjim' came from a *Bulletin* competition to find a popular name for the Australian soldier that would be the equivalent of the British 'Tommy'. ('Billjim' had been used facetiously in the *Bulletin* since the 1890s to describe the bush everyman.) On the same page another claimed that the *Bulletin* invented 'Billjim' to describe the 'average bushman long before Wilhelm broke loose'. See also discussion of 'digger' in A.G. Butler, *The Digger*, Sydney, 1945; in R. Fair, *A Treasury of Anzac Humour*, Brisbane, 1965, p. 13; and in W.S. Ramson, (ed), *Australian National Dictionary*, Melbourne, 1988.

35. See T. King, 'On the Definition of Digger: Australia and its Returned Soldiers, 1915–1920', PhD thesis, La Trobe University, 1988, pp. 75–6 for use of the term 'digger' to describe AIF members of non-officer status.

36. P. Fussell, *The Great War and Modern Memory*, New York and London, 1975, has a perceptive discussion of the importance of orality and, in particular, the significance of rumour and 'legend', pp. 114–125.

37. Thomson, *Anzac Memories*, op. cit.

38. ibid., pp. 233–4.

39. ibid., p. 7.

40. It should be noted that 'bon' was already in use in Australian vernacular forms such as 'bong tong', 'bontosher', and 'bonz(s)er' at least as early as the 1890s.

41. C.G. (Lt.) Prescott, 'Anzac Vocabulary', in Stephens, *Anzac Memorial, op. cit.*, pp. 300–5. See also Downer, *Digger Dialects*, Melbourne, 1919 and expanded by W.S. Ramson and J. Arthur, under the same title, Melbourne, 1990; also the various editions of Brophy and Partridge.

42. *The Rising Sun*, no 13, February 8, 1917, p. 3. (There are some peculiarities in the dating of this weekly paper, which began on 25 December 1916 and appears to have reached no15 by February 15, 1917.) Other examples of this genre in *The Digger*, vol 1, no 5, September 1 1918, p. 1, 'A Digger's Alphabet'; *The Desert Dust-Bin*, vol 1, no 1, 26 April 1916, p. 3 'The Corps Alphabet'; *Honk!* no 11, 7 December 1915, 'ABC of the Australian Ammunition Park'; *The Rising Sun*, no 12, February 5, 1917, p. 3, 'A Soldier's Alphabet'; *The Rising Sun*, no 17, 22 February 1917, p. 4; two more in *The Anzac Book*.

43. *Aussie*, no 1, January 18, 1918, p. 10. On p. 11 it was noted that 'digger' had replaced 'cobber'. See also item titled 'Lingua-Franca of the Trenches', *The Anzac Bulletin*, no 64, March 29, 1918, p. 11.

44. *Honk!* no 9, 29 August 1915, p. 2; reprinted *Aussie*, 15 April 1920, p. 21; similar in A.H. Cooper (comp), *Character Glimpses: Australians on the Somme*, Sydney, nd, p. 5 (pagination imperfect). See also 'Introduction' to G. Moorhouse, *Hell's Foundations: A Town, its Myths and Gallipoli*, London, 1992, pp. 8–12.

45. Bean, *Official History, op. cit.*, vol 6, pp. 8–18. Although D. Winter, *Making the Legend: The War Writings of C.E.W. Bean*, St Lucia, 1992, p. 239, credits this

description to Bean, it is not clear from Bean's introduction of the passage in the *Official History* that he was the original author.

46. Bean, ibid., pp. 16, 10–11. See also Winter, *Making the Legend, op. cit.*, p. 243, for another entry from Bean's diaries (1/12/16) showing the relationship between bad language and belligerent Australianism.

47. See G. Seal, 'Written in the Trenches: Trench Newspapers of the First World War', *Journal of the Australian War Memorial*, no 16, April 1990.

48. C.F. Laseron, *From Australia to the Dardanelles*, Sydney, 1916, p. 30.

49. *First Aid Post*, August 11, 1915.

50. 'Anzac', *op. cit.*, p. 74. See also Anne Donnell, *Letters of an Army Sister*, Sydney, 1920, pp. 106–7 on 'fresh rumours'; the diary of H.P. Demasson in R. Christensen (ed), *To All My Dear People: The Diary and Letters of Private Hubert P. Demasson 1916–1917*, Fremantle, 1917, p. 21.

51. 'B. Bowyang' (Vennard/Reid), 'Furphies', *The Kia Ora Coo-ee*, September 15, 1918, p. 17.

52. F.H. Allport and L. Postman, *The Psychology of Rumour*, New York, 1947.

53. *ibid.* There is also a considerable literature on rumour and 'urban legends' that generally supports these observations, see Introduction to G. Seal, *The Cane Toad High: Great Australian Urban Myths*, Sydney, 2001.

54. 'Bowyang', *op. cit.*

55. L. Degh and A. Vazsonyi, 'The Hypothesis of Multi-Conduit Transmission in Folklore', in D. Ben-Amos and K. Goldstein (eds), *Folklore: Performance and Communication*, The Hague, 1975; T. Caplow, 'Rumors in War', *Social Forces*, no 25, 1947.

56. T. Shibutani, *Improvised News*, Indianapolis, 1966; R. Rosnow and G. Fine, *Rumour and Gossip: The Social Psychology of Hearsay*, New York, 1976.

57. See Appendix.

58. *The Dinkum Oil*, June 11, 1915, np.

59. ibid.

60. *The 7th Fab Yandoo*, vol 3, no 5, Christmas 1917, p. 86. Printed 'in France'.

61. Diary of A.J. Stoppard (7337), 5th AA Brigade, AIF, 2nd, Div.

62. 'Bowyang', *op. cit.*

63. See discussion in J. Terraine, *Smoke and Fire: Myths and Anti-Myths of War, 1861–1945*, London, 1980, pp. 17–21; and in Fussell, *op. cit.*, pp. 115–16. Also K. McClure, *Visions of Bowmen and Angels: Mons 1914*, St Austell, Cornwall, 1992.

64. *Honk!* no 10, September 30 1915, p. 6. A similar proto–legend is that of the last man off Gallipoli ('Young' Pollack of Cowra, NSW), *Smith's Weekly*, December 6, 1924. A West Australian variant claims this honour for Col. George Shaw, *West Australian*, August 20, 1984, p. 3.

65. Reprinted from *Southward-Ho*, written aboard the *Suevic* on the voyage home, commencing May, 1917 and reprinted in *Aussie*, 15 December 1920, p. 63.

66. 'Digger's Diary', *Western Mail* December 5, 1929 refers to the persistence of

this folk belief among diggers in the post-war period, concluding with the accurate statement 'The old superstitions die hard'.

67. See G.P. Cuttriss, *'Over the Top' with the Third Australian Division*, London, nd [c1918] pp. 49ff.

68. See R. Linton, 'Totemism and the AEF', in W.A. Lessa and E.Z. Vogt (eds), *Reader in Comparative Religion*, 2nd edition, New York, Evanston and London, 1965 and E. Oring, 'Totemism in the AEF', *Southern Folklore Quarterly*, vol 41, no 1; vol 41, no 2, 1977. This story is recounted in 'Digger's Diary', *Western Mail*, May 1, 1930. The incident allegedly took place at Armentieres, in this version, in B Co, 44Bn. For the quantity and variety of mascots at Gallipoli, see also J. Gallishaw, *Trenching at Gallipoli*, New York, 1916, pp. 31–2. Also pp. 83ff and 138ff for related information (spurious) about Simpson and his donkey.

69. See E. Leed, *No Man's Land: Combat and Identity in World War One*, Cambridge (England), 1979, pp.127–9, 144–5; Fussell, *op. cit.* chapter 4, pp. 124–135.

70. 'Digger's Diary', *Western Mail*, May 22, 1930 carried a typical 'miraculous escape' story. Instead of the usual Bible, the lucky digger was spared by a tin of bully beef.

71. Cuttriss, *op. cit.*, pp. 56–7.

3. The Anecdotal Republic

1. R. Edwards, *The Australian Yarn*, Adelaide, 1977. Also R. Edwards, 'Yarns and Contemporary Legends: A Reassessment' in R. Edwards (ed), *Proceedings of the 3rd National Folklore Conference*, Canberra, 1988; R. Edwards, *Fred's Crab and Other Bush Yarns*, Kuranda, 1990. There are, of course, many other collections of yarns, but Edwards is the only writer to attempt a serious classification and definition of this elusive genre of folk expression, though he does not consider digger yarns. See also J.S. Ryan and G. Seal, 'Folk Tales' in G. Davey and G. Seal (eds), *The Oxford Companion to Australian Folklore*, Melbourne, 1993.

2. An unattributed version of this is given in Robson 'The Australian Soldier', *op. cit.*, p. 328. An earlier occurrence is in Anon., *Digger Aussiosities: Collected by 'Aussie' During the Last Five Years*, Sydney, 1927, p. 122. Also in B. Wannan, *Come in Spinner*, (1964 as *Fair Go, Spinner*), Melbourne, 1979, p. 188 (from a NT informant) and in *Smith's Weekly*, May 9, 1925 (set in Palestine, 1917).

3. M. Field, *Dinkum Aussie Yarns: Tall Tales from the Bush*, Melbourne, nd, p. 19. On the same page, Field also relates the yarn of a digger who refuses to salute a British officer in Cairo because the officer is 'not one of our mob'.

4. A. Facey, *A Fortunate Life*, Ringwood, 1984, p. 264. See also J. Newman, 'Facey's Folkloric History', *Australian Folklore*, no 4, March 1990.

5. See P. Stanley, 'Paul the Pimp Re-considered: Australian "G" Staffs on the Western Front and the "Kiggell Anecdote"', unpublished paper to AWM History Conference, 1987 for details of this well-known anecdote. See also B. Liddell-Hart, *History of the First World War*, London, 1971, p. 434; Fussell, *op. cit.*, pp. 83–5;

Digger Aussiosities, op. cit., p. 124, for another yarn in which 'Billzac' cheekily salutes a British officer who complains that Australians are more trouble to them than all rest of British army. The Australian replies: 'That's exactly what General Hindenberg is saying'.

6. Cooper, *op. cit.*, p. 13.

7. Wannan, *Come in Spinner*, op. cit., p. 185; E. Nally, 'Hopping Mad', *Lest We Forget: Digger Tales, 1914–18, 1939–42*, Melbourne, nd (c1942).

8. *Digger Aussiosities*, op. cit., p. 115.

9. Field, op. cit., p. 42. Also in Wannan, *The Australian*, op. cit., p. 81 (from *Australasian Post*, April 26, 1956). This is a World War Two version.

10. F. Mills (comp), *Square Dinkum*, Melbourne, 1917, pp. 20–212. Another in W. Wannan, *A Dictionary of Australian Folklore*, Ringwood, 1987 (1970), p. 508 (also in his *The Australian*, p. 80). See *Aussie*, June 15, 1920, pp. 21 and 64 for other examples.

11. Fair, *op. cit.*, p. 12; also in J.J. Kennedy, *The Whale Oil Guards*, Dublin, 1918. See C. Atkinson, 'The Whale Oil Guards: A Plain Tale from France', *The Anzac Bulletin*, no 64, March 29, 1918, p. 13; C. Davies, *Ethnic Humour Around the World*, Bloomington, Ind., 1990, p. 266; *Smith's Weekly*, August 15, 1925. (This version appears without the motif of Birdwood telling the story after the war to amazed British officers. The dominant aim is to establish Birdwood's egalitarianism and common sense, or 'nous', while in the later versions, there is the additional fillip of rubbing the noses of the British officer class in Australian egalitarianism.)

12. In Fair, op. cit., p. 11, and also occurs in other versions. See Wannan, *Dictionary*, op. cit., p. 184.

13. *Digger Aussiosities*, op. cit., p. 7. Wannan, *Dictionary*, op. cit., p. 60.

14. Fair, op. cit., p. 11.

15. Nally, op. cit., np titled 'Slight Mistake'.

16. 'Semaphore', *Digger Yarns (and some others) to Laugh At*, Melbourne, 1936, pp. 31–2. Quoted in chapter 8. A version in *Digger Aussiosities*, op. cit., np.

17. Robson, 'The Australian Soldier', op. cit., p. 328 (sourced as 'traditional').

18. ibid.

19. Fair, op. cit., p. 11.

20. *The Listening Post*, August 17, 1923, p. 21.

21. *Lest We Forget*, op. cit. np. Also in Wannan, *Dictionary*, op. cit., p. 183; Field, *op. cit.*, p. 19; Fair, op. cit., p. 12; and E. Nally, *Digger Tales 1914–1918, 1939–1942*, nd (c1942), titled 'He Could Tackle It'. Accounts of digger nonchalance and humour under fire typically spice unofficial and semi-official unit histories, see for example W. (Captain) Belford, '*Legs-Eleven': Being the Story of the 11th Battalion (AIF) in the Great War of 1914–1918*, Perth, 1940, pp. 321–2.

22. Cooper, *op. cit.*, p. 13. (For photographic evidence of Australians playing two-up under fire at Gallipoli, see Robertson, *Anzac and Empire, op. cit.*, p. 175.)

23. *Herald* (Melbourne), February 27, 1956. (Quoted in Wannan, *Dictionary*, op. cit.,

p. 533. Also in B. Beatty, *A Treasury of Australian Folk Tales and Traditions*, Sydney, 1960, pp. 118–119.

24. *Australian Corps News Sheet*, November 6, 1918, p. 2.

25. Wannan, *Come in Spinner*, op. cit., p. 188; Field, op. cit., p. 42. See also Cuttriss, *op. cit.*, pp. 97–8 for the Digger smashed into a dugout wall by shell-blast — 'Are you hurt?', asks the NCO. 'Only my feelings', comes the reply.

26. Nally, *Lest We Forget*, op. cit., np.

27. W. Wannan, *Crooked Mick of the Speewah and Other Tales*, Melbourne, 1965. From Ian A. Hamilton. See also Wannan, *Dictionary*, op. cit. pp. 505–6. Also Field, op. cit., p. 42.

28. Cartoon version *Port Hacking Cough*, produced aboard homeward bound troopship, *Port Hacking*, December 1918 — January 1919. Reprinted *Aussie*, June 15, 1920, p. 21.

29. Cooper, *op. cit.*; Nally, *Lest We Forget*, op. cit. (Copy in La Trobe Library, Melbourne titled 'The Poor Cook'. Variant involving bag-piper in *Lest We Forget*.); 'Digger's Diary', *Western Mail*, January 2, 1930 and October 30, 1930; *Smith's Weekly*, June 6, 1925 (Variant involving digger being questioned by officer in charge of his court-martial: 'Did you call the cook a …____?' 'No', the digger answers, 'but I could kiss the …____ who did!').

30. Bean, *Official History*, op. cit., vol 6, p. 10.

31. E. Wells, *An Anzac's Experiences in Gallipoli, France and Belgium*, Sydney, 1919 (np); C. Longmore (ed), *Carry On! The Traditions of the AIF*, Perth, 1940, pp. 81–2. In this version it is a German officer at Beersheba who recognises the Australians by their language.

32. Quoted in Robertson, *Anzac and Empire*, op. cit., pp. 43–4, from letter of a New Zealand soldier, W. Fairbairn, March 1915; Robertson, *Anzac and Empire*, op. cit., p. 280, notes a variant in Godley correspondence, August, 1915. Variants (using Australian place-names instead of swearing) in 'Digger's Diary', *Western Mail*, September 25, 1930; *Smith's Weekly*, November 21, 1925 (names of Sydney suburbs); *Smith's Weekly*, August 29, 1925 ('a pot of Carlton'). See also *Honk!* no 11, December 7, 1915, p. 2 for a digger who 'wastes' bad language on a Belgian. See also chapter 6 of this volume.

33. *Honk!* no 11, December 7, 1915, p. 1.

34. Cuttriss, *op. cit.*; Wannan, *Come in, Spinner*, op. cit., p. 186.

35. Wannan, *Come in, Spinner*, op. cit. p. 186.

36. Wannan, *Dictionary*, op. cit., p. 554–5 prints a version much like the *Overland* one, notes others and claims for Boer War origin.

37. See *Overland*, July 1956; Fair, op. cit., pp. 42–3, titled 'How Would I Be?' and Field, op. cit., pp. 60–1. See *The Digger*, vol 1, no 6, September 8, 1915, p. 4 for a yarn titled 'The Senior Soldier' which, although it has a different point, has a very similar narrative structure to 'The Whinger'.

38. *Digger Aussiosities*, op. cit., p. 109; Wannan, *Dictionary*, op. cit., p. 183.

39. *League Post*, October 1, 1932, p. 3; 'Diggers' Diary', *Western Mail*, August 29, 1929.

40. *The Digger,* vol 1, no 6, September 8, 1918, p. 4; Field, op. cit., p. 19 (World War Two version — Western Desert).

41. *Aussie*, April 15, 1920, p. 20. Reprinted from *The Cacolet*, nd.

42. Wannan, *Come in, Spinner*, op. cit. p. 183.

43. The troops usually Shortened 'Anzac Cove' to 'Anzac'. The term was used colloquially, and this usage is preserved in *Inventing Anzac.*

44. *Aussie*, October 15, 1920, p. 22. Reprinted from *The Karoolian*, written aboard homeward bound *Karoola*, April 1919. Robson, op. cit., p. 320 for a similar story about Kitchener during the Boer War, when an Australian asked 'Mr Kitchener, when are you going to let us blokes go home? You know we only signed on for twelve months'.

45. For instance, 'Long Jack' (the stutterer) of Third Battalion yarns, *Aussie*, December 15, 1920, p. 66, and Smith's *Weekly*, April 25, 1925, in 'The Unofficial History of the AIF'; the drunken digger who attempts to obtain rations from Tommies with a false signature of 'Lt. Wank' in *Aussie*, Thursday, April 15, 1920, p. 20. Reprinted from *Headin' South*, August 1919 and the diggers who fool the sentry into thinking they are leaving camp by walking backwards when returning late from leave, in *Aussie*, December 15, 1920, p. 21 and *Digger Aussiosities*, op. cit., p. 19.

4. The Singing Soldiers

1. *Patches*, Adelaide, 1938 (Australian Army Medical Corps Interstate Reunion souvenir booklet) p. 47. Mainly a marching song. Only sources for versions quoted are provided here. For full comparative sources and notes see G. Seal, *Digger Folksong and Verse: An Annotated Anthology*, Perth 1991.

2. *Re-Union Songs*, Adelaide, nd [1920s], np (non-coms: Non-commissioned offi-cers). These verses are also sometimes found attached to versions of 'One For His Knob' ('Horseferry Road').

3. D. Winter, *25 April 1915: The Inevitable Tragedy*, St Lucia, 1994, p. 70.

4. W. Gammage, *The Broken Years: Australian Soldiers in the Great War*, Canberra, 1974, p. 126. (*Gyppo's*: Egypt's, and so '*Gyppo*' for an Egyptian; *Fritzie*: German soldier; *spielers*: swindlers, especially at gambling; *saida Wallahed*: Saida is an Arabic greeting, used colloquially by Australian troops as 'goodday'. The term was also used to denote a prostitute, hence '*saida bint*', a 'goodday girl'.

5. *Digger's Smoke-O War Songs*, Devonport, nd [1920s], np. Parody of the popular song 'We're All Waiting for a Girl'. (*Whizz-bang*: shell from a light field gun; *Five-nine*: artillery shell; *Nine-two*: artillery shell.)

6. Gammage, *The Broken Years*, op. cit., p. 163.

7. Anon., *Re-Union Songs*, Adelaide, nd. It seems that the song originated in the

Boer War, according to the compiler of B. Reardon, *With the Diggers, 1914–1918*, Sydney(?), 1935, p. 60.

8. Such as *4th and 56th Battalions* [sic] *Reunion*. (AWM Leaflets File 23753), p. 17 and ibid.

9. *Remnants from Randwick*, 1918, p. 13. Contributed by 'Punch' of the 9th Field Ambulance, this is an early printed version of 'Down in the Old Front Line'. The tune given is 'In Tennessee' [sic]. The hit song 'Down (or 'Back') Home in Tennessee' was composed by W. Jerome and W. Donaldson in 1915.

10. *Remnants from Randwick 2*, 1919, p. 27. Credited to 'N.D.M.C.' and titled 'One for His Nob', this World War One item was also well known in the 1939–45 war. *Shirker*: one who avoids responsibility or danger; *soft snap*: an easy and a safe occupation. The earliest text of this song is in *Aussie*, no 7, September 1918, p. 10.

11. *Re-Union Songs*, op. cit.

12. *Digger's Smoke-O War Songs*, op. cit. To the tune of 'Home, Sweet Home' (composed 1823: w. John Howard Payne, m. a 'Sicilian air' arranged by Sir Henry Rowley Bishop). (*Chats*: body lice.)

13. From an 'Ex-Bendigoian', VIC (Seal collection). Similar to that in *With the Diggers*, op. cit., p. 24. (*Jack Johnstons*: shells that burst with a great amount of black smoke, prompting the diggers to call them after the famous Negro boxer of the time, Jack Johnston; *Nappers*: heads; *Bully*: bully beef; canned meat.)

14. This version from F. Nettleingham (ed), *Tommy's Tunes*, London, 1918, p. 43. (*Sells*: cheats, liars; '*Six bob a day*' refers to the basic pay of an Australian soldier at this time, hence the term 'six bob a day tourists' sometimes applied by and to the AIF.)

15. An early (the first?) Australian version, reported as sung on Gallipoli by the *Sunday Times* (Sydney), July 11, 1915, p. 14 (a reference for which I am indebted to Peter Cochrane). Essentially the same text in Laseron, op. cit., p. 59, where he claims that the song was sung by Australians in Egypt before the Gallipoli landing. In his *On the Anzac Trail*, op. cit., p. 73, 'Anzac' says that 'Ragtime Army' was a common term for the AIF while in Egypt, again before the April 25 landing. On April 29, four days after the initial landings, the term 'ragtime army' was used by an Australian soldier to describe the Australian troops. Welborn, op. cit., p. 68. Welborn is quoting from the diary of West Australian Murray Aitken, waiting on Lemnos Island to join the attack as a member of the 3rd Brigade, 11th Battalion.

16. D. See Holloway (ed), *Dark Somme Flowing: Australian Verse of the Great War 1914–1918*, Malvern, Vic., 1987, for a representative sampling of this poetic material.

17. 'Corporal Geebung', 'The Songs We Sing', *The Kia Ora Coo-ee*, September 15, 1918, p. 18.

18. See 'Old Soldiers Never Die' in Seal, *Digger Folksong*, op. cit.

19. 'Corporal Geebung', op. cit.

20. Christensen, op. cit., pp. 21, 24, 27, 85–6 (poetry).

21. Quoted in Gammage, *The Broken Years*, op. cit., p. 201.

22. ibid., p. 227.

23. All quotations from C.J. Dennis, *The Moods of Ginger Mick*, Angus and Robertson, Sydney, 1916.

24. C.J. Dennis, *The Moods of Ginger Mick*, Sydney, 1916.

25. Winter, *25 April 1915,* op. cit., p. 155 (letter from A. Darnell). See also Welborn, op. cit., chapter 7 and pp. 68–8, 82 for singing amongst diggers. Australian War Memorial Leaflets file 23753 for a wartime printing of the lyrics of this song under the heading 'Your mates are done up! Will you look on?' According to what Nurse Olive Haynes heard from the Gallipoli wounded back at No 2 AGH, Mena, the Anzacs sang 'Tipperary' — M. Young (ed), *'We Are Here, Too': Diaries and Letters of Sister Olive L.C. Haynes No 2 A.G.H. November 1914 to February 1918*, Adelaide, 1991, p. 39.

26. Letter quoted in Tony Mathews, *Crosses: Australian Soldiers in the Great War 1914–18*, Brisbane, 1987, p. 80. On the progress of soldier songs from vainglory to sentimentality within a few weeks of arriving at the front (in this case, Gallipoli) see J. Gallishaw, *Trenching at Gallipoli: A Personal Narrative of a New-foundlander* p. 137.

27. *Patches*, op. cit.

28. Letter from Western Front, August 1916, quoted in Mathews, op. cit., pp. 61–2.

29. Many writers on war songs deal with the widespread nature of parody. See, for instance, Donald Sankey, *A Student in Arms*, London, 1918, p. 27 (British army); Brophy and Partridge, 'Introduction', *The Long Trail: What the British Soldier Sang and Said in the Great War of 1914–18*, London, 1965; and C.R. Collins, 'Songs of the Great War', in *The WA Digger Book, 1929*, Perth, 1929. A valuable treatment of parody in folksong is I. Russell, 'Parody and Performance' in M. Pickering and T. Green (eds), *Everyday Culture: Popular Song and the Vernacular Milieu*, Milton Keynes and Philadelphia, 1987. For primary accounts of the process of song parodisation by World War One Australian troops see 'A. Tiveychoc' (pseud: R.E. Lording), *There and Back: The Story of an Australian Soldier, 1915–1935*, Sydney, 1935, p. 261; Adcock, op. cit., p. 11; Fair, op. cit., pp. 111–2, 'A Concert at the Front'.

30. Zelman. Other versions in *Patches*, op. cit., p. 50; *With the Diggers*, op. cit., p. 33 and (British) in Brophy and Partridge (1965), op. cit., p. 54.

31. W.R. Williams (Rossiter), 1910.

32. 'M.H.M', *Listening Post*, January 20, 1937, p. 5. See also *Digger's Smoke-O War Songs*, op. cit.

33. *Patches*, op. cit.

34. A. Zelman, *Digger Songs*, Allan's Music Publishers, Sydney, 1935.

35. Collins, op. cit., p. 61.

36. *Aussie*, May 15, 1920, p. 13. The terms 'bloody' and 'bastard' are occasionally printed in publications of the war, see for instance, Bean writing on the Messines

attack in the *Anzac Bulletin*, no 23 (new series), June 13, 1917, p. 6 and again in no 64, March 29, 1918, p. 13.

37. J. Brophy and E. Partridge (eds), *Songs and Slang of the British Soldier 1914–1918*, London, 1930.

5. Transforming a Tradition

1. See R. Nile, 'Orientalism and the Origins of Anzac' in A. Seymour and R. Nile (eds), *Anzac: Meaning, Memory and Myth*, London, 1991, p. 37. In his *Anzac and Empire*, op. cit., p. 60, Robertson quotes a digger referring to 'the 3rd class nigger carriages' of the Egyptian railways.

2. See K. Fewster, 'The Wazza Riots, 1915', *Journal of the Australian War Memorial*, no 4, 1984; Robertson, *Anzac and Empire*, op. cit., pp. 59–60, for the Wazza/Wassir/Wassa Riot in Cairo, Good Friday, 1915. Also Gammage, *The Broken Years*, op. cit., pp. 39–40 and on other AIF rioting, pp. 28, 34–5, 234–5, 237–8, 264.

3. Gammage, ibid., p. 91.

4. C.J. Dennis, 'A Gallant Gentleman' from *The Moods of Ginger Mick*, Sydney, 1916.

5. A.T. Yarwood and M.J. Knowling, *Race Relations in Australia: A History*, Sydney, 1982; D. Cole, 'The Crimson Thread of Kinship: Ethnic Ideas in Australia 1870–1914', *Historical Studies*, vol 14, no 56, 1971.

6. On the role of the clergy, see M. McKernan, 'Clergy in Khaki: The Chaplain in the AIF, 1914–1918', *Journal of the Royal Australian Historical Society*, vol 64, no 3, 1978.

7. Robertson, *Anzac and Empire*, op. cit., pp. 59–60. On the indiscipline, venereal infection and related problems among the AIF, see chapters 6 and 8, respectively titled 'Painting Cairo Very Red' and 'The Wild Colonial Corps Has Left Cairo'.

8. Mathews, op. cit., p. 80.

9. Cochrane, op. cit., p. 111.

10. See D. Holloway (ed), *Dark Somme Flowing: Australian Verse of the Great War 1914–1918*, Malvern, Vic., 1987 for numerous examples of this. Also relevant is Kent, 'The Anzac Book', op. cit.

11. See, for example, those quoted in Welborn, *op. cit.*, passim.

12. Ambrose Cull, recollecting his experience as an officer in the lead-up to Pozieres, writes of the general tone of the letters it was his duty to censor: 'The key-note was ever the same, and I make no apology for breach of trust in revealing it. "My dear mother, this is the eleventh hour"'. A. Cull, *At All Costs*, Melbourne, 1919, p. 52. See also Cochrane, op. cit., on the relationship between the 'feminine' element of the digger and the Simpson story.

13. D. Kent, *From Trench and Troopship: The Experience of the Australian Imperial Force 1914–1919*, Hale and Iremonger, Alexandria, 1999.

14. See also David A. Kent, 'Troopship Literature: A Life on the Ocean Wave,

1914–19', *Journal of the Australian War Memorial*, no 10, April 1987; G. Seal, 'Written in the Trenches', op. cit.

15. For these reasons, those publications, such as *Sai-eeda* and the *Anzac Bulletin*, are not treated as trench journals, as they were published in England. See Kent, 'Troopship Literature', op. cit., and 'Introduction' to D. Kent (ed), *The Kia Ora Coo-ee*, Sydney, 1981 (reprint).

16. C.E.W. Bean (comp), *The Anzac Book*, London, 1916. See also Kent, 'The Anzac Book', op. cit.

17. According to Bean's diary, the suggestion was made to him on November 12, 1915; in Fewster, *Gallipoli Correspondent*, op. cit., p. 179. See also Bean, *Official History*, op. cit., vol 2, p. 384, where he makes an explicit distinction between General Headquarters publications like *The Peninsula Press* and 'A journal of a different order, *Dinkum Oil*'.

18. *The Bran Mash* 1, June 15 1915 (Australian War Memorial S114).

19. ibid.

20. *The Dinkum Oil*, nos 1–7, 1915. Handwritten, drawn and stencilled on one side of foolscap sheet. (Australian War Memorial 419/46/30 Acc 21435).

21. Bean, June 7, 1915, in Fewster, *Gallipoli Correspondent*, op. cit., p. 126. It is worth noting that this appears to be — so far — the earliest recorded use of 'furphy', pre-dating the earliest entry cited in Ramson, *The Australian National Dictionary*, op. cit. by three weeks.

22. *Honk!* no 10, September 30, 1915 (Australian War Memorial S508).

23. Both *Aussie and The Kia Ora Coo-ee* have been reprinted for a general readership since 1919. Some, such as *The 7th FAB Yandoo* (in September, 1919) were reprinted in omnibus form as souvenirs for veterans and their families, and so privately distributed.

24. *The Digger*, publication of the Australian Base Depots, France (Australian War Memorial S186).

25. See, for instance, *The Digger*, vol 1, no 24 — vol 1, no 26, January 1919; and *Aussie*, nos 2–4, February–April 1918 and again in nos 7–10, September 1918–January 1919. For a discussion on the term 'digger', see also Ramson, *The Australian National Dictionary*, op. cit.; Partridge, *Frank Honeywood,* op. cit., p. 71, and discussion elsewhere in this book.

26. See Australian War Memorial 3DRL 8044 for list of rejected *Anzac Book* mss and notations on which were later used for *The Rising Sun*: not entirely accurate. See also letter from A.W. Bazley, Bean's assistant, to the publication *Stand-To*, 9–12–63, regarding the rejected mss and the circumstances surrounding the editing of *The Rising Sun* — Australian War Memorial 3DRL 8044.

27. Australian War Memorial 3DRL 606, Item 68, p. 17.

28. B. Watts, 'Introduction' to *Selected Works of C.J. Dennis*, Sydney, 1988, p. 11. See H. McQueen, 'Sentimental Thoughts of "a Moody Bloke": C. J. Dennis', in the author's *Gallipoli to Petrov: Arguing With Australian History*, N. Sydney, 1984.

29. Alomes, op. cit., p. 57 on the sporting language and understanding which many

Australians applied to the war. On the broader relationship between sport, language and war see Fussell, op. cit., pp. 25–9.

30. See D. Blair, *Dinkum Diggers: An Australian Battalion at War*, Melbourne University Press, Melbourne, 2001, for a study of the disjunctures between the stereotype of the digger and the reality, as evidenced in the 1st Battalion.

31. See letter of Corporal H. Brewer in Stephenson, op. cit., pp. 288–92 regarding his and others' (veiled) experiences in France.

32. K. Theweleit, *Male Fantasies* (1977), trans. C. Conway, et al., 2 vols, Cambridge/Oxford, 1987. For critiques of the Anzac and digger traditions from a feminist viewpoint see C. Shute, 'Heroines and Heroes: Sexual Mythology in Australia 1914–1918, *Hecate*, 1975; M. Dixson, *The Real Matilda: Women and Identity in Australia 1788–1975*, Ringwood, 1976; A. Summers, *Damned Whores and God's Police*, Ringwood, 1975, especially pp. 380–87; and A. Howe, 'Anzac Mythology and the Feminist Challenge', *Melbourne Journal of Politics*, no 15, 1983. See also D. Buchbinder, 'Mateship, *Gallipoli* and the Eternal Masculine', in P. Fuery (ed), *Representation, Discourse and Desire*, South Melbourne, 1994.

33. J. Carroll, 'Mateship and Egalitarianism: The Failure of Upper Middle-Class Nerve', in Carroll, *Intruders in the Bush*, op. cit., pp. 146–7. Although relating to World War Two, the results of a survey reported in J. Barrett, *We Were There: Australian Soldiers of World War II Tell Their Stories*, Ringwood, Vic., 1987 tend to support this observation.

34. D. Hankey, *A Student in Arms*, London, (c1916), 4th edition, 1918, pp. 234–5. See also Thomson, *Anzac Memories,* op. cit., p. 42, where it is observed that the comradeship referred to as 'mateship' in the Australian context was not unique to the AIF; see also p. 94.

35. Carroll, 'Mateship', op. cit., for oral reminiscences; Cull, op. cit. and Blair, op. cit., as for examples of the retrospective lauding of mateship at war.

36. Mosse, op. cit.

37. Cull, op. cit., p. 32.

38. ibid., p. 54.

39. ibid., p. 55.

40. ibid.

41. ibid., p. 53.

42. ibid., p. 69.

43. For a full account of the activities of the Round Table Movement see L. Foster, *High Hopes: The Men and Motives of the Australian Round Table*, Melbourne, 1986. C.E.W. Bean was a member of the Sydney Round Table group — pp. 40, 192, 245.

44. It was the policy of the Round Table Movement that most 'general' (as opposed to 'special') contributions to their journal should be anonymous, Foster, op. cit., pp. 3–4.

45. *Round Table*, vol 9, no 34, March, 1919, pp. 388–401.

46. ibid.

47. ibid.
48. ibid.
49. ibid., p. 401.

6. The Echo of an Anzac's Cooee

1. See R. Gerster, *Big-Noting: The Heroic Theme in Australian War Writing*, Melbourne, 1987, pp. 118ff, 129 for the post-war concern of diggers with their own image and their exclusivity, in relation to literary output.

2. Robertson, *Anzac and Empire*, op. cit.; Wannan, *Dictionary*, op. cit.; 'Digger's Diary' in the *Western Mail*, 1929–1931 and later. See also C. Longmore, *Carry On!* op. cit. (Longmore, under the pen-name 'Non-com', had run the 'Digger's Diary' column). It seems that there was also considerable plagiarism or multi-state cooperation between Victorian and NSW publishers, at least, with duplication of yarn texts in publications like E. Nally (comp?), *Digger Tales*, np (c1942); and other such ephemeral publications. A similar processs of replication can be seen in the case of the song lyrics printed in many — though not all — reunion songbooks.

3. *Digger Aussiosities*, op. cit. See Fair, op. cit., p. 12; Atkinson, op. cit., p. 13; and Davies, op. cit., p. 266. For the story of Birdwood ducking see Fair, op. cit., p. 11. For an account of Birdwood's morale-boosting 'common touch', see H.B. Collett, *The 28th: A Record of War Service with the Australian Imperial Force, 1915–1919*, vol 1, Perth, 1922, p. 81. Birdwood and other digger yarns are also still circulating in New Zealand: see J. Henderson (comp), *Soldier Country* (1978), revised edition, 1990, pp. 124–29.

4. *Aussie*, December 15, 1920, p. 21.

5. *Digger Aussiosities*, op. cit. This story also appears in 'Semaphore', *Digger yarns (and some others) to Laugh At*, Melbourne, 1936, pp. 31–2.

6. *League Post,* October 1, 1932, p. 3. Also in Wannan, *Dictionary*, op. cit., p. 183. Another variant in *Western Mail*, May 8, 1930.

7. Cooper, op. cit., p. 13.

8. *Australian Corps News Sheet*, no 7, November 6, 1918. Also Wannan, *Dictionary*, op. cit., p. 183; *Herald* (Melbourne), February 27, 1956 (quoted, together with an earlier version of the yarn, in Wannan, op. cit., p. 533 and Beatty, op. cit., pp. 118–119).

9. Versions in Cooper, op. cit.; Nally, *Lest We Forget*, op. cit. (Copy in La Trobe Library, Melbourne titled 'The Poor Cook'. Variant involving bag-piper in *Lest We Forget*); 'Digger's Diary', *Western Mail*, January 2, 1930 and October 30, 1930.

10. Examples in chapter four, also in E. Wells, *Recollections of Gallipoli, France and Flanders*, Sydney, 1919. Other examples in *League Post*, October 1, 1932, p. 3 and Longmore, *Carry On! op. cit.,* pp. 81–2.

11. G.P. Cutriss, *Over the Top With the 3rd Australian Division*, London, nd (1918); Wannan, *Dictionary*, op. cit., p. 186.

12. Mills, op. cit., pp. 20–1. Others in Wannan, *Dictionary*, op. cit., p. 508; in Wells, op. cit., np.

13. See Seal, *Digger Folksong and Verse*, op. cit.

14. See *The WA Digger Book, 1929*, for instance, as well as occasional columns in *The Listening Post* and Perth newspapers.

15. On this point see Thomson, *Anzac Memories*, op. cit., p. 44 — 'Most of the men I interviewed referred to themselves as 'diggers' and not 'Anzacs'.

16. *Listening Post*, April 24, 1931, p. 21. ('Eggsers' refers to the folk name/battle cry of the 28th Bn. 'Eggs-a-cook', apparently derived from the cry of Egyptian egg-sellers). Collins had been a member of 14th Brigade, AIF, and was now a Captain in the AMF. He was also the author of an article titled 'Songs of the Great War' in *The WA Digger Book, 1929*.

17. *Listening Post*, September 17, p. 14.

18. *Listening Post*, May 20, 1927, p. 23, originally published in *Aussie*.

19. *Listening Post*, March 18, 1927, p. 15. 'The Long, Long Trail' (King/Elliott, 1913), popularised by the Canadians in England and, according to Masefield in his *Gallipoli*, London, 1916, first heard by Australians around February, 1916.

20. *Listening Post*, January 25, 1929, p. 14.

21. *Aussie*, April–December, 1920.

22. See, for instance, the program for 'The Western Mail Digger Diarist's, High-waymens [sic] and Virgilians' Dinner, October 10 (c1929), Battye PR9414. On July 31 'A Digger's Diary' printed a version of 'Mademoiselle from Armentieres', declaring it to have been 'the best item on the programme at a diggers' "smoko" the other night'. The Beverley AGM and 'smoke social' of the League took place at the White Hart Hotel on Saturday July 7, 1923 'in accordance with the best traditions of the AIF' and a band 'raised the spirits of the crowd to a most jubilant plane and songs — interspersed with toasts and yarns, made the function most enjoyable'. *Listening Post*, July 20, 1923, p. 8.

23. G.L. Kristianson, *The Politics of Patriotism*, Canberra, 1966. For a general history of the League, see P. Sekuless and J. Reece, *The History of the Returned Services League, 1916–1986*, Sydney, 1986.

24. *League Post*, October 1932. See Thomson, *Anzac Memories*, op. cit., pp. 120ff. for the social importance of the RSSILA for diggers. It is important to note that while the League itself may well have been unrepresentative of the political and economic aspirations of its rank and file, its social and cultural characteristics and functions were very much of the digger.

25. *Western Mail*, September 19, 1929.

26. *Western Mail*, November 7, 1929.

27. *Western Mail*, October 3, 1929.

28. ibid., and August 21, 1930.

29. *Western Mail*, October 3, 1929. Other reports of reunions refer to the singing, the furphies and consumption of food and drink — *Western Mail,* May 22,

1930. See also M. Wilson, 'The Making of Melbourne's Anzac Day', *Australian Journal of Politics and History*, vol 20, no 2, 1974.

30. Kristianson, op. cit.

31. See Australian War Memorial Leaflets File 23753 *4th and 56th Battalions* [sic] *Reunion.*

32. Reported, as an event worthy of note, in 'Digger's Diary', September 26, 1929.

33. There were also the occasional 'Anzac Eve' reunions, such as that in Melbourne, 1928, noted in Wilson, op. cit., p. 207.

34. A certain E. Wells (No 302, 2nd Pioneer Battalion) published his *Recollections of Gallipoli, France and Flanders* (By A Returned Soldier) in Sydney, 1919. It was also published at the same time and place as *An Anzac's Experiences on Gallipoli, France and Belgium* and as *Fragments from Gallipoli and France* in Sydney, Perth, Brisbane and elsewhere in 1920, 1921 and 1922, usually with some textual variation. Under the authorship of a 'V. Pretty', *Fragments from Gallipoli and France* was published in 1922, 1923 and 1926.

35. H. Anderson, 'On the Track with Bill Bowyang', *Australian Folklore*, no 6, September 1991.

36. For example, a compilation by E. Nally, or T. Carlyon re-published under different titles (*Digger Tales; Lest We Forget; Marching On: Tales of the Diggers*) after the first war and during the second, usually bore the imprint of *The Advertiser*, Footscray, Vic., or Geo. E. Nye Printing Service, Petersham, NSW).

37. See Kent, *The Kia Ora Coo-ee*, op. cit.

38. Anderson, op. cit., pp. 10–11.

39. From *The Dinkum Diggers* by A Returned Soldier, Melbourne, (nd late 1920s-early 1930s). This compilation also included a number of patriotic poems, including one beginning 'Sons of Australia! — Patriots all — /Nobly you answered your Country's call …'

40. *Listening Post*, January 24, 1930, p. 10.

41. *Listening Post*, June 20, 1930, pp. 3–5.

42. Alomes, op. cit., pp. 62–6; H. McQueen, 'New Guard', in his *Gallipoli to Petrov: Arguing with Australian History*, Sydney, 1984, p. 212.

43. Souter, op. cit., p. 281.

44. McQueen, 'New Guard', op. cit., pp. 200, 216–17.

45. Serle, op. cit., p. 156.

46. G. Blaikie, *Remember Smith's Weekly?*, Adelaide, 1966, pp. 15–19.

47. ibid.

48. *Smith's Weekly*, April 26, 1921, p. 9.

49. Blaikie, op. cit., p. 154.

50. Blaikie, ibid. and pp. 153, 111.

51. Wilson, op. cit.; M. Lake, 'The Power of Anzac', in M. McKernan and M. Browne (eds), *Australia Two Centuries of War and Peace*, Canberra/Melbourne, 1988; Kristianson, op. cit.

52. *Smith's Weekly*, July 9, 1921.

53. Blaikie, op. cit., p. 161, incorrectly gives October as the first appearance of this feature.

54. *Smith's Weekly*, September 13, 1924.

55. Blaikie, op. cit., p. 161.

56. *Smith's Weekly*, April 11, 1925.

57. Blaikie, op. cit., p. 161.

58. Quoted in ibid., p. 162.

59. *Aussie*, November 25, 1920, p. 23; April 15, 1920, p. 19; June 15, 1920 pp. 19, 21.

60. Such as *Headin' South* written on board the *Chemnitz*, homeward-bound, August, 1919 and printed in Durban, South Africa; *The Maltese Roller*, written aboard the *Malta*, homeward-bound August–September, 1918 and printed at Capetown; and *The Takadaussie*, written aboard the *Takada*, homeward-bound, July–September, 1919, and printed in Sydney. See also Kent, *From Trench and Troopship*, op. cit.

61. *Aussie*, November 15, 1920, p. 23; December 15, 1920, pp. 21, 66, 65.

7. The Fifty-third Sunday

1. RSSIL, *Anzac Day Commemoration Concert Souvenir Programme*, Sydney, 1921.

2. Though, as reported in the Adelaide *Express and Telegraph*, April 26, 1916, there was unhappiness among the Anzac ranks as only 'the giants were included' in the procession — the smaller Australians had to stay in camp.

3. Robertson, *Anzac and Empire,* op. cit., p. 247.

4. Stephens, *Anzac Memorial*, op. cit., p. 14.

5. See Wilson, op. cit., p. 203.

6. See L. Hills, *The RSSILA. Its Origin, History, Achievement and Ideals*, Melbourne, 1927, pp. 56–8.

7. Sekuless and Reece, op. cit., p. 48. See also Australian War Memorial Research Note No 546 (2nd series), 2 April 1952.

8. *Aussie*, vol 2, no 15, May 15, 1920, p. 12.

9. Reported in detail in *Listening Post*, September 15, 1922, p. 13. On the policies of the national body, generally mirrored by the WA RSSILA; see also Kristianson, op. cit.; and Lake, 'The Power of Anzac', op. cit.

10. *Listening Post*, October 26, 1923, p. 3.

11. *Listening Post*, December 21, 1923, p. 3.

12. *Listening Post*, October 24, 1924, p. 14 (inside back cover).

13. *Listening Post*, August 2, 1925. For financial membership figures for the League see Kristianson, op. cit., pp. 234–5; this shows that membership in WA remained strong while declining in most other states during the 1920s.

14. Lake, 'The Power of Anzac', op. cit., p. 212. See also Wilson, op. cit.

15. *Listening Post*, April 19, 1929, p. 18. The monument was finally unveiled in November, 1929. See the *Western Mail*, November 28, 1929, p. 1.

16. *Age*, April 25, 1916.

17. *Age*, April 26, 1916.

18. *The Anzac Bulletin*, no 17, May 2, 1917, p. 10 (new series).

19. Wilson, op. cit., after Kristianson, op. cit. Membership of the RSSILA, from around 150,000 in 1919, had dropped to 50,000 by the end of 1920. By 1924 membership was less than 24,000, with Victorian branches being hardest hit as only 7 per cent of potential members were financial. On the development of Anzac Day in Melbourne see Robertson, op. cit., pp. 246, 250, 253–4.

20. Despite the apathy regarding public spectacle, a uniquely Melburnian response at this time, Anzac Day services of various kinds were regularly held in churches throughout the city.

21. Wilson, op. cit., p. 206.

22. ibid., p. 208.

23. *Age*, April 25, 1929, p. 8.

24. *Age*, April 26, 1929, p. 10.

25. The strongly Protestant Melbourne establishment effectively monopolised the religious aspects of Anzac Day, a matter of increasing Roman Catholic dissatisfaction. This sectarian conflict, however, did not result in confrontation until 1938. See K. Inglis, 'Memorials of the Great War', *Australian Cultural History*, no 6, 1987, pp. 14–15.

26. *Age*, April 25, 1929, pp. 9–10 and *Age* April 26, p. 9.

27. *Age*, April 25, 1929, pp. 9–10.

28. H. Diddams (comp), *Anzac Commemoration 1921*, Brisbane, 1921, pp. 7–8. The organisation continues to this day.

29. As the second proposal of the original meeting put it. ibid., p. 8.

30. ibid., pp. 8–9.

31. On this point see King, op. cit., passim and especially chapter 5, 'Class, Rank, and the Digger'.

32. Diddams, op. cit., p. 10. A point of view echoed at length in the sermon of Rev. Father Paul Lynch, Chaplain-Captain AIF, preached in Roma, ibid., pp. 73ff.

33. ibid., p. 11

34. ibid., pp. 9, 10. Also photograph p. 5 (np).

35. ibid., p. 7.

36. For specific information on the role of women see M. McKernan, *The Australian People and the Great War*, West Melbourne, 1980, especially chapter 4 'To Wait and Weep': Australian Women at War', and chapter 6, 'From Hero to Criminal: the AIF in Britain, 1915–19'. Rates of venereal infection among Australian soldiers were well-known: see for instance, McKernan, *The Australian People*, op. cit., p. 92; Gammage, *The Broken Years*, op. cit., pp. 36, 37, 120, 123. On the murder of prisoners by Australian troops see D. Hawken, 'Letters and Diaries from Gallipoli', *Journal of the Australian War Memorial*, no 16, April, 1990, pp. 74–5.

37. Diddams, op. cit., p. 10. The sermons and addresses were by Roman Catholic, Presbyterian, Methodist, Baptist, Anglican, and Salvation Army clergy.

38. *League Post*, October 1, 1932, p. 23.

39. Quoted from the proceedings of the conference by Robertson, op. cit., p. 250.

40. Robertson, op. cit, p. 254.

41. *Sydney Morning Herald*, April 26, p. 14; 25 April, p. 10; 23 April, p. 15 (for list of clergy). A memorial tablet to Roman Catholic soldiers killed in the war was unveiled at the Catholic Club in Castlereagh Street at 3pm, *Sydney Morning Herald*, April 24, 1929, p. 18; April 25, 1929, p. 10; April 23, 1929, p. 10; April 26, 1929, p. 14.

42. See Australian War Memorial Research note No 546 (second series), 2 April, 1952. Also Hills, op. cit., pp. 56–8; *League Post*, October 1, 1932, p. 23, discussing Anzac Day celebrations in Queensland from 1930. South Australia had instituted the Anzac Day holiday in 1922, by accident, it seems. See Robertson, *Anzac and Empire*, op. cit., p. 251.

43. For the extent to which Anzac Day observance varied in the early years of its history, see Wilson, op. cit. and P. Kitley's description of Anzac Day in Toowoomba, Qld., in his 'Anzac Day Ritual', *Journal of Australian Studies*, no 4, 1979. Also L. Sackett, 'Marching Into the Past: Anzac Day Celebrations in Adelaide', *Journal of Australian Studies*, no 17, November 1985 and, more diffusely, C. Flaherty and M. Roberts, 'The Reproduction of Anzac Symbolism', *Journal of Australian Studies*, no 24, May 1989. McKernan, op. cit., p. 214, states that 'in 1928 'the march' was a universal way of commemorating the Anzacs', though his focus is mainly on Sydney and Melbourne.

44. C.E.W. Bean, 'Sidelights of the War on Australian Character', *Royal Australian Historical Society Journal*, vol 13, no 4, 1927.

45. See Thomson, *Anzac Memories*, op. cit., chapter 2, especially p. 70 for Bean's work on the *Anzac Book*.

46. A. Millar, 'Gallipoli to Melbourne: The Australian War Memorial, 1915–19', *Journal of the Australian War Memorial*, no 10, April, 1987. See also K. Inglis, 'A Sacred Place: The Making of the Australian War Memorial', *War and Society*, vol 3, no 2, 1985.

47. Quoted in Millar, op. cit., p. . 38.

48. ibid., p. 41.

49. *Canberra Times*, April 25, p. 1 and April 26, p. 1. See also *West Australian*, April 26, 1929, p. 19.

50. ibid.

51. See McKernan, M., *Here is Their Spirit: A History of the Australian War Memorial, 1917–1990*, St Lucia, Qld., 1991 for the details of the Memorial's history. The symbolism of the designs of the East and West windows of The Hall of Memory is important here. Both these are dedicated to the AIF (men and women), with the West window embodying the social qualities of Australian service men and women — 'comradeship', 'ancestry', 'patriotism', 'chivalry' (to the defeated) and

'loyalty'. The east window represents AIF fighting qualities — 'coolness' (in action), 'control' (of self and others), 'audacity' and 'decision'. From AWM, *The Hall of Memory*, Canberra (1961), 1984. The essentials of the Anzac tradition are clearly rendered here in the centre of the shrine.

8. The Great Spectacle

1. B. Kapferer, *Legends of People: Myths of State*, Washington, 1988, p. 147.
2. *Western Mail*, May 2, 1929, p. 25. The account of Anzac Day given here is derived initially from the *Western Mail* article. The details have been confirmed from other sources, including the *Sunday Times*, *The Listening Post*, the *West Australian* and *The Daily News*. See also *Anzac Day 1929 Order of Service*, Battye PR 8891/3, and also a motion picture of segments of the event by J. Finney, State Library of WA Film Collection.
3. *Listening Post*, April 19, 1929, p. 18 and May 24, 1929.
4. Also 'unfinished', in the sense that it had not yet fully grown, was the King's Park Honour Avenue. This memorial had been dedicated on August 3, 1919. See Honour Avenue Committee, *History of the King's Park Honour Avenues*, Highgate RSL sub-branch, nd.
5. Use of this and related terms discussed below derives from the symbolic anthropology of Victor Turner, based in turn on the pioneering work of the Belgian folklorist Arnold van Gennep in his *Les Rites de Passage*, Paris, 1909.
6. The event is referred to as the 'Dawn Service' in the *Sunday Times*, April 28, 1929, p. 3, which continued to use the term the following year — *Sunday Times*, April 27, 1930, p. 3. See also discussion below on the origins of this element of the Day.
7. Cole, op. cit.
8. A. Falassi (ed) *Time Out of Time: Essays on the Festival*, Albuquerque, 1987.
9. ibid., p. 2.
10. ibid., p. 4. For a rather different approach, see M. Ozouf, *Festivals and the French Revolution* (1976), trans. A. Sheridan, Cambridge, Mass./London, 1988.
11. ibid.
12. ibid., p. 5. On 'communitas', see V. Turner, *The Ritual Process: Structure and Anti-Structure*, London, 1969 and *Dramas, Fields and Metaphors: Symbolic Action in Human Society*, Ithaca/London, 1974 amongst others of his works that utilise the notion of communitas and structure. Turner introduced these notions in his 1969 work *The Ritual Process*. Communitas is the opposite of 'structure' — the official framework of law, institutions and norms. 'Structure is all that holds people apart' — *Dramas, Fields and Metaphors*, pp. 46–7. By contrast, communitas involves, and depends on, sharing.
13. Falassi, op., cit., p. 6 .
14. ibid.
15. See Turner, *The Ritual Process*, op. cit.

16. The following year, the daughters of the war dead were also allowed to march in Perth. *Sunday Times*, April 27, 1930, p. 3.

17. A. Van Gennep, op. cit.

18. See Kitley, op. cit., p. 59 on the 'Old Soldiers Fade Away' ritual in Toowoomba from at least 1934.

19. *The Daily News*, April 25, 1921, p. 6.

20. Diddams, op. cit., p. 3.

21. *Western Mail*, May 2, 1929. The allegedly unique nature of the Anzac's sacrifice was, apparently only able to be appreciated by men. See also ibid.

22. See *Listening Post*, May 24, 1929, p. 7. The 'Dawn Service' is usually said to have originated in Sydney in 1927, Robertson, *Anzac and Empire*, op. cit., p. 254 and Inglis, *Sacred Places*, op. cit., pp. 329–32, 423–5 and note 330. However, it is also widely believed, especially in Western Australia, that a Reverend White held the first dawn service in Albany, WA, in 1923, see 'Our First Dawn Service', *Willoughby* (NSW) *Legion Club News*, April/May, 1989, pp. 22–3. *The Albany Advertiser* for April 21 and April 28, 1923, makes no mention of this event as part of the official Anzac observances, though a small, spontaneous and folkloric activity would perhaps not have left many public traces. There is a commemorative marker of this event at the alleged site in Albany, and the belief is perpetuated in information displayed at Albany's 'Friendly Forts' heritage site. It is likely that news of this first dawn service spread by word of mouth, inspiring emulation and leading eventually to the event being accepted as part of Anzac Day. On this, again see Inglis.

23. *Age*, April 25, 1929, pp. 9–10.

24. ibid. and *Age*, April 26, 1929, pp. 9–12.

25. Sackett, op. cit.; *The Observer*, April 27, 1929, p. 49 (also p. 10).

26. *West Australian*, April 26, 1929, p. 19.

27. *Sydney Morning Herald*, April 25, 1929, p. 10.

28. *Sydney Morning Herald*, April 23, 1929, p. 15. The ferries were free to marchers wearing a badge.

29. ibid.

30. *Canberra Times*, April 17, 1929, p. 1; April 23, p. 1; April 25, p. 1 and April 26, p. 1.

31. See F. Crowley (ed), *A Documentary History of Australia, Vol 4, Modern Australia 1901–1939*, West Melbourne, 1973, pp. 252–4.

32. King, op. cit., deals with aspects of this problem.

33. The effect of the various War Precautions Acts from 1914 to 1918 was to suspend the usual constitutional limitation of the Commonwealth powers and to effectively restrict the legislative functions of Parliament.

34. Souter, op. cit. pp. 290–294.

35. ibid., pp. 307, 228–30.

36. *History of the King's Park Honour Avenues*, op. cit. Symbolically, the English oaks died, having to be replaced with eucalypts in 1941–2.

37. Robertson, *Anzac and Empire*, op. cit., p. 251.

38. S. Firth and J. Hoorn, 'From Empire Day to Cracker Night', in P. Spearritt, and D. Walker (eds), *Australian Popular Culture*, Sydney, 1979.

39. Diddams, op. cit., p. 3.

40. See Souter, op. cit., p. 223.

41. See Inglis, *Sacred Places*, op. cit. for some indication of the local variations of observation, pp. 422–40.

42. Kitley, op. cit.

43. R. White, 'War and Australian Society', in M. McKernan and M. Browne (eds), *Australia Two Centuries of War and Peace*, Canberra/Melbourne, 1988, p. 417. See also Inglis, *Sacred Places,* op. cit.

44. *Listening Post*, May 24, 1929, p. 7. 'It needs the pen of a master to portray the strange wonderment of scene and the deep impression created [by the dawn laying of wreaths]. One had to be there to understand. It was expected that a few representative war veterans only would be present to lay wreaths, but diggers and the public turned up in their thousands. The ceremony at dawn has not only come to stay, but it is our opinion that next year it will be extended throughout the country …'

45. Mosse, op. cit., discusses the transformation of the reality of war into the 'Myth of the War Experience, which looked back on the war as a meaningful and even sacred event'. In the Australian context, while the Anzac tradition sought to sacralise the war in the same way as the official traditions of European countries, the digger tradition sought to secularise it within the context of a populist Australian nationalism.

46. This struggle continued in the years after 1929. In 1930, due to the large numbers who attended the ceremony at dawn, it was found necessary to organise a 'procession from the gates of King's Park to the now-completed War Memorial. Military ceremonial further eroded communitas with the introduction of 'a muffled kettle drum' to accompany the procession — 'A Digger's Diary', *Western Mail*, April 3, 1930.

47. Inglis and Brazier recorded 1455 World War One memorials, though if the honour rolls and commemorative boards and other less public commemorations in country halls, schools, returned soldiers' clubs, etc. are also considered 'memorials' the number is dramatically higher, Inglis, *Sacred Places*, op. cit., p. 485.

48. Sir John Monash, letter from Serapeum, May 10, 1916, quoted in *Despatch*, vol 7, no 12, June 1972, p. 179. See also Inglis writing in *Age* and *Sydney Morning Herald*, Anzac Day, 1964, quoted in Sekuless and Rees, op. cit., p. 46. See also Donnell, op. cit., p. 94. The predominantly festive nature of the AIF observance of Anzac Day was again in evidence in France in 1919, where diversions included track events, tug of war, pillow fights and 'gymnastic entertainers' — see *Anzac Day 1919: Australian Base Depots, France. Souvenir Programme.*

49. Monash, op. cit. See also letter of W.O.C. Newman, 4th Division Ordinance, written from Serapeum on 26 April, 1916, describing the same events, quoted

in *Despatch*, vol 8, no 10, April, 1973, pp. 148–9. Newman also describes the Anzac night dinner at which he was 'the only one that did not open my bottle of beer — Of course someone else soon opened the bottle set for me' (p. 149).

50. Monash, op. cit.

51. Inglis in Sekuless and Rees, op. cit.

52. *Aussie —* 'The Cheerful Monthly' and also 'The Organ of Australianism', May 15 1920, p. 12. This was a commonly expressed point of view regarding the dawn service, see Sekuless and Rees, op. cit., p. 49; *The Listening Post*, May 24, 1929, p. 3; *Sunday Times* (Perth), April 28, 1929, p. 3; *Daily News*, April 25, 1929, p. 1.

53. *Toowoomba Chronicle*, April 20, 1916, p. 4, quoted in Kitley, op. cit., p. 58. It is instructive to contrast the Toowoomba, 1916, gastronomic experience with that recorded in the diary of Sergeant-Major T. Murphy, No 36, 1st Battalion AIF, homeward bound on the same day: '24/4/'16 — Anzac Day, first Anniversary of Landing. Saloon food to all ranks supposed to be issued, but does not appear. Officers have ten-course dinner …' Quoted in Stephens, *Anzac Memorial*, op. cit., p. 330.

54. Sackett, op. cit., p. 19.

55. *Listening Post*, July 20, 1923, p. 8.

56. ibid.

57. ibid.

58. *Anzac Bulletin* no 17, May 2, 1917, p. 10 (new series). Sports were also played aboard homeward-bound transports on Anzac Day, 1916. See Stephens, op. cit., p. 330.

59. *Listening Post*, May 19, 1922, p. 12; also September 15, 1922, p. 13. On October 20, 1922, p. 9, *Listening Post* reported the resolutions of the federal Congress regarding Anzac Day. In part 'the afternoon be devoted to sports and carnivals of a national character, designed to inculcate in the rising generation the highest national ideals'. What these sports might be was not specified, though the frequency of reports about tennis and bowls suggests that the less physical, non-contact sports were favoured.

60. C.H. Thorp, *A Handful of Ausseys*, London, 1918, pp. 33, 247–8. See also P. Charlton, *Two Flies up a Wall: The Australian Passion for Gambling*, North Ryde, 1987, pp. 257ff for a discussion of the popularity of two-up during the war.

61. Stephens, op. cit. p. 273. See also Laseron, op. cit., p. 25; 'Tiveychoc', op. cit., p. 44; Christensen, op. cit., p. 27. 'Anzac', unfortunately not always a reliable source, in his *On the Anzac Trail* also describes gambling and claims that the Anzacs took bets on who would live and who would die, which would go to heaven and which to hell, during the Gallipoli landing (p. 114). Even if untrue, this accords with what the Anzacs were expected to do.

62. Bean, *Official History*, op. cit., vol 6, p. 15.

63. ibid., p. 16.

64. All noted by Bean as extremely popular, ibid.

65. The practice of 'dicing with death' is often reported from the front lines where those already marked for death and presumably having reconciled themselves to eventual extinction, would deliberately expose themselves to sniper or other enemy fire. See Stephens, op. cit., p. 385. Also relevant is the extent to which the official language of war, as used by generals, politicians and reporters, frequently referred to the event as a 'game' which had to be 'played' — 'They played the game', wrote an anonymous author describing the behaviour of Australian troops in France, up to 1917, in Stephens, op. cit., p. 397.

66. Collett, op. cit., vol 1, p. 116. Collett also notes that substantial sums of money were involved in two-up games. See also yarns concerning two-up.

67. See Roberston's, *Anzac and Empire*, op. cit., p. 175. A certain F.J. Miles (DSO) addressed an Anzac Day service in the Central Hall, Westminster, London in 1918, claiming that he had witnessed diggers at the Gallipoli landing playing cards in the lighters that carried them towards the beach. Another group, whose lighter had been blown into the water 'vigorously expressed resentment against the man who had failed to salve their crown and anchor board'. *Anzac Bulletin*, no 69, May 3, 1918, p. 6.

9. Community and Nation

1. Supplied by Mr M. Robinson (Tas.), Seal Collection.
2. Collected from Mr Paddy Fosch, Hornsby, NSW by author, 1982.
3. Wannan, *Come in Spinner*, op. cit., p. 189.
4. *The Digger*, vol 1, no 6, September 8, 1918, p. 4 and Field, op. cit., p. 19 (World War Two version — Western Desert).
5. *Daily News* April 25, 1916, p. 8.
6. G.D. Snooks, 'Development in Adversity 1913–1946' in C.T. Stannage (ed), *A New History of Western Australia*, Nedlands, 1981.
7. From Mrs M. Ryan (NSW), Seal collection. Another version from Mrs T. Kennedy, set in Perth and another in L. Cleveland, 'When They Send the Last Yank Home', *Journal of Popular Culture*, vol 18, no 3, Winter 1984, p. 34.
8. E. and A. Potts, *Yanks Down Under, 1941–45*, Melbourne, 1985, p. 295. Also an oral version Seal Collection, op. cit.
9. K. Darian-Smith, 'War and Australian Society', in J. Beaumont. (ed), *Australia's War, 1939–1945*, St Leonards, 1996.
10. Kristianson, op. cit., Appendix B.
11. J. Barrett, *We Were There*, op. cit., pp. 185–7.
12. Extreme loyalty to comrades-in-arms and to the fighting unit or group is a constant factor noted by students of military psychology and sociology, and by the participants themselves. See S. Bidwell, *Modern Warfare: A Study of Men, Weapons and Theories*, London, 1973, especially the chapters titled 'Military Groups', 'Military Leadership' and 'The Stress of Battle'. For a participant-ob-

servation of 'mateship' amongst British 'Tommies', the equivalent of the digger, on the western front see Hankey, op. cit., pp. 234–5.

13. Blair, op. cit., *passim* and especially chpt 6 and Conclusion.

14. M. Johnston, *At the Front Line: Experiences of Australian Soldiers in World War II*, Melbourne, 1996, pp. 196–9. See also a letter on p. 187 that refers to the Second AIF as 'the big bronze [sic] Anzacs', an explicit recognition of their inheritance of the digger tradition.

15. ibid., chpt 10, 'A Band of Brothers?'

16. Blaikie, op. cit., p. 19.

17. Kristianson, op. cit., Appendix B. There was a slight rise in the 1960s, but the League would never again achieve its 1946 membership high.

18. There were 43 Army Nurses and 105 RAAF nurses on active duty in Vietnam, J. Grey, 'Vietnam, Anzac and the Veteran' in J. Grey (ed), *Vietnam Days: Australia and the Impact of Vietnam*, Ringwood, 1991, p. 91.

19. M. Cameron, *A Look at the Bright Side*, Richmond, Vic. 1988, np.

20. ibid., np.

21. *Australian Folklore Society Journal*, no 37, September 1997, p. 831.

22. ibid.

23. ibid.

24. Grey, op. cit., p. . 87.

25. ibid.

26. More than this number have since died of causes probably related to their war service, ibid., p. 279.

10.   The Lost Memorial

1. See Peter Cochrane's exposure of the manufactured legend of Simpson and the Donkey in his *Simpson and the Donkey: The Making of a Legend*, Melbourne, 1992.

2. See R. Ely, 'The First Anzac Day: Invented or Discovered?', *Journal of Australian Studies*, no 17, 1985.

3. *The Daily News* (Perth) April 14, 1916, p. 1.

4. *Anzac Bulletin* no 1, July 8, 1916, p. 4. Also covered in the *War Precautions Act Repeal Act 1920*, the *Crimes Act 1914* by substantial fines and gaol terms of up to 12 months. Also relevant to Anzac Day as official observance is the *Anzac Day Act 1995*, see B. Topperwien, 'The Word "Anzac"', *Sabretache* vol XXXVIII September 1997, pp. 33–36.

5. Quoted in W. Gammage, 'Anzac's influence on Turkey and Australia', paper presented at Australian War Memorial History Conference, July, 1990, p. 3.

6. *Anzac Bulletin*, no 9, July 28, 1916, p. 2. At a less exalted, but nonetheless revealing level, a proposal was made in August to change the name of the Tasman Sea to the 'Anzac Sea'. *Anzac Bulletin*, no 22, August 28, 1916, p. 3.

7. Mt Hawthorn Progress Association Constitution and Rules, 1916 (Ministry of

Fair Trading microfiche A17001), Objects 2e and 2f. An 'Affidavit Verifying Memorial' and incorporating the Association was signed by Frank Kelsall and John Beveridge on January 22, 1917. Beveridge was living in Kalgoorlie Street in 1915 and in 1916 moved to Anzac Road, according to the relevant editions of *Wise's Western Australian Post Office Directory*.

8. *Westralian Worker*, 17 December 1915, p. 5.

9. ibid. It is also noted here that 'A suggestion was made to the Progress Association that an endeavour be made to provide Mr Porter with a home'. The 'Mt Hawthorn Notes' column of this weekly ALP newspaper was written by 'Advance', clearly a member of the Progress Association, almost certainly Frank Kelsall, a local resident, linotype operator at the *Westralian Worker*, President of both the Association and of the Anzac Cottage Committee. Kelsall had emigrated to WA from New Zealand in 1896 and began living in (Mount) Hawthorn in 1913. He died in South Perth during the 1950s. (Interview with Frank Kelsall's grandson, Gordon Kelsall, 25/4/97) Kelsall always wrote his occupation as 'journalist' in legal documents relating to the Progress Association and Anzac Cottage.

10. It seems that the Progress Association was not incorporated until 1917, see 'Affidavit Verifying Memorial' by Frank Kelsall and John Beveridge, 23 January 1917.

11. This happened in 1916. *Wise's Western Australian Post Office Directory*, 1916 and 1917.

12. *Westralian Worker*, 11 February 1916, p. 3.

13. *Westralian Worker*, 28 January 1916, p. 2.

14. *Anzac Cottage Souvenir of the Monument Erected at Mt Hawthorn*, 1916, (2nd edn), np. The quotations and much of the information related to Anzac Cottage are taken from this and from the extensive pictorial and textual coverage given to the event by *The Western Mail*, February 4, 1916, p. 29; February 11, pp. 20, 28; February 18, p. 25. See also *Western Mail*, April 23, 1955; *West Australian*, April 25, 1963; April 26, 1963; April 14, 1964; and *The Westralian Worker*, December 1915–April 1916. There is no record of the fate of the 'decoction'.

15. *Westralian Worker*, December 4, 1916, p. 3.

16. *Western Mail*, 18 February 1916.

17. Broken and lost in the 1950s–60s (information from Mr Wayne Belcher), this tablet obviously (and typically) overlooks the New Zealand participation in the landing and the name 'ANZAC'.

18. *Westralian Worker*, December 4, 1916, p. 3.

19. *Anzac Cottage Souvenir of the Monument Erected at Mt Hawthorn*, 1916 (2nd edtition), np. Though the *Western Mail* report put the figure at 2,000.

20. *Western Mail*, 18 February 1916.

21. *Westralian Worker*, February 11, 1916, p. 2.

22. The external walls were substantially finished, with the rest of the work

completed over the next few weeks, see Anzac *Cottage Souvenir of the Monument Erected at Mt Hawthorn*, p. 3, and *Westralian Worker*, February to April, 1916.

23. *Western Mail*, 18 February 1916, p. 2.

24. *Westralian Worker,* March 3, 1916.

25. See M. Pitt Morison and J. White, 'Builders and Buildings' in C.T. Stannage (ed), *A New History of Western Australia*, UWA Press, Perth, 1981, p. 546.

26. Reported in the *West Australian*, March 25, 1916, p. 8. The MLA, Veryard, had emphasised that Mt Hawthorn was 'one of the most eligible residential districts in the neighbourhood of the city'.

27. *Westralian Worker*, 14 March 1916, p. 2.

28. *Westralian Worker*, 21 April 1916, p. 2.

29. *West Australian*, April 17, 1916, p. 7.

30. *Anzac Cottage Souvenir*, p. 3.

31. *West Australian*, April 17, p. 7.

32. There was also a later art union for a block of land donated to the fund, drawn at the May 23rd meeting of the Progress Association. It is not clear whether this was one of the previously sold blocks or yet another slice of land. *Westralian Worker,* 12 May, 1916, p. 2.

33. *Westralian Worker*, 21 April 1916, p. 2

34. *Daily News*, April 14, 1916, p. 1.

35. For a broader discussion of the World War One memorial movement see Inglis, *Sacred Places*, op. cit., chapter 4 and *passim* for the significance of war memorials, though Anzac Cottage is not mentioned.

36. Anzac Cottage Restoration 95 Committee Newsletter 1, 1994.

37. The work was organised and co-ordinated by a volunteer committee, with heritage specifications overseen by Laura Gray, who authored the Heritage Conservation Plan on the Cottage.

38. The Lone Pine seedlings are a recurrent and symbolically significant element in the undergrowth of the Anzac mythology in which they hold a position akin to that of pieces of the True Cross in Christian belief. There are numerous stories about how the seedlings were brought to Australia — and New Zealand — and by whom. None of them seems to have any historical foundation, a fact that has had no effect whatsoever on the persistence and potency of the story and its physical manifestations. The seedlings surface from time to time in newspaper correspondence; see, for example, the *Weekend Australian*, 10–11 August 1996 for a letter on the subject by military historian David H. Dial who outlines the (negative) results of his research into this topic.

11. True Inventions

1. E. Hobsbawm, 'Mass Producing Traditions: Europe 1870–1914' in E. Hobsbawm and T. Ranger (eds), *The Invention of Tradition*, Cambridge, Cambridgeshire, 1983, p. 307.

2. G. Seal,'Two Traditions: The Folklore of the Digger and the Invention of Anzac', *Australian Folklore* 5, 1991.

3. The processes by which the official tradition of Anzac and the folk tradition of the digger intermingle are not unique to those particular cultural formations. Similar processes can be discerned in the creation of other mythologies, such as that surrounding the progress of Ned Kelly from local outlaw to national hero, a set of discourses almost as riddled with ambivalence, contradiction and disjuncture as those of Anzac and the digger. See G. Seal, *'Tell 'em I Died Game': The Legend of Ned Kelly*, Melbourne, 2002.

4. Military activity and attack in Australia includes attacks on Indigenous people, the suppression of the Eureka Stockade and the Japanese bombing of World War Two. However important these events, they are not typical of the mass conflicts and mobilisation of civilians that characterise twentieth-century conflicts and which have been the basis of the mythology discussed in this book.

5. Thought to have been first enacted in Australia in 1952 at St Andrew's Anglican Cathedral, Sydney, and derived from an English observance for Armistice Day, Inglis, *Sacred Places*, op. cit., pp. 432–5.

6. G. Seal, 'Anzac Cottage: Australia's First Great War Memorial', *Simply Australia*, (online magazine) June 2002.

7. Inglis, *Sacred Places*, op. cit., for a broad survey of the number and variety of war memorials.

Appendix

1. L.L. Robson, 'The Origin and Character of the First AIF, 1914–1918: Some Statistical Evidence', *Historical Studies*, vol 15, no 61, October 1973. Also his *The First AIF: A Study of its Recruitment, 1914–1918*, Melbourne, 1970.

2. Robson, 'Origin', op. cit., p. 738.

3. Though by 1919 this proportion had dropped to 12 per cent. Souter, op. cit., p. 284.

4. ibid., p. 744.

5. Bean was of the opinion that 73 per cent of the first contingent of the AIF was born in the United Kingdom. This seems rather too high, though may have been encouraged by the high percentage of British in some sectors of the AIF, such as the 1st Brigade, whose recruiting showed a figure of around 60 per cent British-born. See Winter, *25 April 1915*, op. cit., pp. 31–2.

6. Robertson, *Anzac and Empire*, op. cit., p. 22.

7. Robson, *The First AIF*, op. cit., p. 52.

8. ibid., *passim*.

9. ibid., p. 37. The 1st Light Horse had a slightly higher proportion of Australian-born (79 per cent).

10. Robson, 'Origin', op. cit., p. 738.

11. ibid., p. 280. Robertson presumably means that the majority of Roman Catholics

were 'working class'. Though, by the same logic, this would imply that the vast majority of the AIF ranks were not working class.

12. Robson, 'Origin', op. cit., p. 749.

13. ibid. Interestingly, for the purposes of the present work, Robson concludes that 'reasons for this [disparity of religious affiliation and officer status] provide material for speculation about the 'democratic' character of Australian society but evidently have not interfered with the transmission of the democratic legend'. It seems fair to observe, as Robson implies, that this marks the point at which statistical analysis ceases to be useful for the investigation of socio-cultural processes.

14. McQueen, 'New Guard', op. cit., p. 212.

15. Gammage, *The Broken Years*, op. cit., pp. 280–3.

16. Those given here follow Gammage and are based upon *The Official History*, the *Official Medical History*, AWM, AIF and War Office sources.

17. Robson, *The First AIF*, op. cit., p. 203.

18. McQueen, 'New Guard', op. cit., p. 200. McQueen arrives at this figure by extrapolating backwards from the 1933 Census, which showed 226,438 males who had served overseas still living. While this is a statistically dubious method, it is sufficient to give an approximate figure of living diggers.

19. See Kristianson, op. cit., Appendix B for League membership figures. The 1919 figure is that claimed by the League; no accurate figures are available for this year's membership. From 1926, national League membership rose steadily from 30,346. There was a very slight decline in 1927, but by 1929 it stood at 41,417, according to Kristianson.

Select Bibliography

PRIMARY SOURCES
Libraries, Archives, Collections, etc.
Australian Archives

Australian Defence Force Academy Library, Canberra

Australian War Memorial, Canberra

Centre for English Cultural Tradition and Language, Sheffield University, Sheffield

Mitchell Library, Sydney

La Trobe Library, Melbourne

National Library of Australia, Canberra, (Manuscripts, Sheet Music, Oral History)

Battye Library, Perth

Western Australian Folklore Archive, Curtin University, Perth.

Trench Journals and Related Digger Publications
Aussie, from no 1, January 1918

Brain Wave

First Aid Post

14th Company Magazine

Ghutz

Honk!

Remnants from Randwick (published in 1918 and 1919 by No. 4 AGH, Randwick, NSW)

Sniper's Shots

The Battalion Buzzer

The Bran Mash

The Cacolet

The Desert Dust-Bin

The Mirage

The Mud Lark (later *Mud Lark's War News*)

The Dinkum Oil

The Kia Ora Coo-ee, 1918

The Kookaburra (1st Div. Base Depot, Tel-el-Kebir, 1916)
The Kookaburra (3rd DAC, 1918)
The Kookaburra (AMT, 1917)
The Rising Sun
The Yandoo (7th Fab Yandoo

Military and Government Periodicals
The Anzac Bulletin (London)
Australian Corps News Sheet
Diggers' Gazette (military)

League and League-related Periodicals
The Australian (AIF Returned Soldiers and Sailors Association of WA)
The Digger's Gazette, vols 1–4, 1919–24
Duckboard
League Post
Mufti
Stand-To
The Listening Post (Perth)
The Queensland Digger (RSSILA — Queensland)
The Digger

Newspapers
Age
Albany Advertiser
Argus
Canberra Times
Northam Advertiser
Smith's Weekly
Sydney Morning Herald
The Daily News (Perth)
The Express and Telegraph (Adelaide), 1916
The Observer (Adelaide)
West Australian
Western Mail (Perth)
Westralian Worker

Other Periodicals
Remnants from Randwick, No. 4 AGH, Randwick, NSW, 1918 and 1919.
Round Table

Memoirs, Reminiscences, Anthologies, etc.

'A Bombardier', *With the 27th Australian Battery in France,* London, 1919.

'A Returned Soldier', *The Dinkum Digger,* Melbourne, nd (late 1920s–early 1930s).

'CNL', 'Songs of the War', *The Listening Post,* Feb. 20, 1937.

'MHM', 'Songs of the War', *The Listening Post,* April 15, 1937.

'Tiveychoc, A'. (pseud: Lording, R.E.) *There and Back: The Story of an Australian Soldier, 1915–1935,* Sydney, 1935.

Adcock, W.F., *Genuine War Letters,* Melbourne, nd. [1919].

Anon. (Longmore, C.), 'Digger's Diary' in the *Western Mail,* 1929–1931.

Anon., 'Digger Journalism on Land and Sea', *Aussie,* April–December, 1920.

Anon., 'Songs of the Great War', *Twenty Years After,* Parts 12, 13, nd (1939?).

Anon., 'Why Do We Still Favour First World War Songs?', *Mufti,* 14:6, June 1949.

Anon., 'Writers of War Songs', *Duckboard,* April 1929.

Anon., *Digger Aussiosities: Collected by 'Aussie' During the Last Five Years,* Sydney, 1927.

Anon., *Lest We Forget: Digger Tales 1914–18, 1939–41,* Melbourne., nd (1941?).

Anon., *Re-Union Songs,* Adelaide, nd.

Anon., *Songs of the 7th Battalion,* Melbourne, 1915.

Anon., *Songs the Soldiers Sang,* New York, 1918.

Anon., *The Airman's Song Book,* nd, np.

Anzac Cottage Souvenir of the Monument Erected at Mt Hawthorn, 1916, (2nd edn).

Anzac, *On the Anzac Trail: Being Extracts from the Diary of a New Zealand Sapper,* London, 1916.

Bean, C.E.W. (ed), *The Anzac Book,* London, 1916.

Bell, A.D., *An Anzac's War Diary,* Adelaide, 1981.

Carson, H., *Battlefield Backwash: A Digger's Memoirs,* Perth, 1929.

Christensen, R. (ed), *To All My Dear People: The Diary and Letters of Private Hubert P. Demasson 1916–1917,* Fremantle, 1988.

Collins, C.R., 'Songs of the Great War', in *The WA Digger Book 1929,* Perth, 1929.

Cooper, Albert Horace, *Character Glimpses: Australians on the Somme,* nd (1919?).

Cull, A., *At All Costs,* Melbourne, 1919.

Cuttriss, George Percival, *'Over the Top' with the Third Australian Division,* London, nd (1918).

Diddams, H. (comp.), *Anzac Commemoration 1921,* Brisbane, 1921.

Digger's Smoke-O War Songs, Devonport (Tas), nd.

Dinning, H., *By-Ways on Service: Notes from an Australian Journal*, London, 1918.

Donnell, Anne, *Letters of an Army Sister*, Sydney, 1920.

Doull, David (Lt.) *With the Anzacs in Egypt*, Sydney, 1916.

East, Sir Ronald (ed), *The Gallipoli Diary of Sergeant Lawrence of the Australian Engineers — 1st AIF 1915*, Melbourne, 1981.

Facey, A. B., *A Fortunate Life*, Fremantle, 1984.

Gallishaw, J., *Trenching at Gallipoli: A Personal Narrative of a Newfoundlander with the Illfated Dardanelles Expedition*, New York, 1916.

Garland, Hugh G., *Vignettes of War* (from the notebook of a journalist in arms), Adelaide ?, nd (1917?).

Graves, R., *Goodbye To All That*, London, 1929.

Greenwall, H.J., 'The Songs They Sang: Some Famous Oldtime Melodies', *The Queensland Digger*, Nov. 1, 1939.

Hankey, D., *A Student in Arms*, London, (1916?), 4th edn. 1918.

Hanman, E.F. ('Haystack'), *Twelve Months with the Anzacs*, Brisbane, 1916.

Harney, W., *Bill Harney's War*, Melbourne, 1983. (adapted from ABC Radio broadcast of same name).

Harris, P., 'The Story of *Aussie*', *The Digger's Gazette*, March 15, 1920.

Hartt, C., *Diggerettes*, Sydney, nd (1917?).

Hiscock, E., *The Bells of Hell go Ting-a-Ling-a-Ling*, London, 1976.

Kent, D., (ed) *The Kia Ora Coo-ee*, Sydney, 1981 (facsimile reprint of *The Kia Ora Coo-ee*).

Knyvett, Capt. R. Hugh, '*Over There' With the Australians*, New York, 1918.

Laseron, Charles F., *From Australia to the Dardanelles: Being Some Odd Pages from the Diary of Charles Francis Laseron*, Sydney, 1916.

Mills, F., '(The Twinkler'), (comp.) *Square Dinkum*, Melbourne, 1917.

Nally, E. (comp.?)*Lest We Forget: Digger Tales 1914–18, 1939–42*, Melbourne, nd (1942?).

Nally, E. (comp?), *Digger Tales*, np, nd, (1942?).

Nettleingham, F. (ed), *Tommy's Tunes*, London, 1918.

Nicholls, H., 'The Anzac's Forebears', in Stephens, A.G. (ed) *The Anzac Memorial*, Sydney, 1917.

tridge, E., writing as 'Frank Honeywood', *Frank Honeywood, Private: A ersonal Record of the 1914–18 War*, [1929] Melbourne University Press tion, 1987.

Adelaide, 1938. (Australian Army Medical Corps Interstate Reunion nir booklet).

C.G. (Lt.), 'Anzac Vocabulary', in Stephens, A.G. (ed), *Anzac Memorial*, , 1917.

Pretty, V., *Fragments from Gallipoli and France*, np, 1922.

Pritchard, Les H. (comp.), *Lest We Forget: Anzac Day Souvenir*, Perth, 1918.

Pulling, C., *They Were Singing and What They Were Singing About*, London, 1952.

Re-Union Songs, Adelaide, nd.

Reardon, B., *With the Diggers, 1914–1918*, Sydney?, 1935.

Sankey, Donald, *A Student in Arms*, London, 1918.

Scanlon, H. (comp.), *Digger Stories*, np (Sydney?), nd (1929?).

Semaphore, *Digger yarns (and some others) to Laugh At*, Melbourne, 1936.

''SJS' (comp.) (Fourth Div. AMC), *With the Diggers, 1914–1918*, np, 1933.

Songs the Soldiers and Sailors Sing, New York, 1918.

Stephens, A.G., (ed) *Anzac Memorial*, 2nd edn. Sydney, 1917.

Sydney University Company, *The Company Songbook*, Sydney, 1918.

Sydney University Student Songbook, Sydney, 1915.

The WA Digger Book, Perth, 1929.

Thorp, C. Hampton, *A Handful of Ausseys*, London, 1918.

Wells, E. (No 302, 2nd Pioneer Battalion), *Recollections of Gallipoli, France and Flanders* (By A Returned Soldier) Sydney, 1919.

Wells, E., *An Anzac's Experiences in Gallipoli, France and Belgium,* Sydney, 1919.

Wells, E., *An Anzac's Experiences on Gallipoli, France and Belgium*, Perth, 1922.

Wells, E., *Fragments from France and Gallipoli by a Returned Anzac*, np, 1921.

Wells, E., *Fragments from Gallipoli and France*, Brisbane, 1920 (also 1921).

Westralia Gift Book, Perth, 1916 (Preface by Walter Murdoch).

White, J. A., *With the Men of the AMP Society in the Great War*, Sydney?, nd.

Wilson, E. H., 'Melody at War: Songs the Soldiers Sang', *The Queensland Digger,* 13:11, November 1937.

Zelman, A., *Digger Songs*, Allan's Music Publishers, Sydney, 1935.

Unpublished Materials and Ephemera (Diaries, Programs, Correspondence, etc.)

Anzac Day 1919: Australian Base Depots, France (program), BL PR 2946.

Anzac Day Order of Service 1923, Perth, 1923 BLPR8891/1–2.

Anzac Day: Orders of Service, Cottesloe, 1928 and 1935. BL PR 5305/1–2.

Anzac Day Souvenir, Geraldton, April 26 [sic], 1920 (lists 'Returned Heroes') BL PR 8891/13.

Anzac Fellowship of Women (records 1918–1967) MS 2864 NLA.

Australian War Memorial Research Notes, 1st and 2nd Series.

Australian War Memorial Special Collections — 'Cigarette Cards — Souvenirs — Leaflets'. Un-numbered black plastic file.

Bazley to James (*Stand-To*) 9–12–63 (letter regarding *Anzac Book* MS) AWM 3DRL/8044.

Bazley, list of rejected MSS of Anzac Book, AWM 3DRL/8044.

Bean, C.E.W., Diary 44, Feb–March 1916; Diary 72, Dec 1916–Jan 1917 and associated papers at AWM 3DRL606.

Benett, T.P., Poems, MS 10138 MSB 173 (La Trobe).

Bostock, H.P., 'The Diary of a Brigade Scout World War 1', typescript BL Q940.415 BOS.

Cleveland, L., 'Soldiers' Songs: The Folklore of the Powerless', unpub. typescript.

Dewar, S., '*Having A Lively Time*': *Australians at Gallipoli in 1915* (Catalogue of Australian MS Collection La Trobe Library), Melbourne, 1990).

Diary of A.J. Stoppard (7337), 5th AA Brigade, AIF, 2nd Div. in possession of Ms. F. Chanter, Berry, NSW.

Finney, J., 'Anzac Day, Perth, 1929', (motion picture) State Library of WA Film Collection.

4th and 56th Battalions [sic] *Reunion*. (AWM Leaflets File 23753).

Garden, F.G., 'History of the Riverston Sub-Branch RSL', Riverston, 1987. (leaflet — BL PR 11030/5).

Harris, Phillip L., (Cpl.), MS 7367 NLA.

Langford, P.C.W., Recollections, MS 11240 MSB 391 (La Trobe).

'Leaflets World War 1' (Wartime issues, poetry and song), AWM.

McPhail, Driver. E., notebook, AWM 3DRL6000.

Morrell, C. F., MS 11202 MSB638 (La Trobe).

Millard, W.G., Copies of Gunner Millard's papers, correspondence, etc. in possession of author.

O'Malley, Cpl., letter AWM PR84/287.

Perkins, Pte. D., Typescript AWM PR88/019.

Rawlinson exercise book AWM 3DRL4162.

Sanders, R., notebook AWM PR88/114.

Seal collection — miscellaneous letters, diaries, reminiscences, verse, songs, etc. from World War One veterans and their families, collected 1980–1990.

RSL — 'Souvenirs' (and Reunions) Nos. 1–2, AWM.

Springthorpe, J.W., Poems, MS9898 Bay 11/4a (La Trobe).

Tickner, F., AWM PR84/105.

Woodman (songs) AWM 3DRL5688.

SECONDARY SOURCES

Books

Allport, G.W. and Postman, L.J., *The Psychology of Rumour*, New York, 1947.

Alomes, S. and Jones, C. (eds), *Australian Nationalism*, Sydney, 1991.

Alomes, S., *A Nation at Last? The Changing Character of Australian Nationalism 1880–1988*, Sydney, 1988.

Australian War Memorial, *The Hall of Memory*, Canberra (1961), 1984.

Barker, M., *Nightingales in the Mud: The Digger Sisters of the Great War 1914–1918*, Sydney, 1989.

Barrett, J., *We Were There: Australian Soldiers of World War II*, Ringwood, 1987.

Bean, C.E.W., *Anzac to Amiens*, Canberra, 1952.

Bean, C.E.W., *Dreadnought of the Darling*, London, 1911.

Bean, C.E.W., (ed) *The Official History of Australia in the War of 1914–18*, 12 Vols, Sydney, 1921–37.

Beatty, B., *A Treasury of Australian Folk Tales and Traditions*, Sydney, 1960.

Beaumont, J., (ed), *Australia's War, 1914–1918*, Sydney, 1995.

Belford, Walter, C. (Capt.), *"Legs Eleven": Being the Story of the 11th Battalion (AIF) in the Great War of 1914–1918*, Perth, 1940.

Blaikie, G., *Remember Smith's Weekly?* Adelaide, 1966.

Blair, D., *Dinkum Diggers: An Australian Battalion at War*, Melbourne University Press, Melbourne, 2001.

Bonaparte, Marie, *Myths of War*, London, 1947.

Brophy, J. and Partridge, E. (eds), *Songs and Slang of the British Soldier 1914–1918*, London, 1930. (Re-published in a number of revised editions, most recently as *The Long Trail: What the British Soldier Sang and Said in the Great War of 1914–18*, London, 1965).

Buley, E. C., *A Child's History of Anzac*, London, 1916.

Buley, E.C., *Glorious Deeds of the Australasians in the Great War*, London, 1916.

Butler, A.G., *The Digger: A Study in Democracy*, Sydney, 1945.

Carroll, J., (ed), *Intruders in the Bush: The Australian Quest for Identity*, Melbourne, 1982.

Cochrane, P., *Simpson and the Donkey: The Making of a Legend*, Melbourne, 1992.

Collett, H.B., *The 28th: A Record of War Service with the Australian Imperial Force, 1915–1919*, Vol. 1, Perth, 1922.

Crowley, F., *Australia's Western Third: A History of Western Australia*, London, 1960.

Crowley, F. (ed), *Modern Australia, 1901–1939*, Vol. 4 of *A Documentary History of Australia*, West Melbourne, 1973.

Damouisi, J. and Lake, M. (eds), *Gender and War: Australians at War in the Twentieth Century*, Cambridge University Press, Melbourne, 1995.

Davies, C., *Ethnic Humour Around the World*, Bloomington, Ind., 1990

Dennis, C.J., *The Moods of Ginger Mick*, Sydney, 1916.

Downing, W.H., *Digger Dialects*, Sydney, 1919.

Edwards, R., *Fred's Crab and Other Bush Yarns,* Kuranda, 1989.

Edwards, R. (ed), *Proceedings of the 3rd National Folklore Conference,* Canberra, 1988.

Edwards, R., *The Australian Yarn,* Adelaide, 1977.

Fair, R. (Comp.), *A Treasury of Anzac Humour*, Brisbane, 1965.

Falassi, A. (ed), *Time Out of Time: Essays on the Festival*, Albuquerque, 1987.

Fewster, K. (ed), *Gallipoli Correspondent: The Frontline Diary of C.E.W. Bean*, Sydney, 1983.

Finnegan, R., *Oral Poetry: Its Nature, Significance and Social Context*, Cambridge, 1977.

Foster, L., *High Hopes: The men and motives of the Australian Round Table*, Melbourne, 1986.

Fraser, E. and Gibbons, J. (comps.), *Soldier and Sailor Words and Phrases*, London, 1925.

Fussell, P., *The Great War and Modern Memory*, New York, 1975.

Gammage, W., *The Broken Years: Australian Soldiers in the Great War*, Canberra, 1974.

Gerster, R., *Big-Noting: The Heroic Theme in Australian War Writing*, Melbourne, 1987.

Goody, J., *The Interface Between the Written and the Oral*, Cambridge, 1987.

Gregory, J. (ed), *Western Australia Between the Wars 1919–1939,* (Studies in Western Australian History XI, June 1990), University of Western Australia, Nedlands, 1990.

Hills, L., *The RSSILA. Its Origin, History, Achievement and Ideals*, Melbourne, 1927.

Hobsbawm, E. and Ranger, T. (eds), *The Invention of Tradition*, Cambridge, 1984.

Holloway, D. (ed), *Dark Somme Flowing: Australian Verse of the Great War 1914–1918*, Malvern, Vic., 1987.

Honour Avenue Committee, *History of the King's Park Honour Avenues*, Highgate RSL sub-branch, nd (1950s?).

Hornadge, Bill, *The Australian Slanguage*, North Ryde, 1980.

Hughes, J. (ed), *Australian Words and Their Origins*, Melbourne, 1989.

Inglis, K., *Sacred Places: War Memorials in the Australian Landscape*, Melbourne, 1998.

Kapferer, B., *Legends of People: Myths of State*, Washington, 1988.

Kent, D., *From Trench and Troopship: The Experience of the Australian Imperial Force 1914–1919*, Alexandria, 1999.

Krantz, F. (ed), *History from Below: Studies in Popular Protest and Ideology*, Oxford, 1988.

Kristianson, G.L., *The Politics of Patriotism: The Pressure Group Activities of the Returned Servicemen's League*, Canberra, 1966.

Laffin, J., *Digger: The Story of the Australian Soldier*, London, 1959.

Layman, L. and Stannage, C.T. (eds), *Celebrations in West Australian History*, Studies in West Australian History X, April, 1989.

Leed, E., *No Man's Land: Combat and Identity in World War 1*, Cambridge, 1979.

Longmore, C. (ed), *Carry On! The Traditions of the AIF*, Perth, 1930.

Longmore, C., *"Eggs-A-Cook!": The Story of the Forty-Fourth*, Perth, 1921.

Longmore, C., *The Old Sixteenth: Being a Record of the 16th Battalion, AIF, During the Great War, 1914–1918*, Perth, 1929.

Lowenthal, D., *The Past is a Foreign Country*, Cambridge, 1985.

Mandle, W.F., *Going it Alone: Australia's National Identity in the Twentieth Century*, (1978) Ringwood, Vic. 1980.

Mathews, Tony, *Crosses: Australian Soldiers in the Great War 1914–18*, Brisbane, 1987.

McCarthy, D., *Gallipoli to the Somme: The Story of C.E.W. Bean*, Sydney, 1983.

McClure, K., *Visions of Bowmen and Angels: Mons 1914*, St Austell, Cornwall, 1992.

McKernan, M and Browne, M. (eds), *Australia Two Centuries of War and Peace*, Canberra/Melbourne, 1988.

McKernan, M., *Here is Their Spirit: A History of the Australian War Memorial, 1917–1990*, St Lucia, Qld., 1991.

McKernan, M., *The Australian People and the Great War*, West Melbourne, 1980.

McLachlan, N., *Waiting for the Revolution: A History of Australian Nationalism*, Ringwood, 1988.

McQueen, H., *Gallipoli to Petrov: Arguing with Australian History*, N. Sydney, 1984.

Meredith, J. and Anderson, H., *Folksongs of Australia, and the men and women who sang them*, Sydney, 1967.

Moorhouse, G., *Hell's Foundations: A Town, its Myths and Gallipoli*, London, 1992.

Mosse, G., *Fallen Soldiers: Reshaping the Memory of the World Wars*, New York, 1990.

Nile, R. and Seymour, A. (eds), *Anzac: Meaning, Memory and Myth*, London, 1991.

Palmer, Roy, *What A Lovely War: British Soldiers' Songs from the Boer War to the Present Day*, London, 1990.

Pickering M. and Green, Tony (eds), *Everyday Culture: Popular Song and the Vernacular Milieu*, Milton Keynes/Philadelphia, 1987.

Ponsonby, A., *Falsehood in War-Time*, London, 1928.

Potts, E. and A., *Yanks Down Under, 1941–45*, Melbourne, 1985.

Powell, C. and Paton, G. (eds), *Humour in Society: Resistance and Control*, London, 1988.

Punter, D. (ed), *Introduction to Contemporary Cultural Studies*, London, 1986.

Ramson, W.S. (ed), *Australian National Dictionary*, Melbourne, 1988.

Robertson, John, *Anzac and Empire: The Tragedy and Glory of Gallipoli*, Port Melbourne, 1990.

Robertson, John, *Australia at War 1939–1945*, Melbourne, 1981.

Robson, L., *Australia and the Great War*, Melbourne, 1969.

Robson, L., *The First AIF: A Study of Its Recruitment 1914–1918*, Melbourne, 1970.

Rosnow, R. and Fine, G., *Rumour and Gossip: The Social Psychology of Hearsay*, New York, 1976.

Ross, J., *The Myth of the Digger. Australian Soldiers in Two World Wars*, Sydney, 1985.

Scott, E. *Australia During the War*. Vol. 2 of *Official History of Australia in the War of 1914–1918*, Sydney, 1937.

Scott, J., *Domination and the Arts of Resistance: Hidden Transcripts*, Yale University Press, New Haven/London, 1990.

Seal, G., (ed) *Digger Folksong and Verse of World War One: An Annotated Anthology*, Perth, 1991.

Sekuless, P. and Reece, J., *The History of the Returned Services League, 1916–1986*, Sydney, 1986.

Shibutani, T., *Improvised News*, Indianapolis, 1966.

Shils, E., *Tradition*, London, 1981.

Skocpol, T. (ed), *Vision and Method in Historical Sociology*, Cambridge, 1984.

Souter, G., *Lion and Kangaroo: The Initiation of Australia 1901–1919*, Sydney, 1976.

Spearritt, P. and Walker, D. (eds), *Australian Popular Culture*, Sydney, 1979.

Terraine, J., *The Smoke and the Fire: The Myths and Anti-Myths of War, 1861–1945*, London, 1980.

Theweleit, K., *Male Fantasies*, (1977), trans. Conway, C., et. al., 2 Vols., Cambridge/Oxford, 1987.

Thomson, A., *Anzac Memories: Living with the Legend*, Melbourne, 1994.

Thompson, E.P., *Customs in Common*, London, 1991.

Turner, V., *Dramas, Fields and Metaphors: Symbolic Action in Human Society*, London, 1974.

Turner, V., *The Forest of Symbols*, Ithaca, NY, 1967.

Turner, V., *The Ritual Process: Structure and Anti-Structure*, London, 1969.

Van Gennep, A., *Rites de Passage*, Paris, 1909.

Vansina, J., *Oral Tradition,* (1961), Harmondsworth, 1965.

Wannan, W., *A Dictionary of Australian Folklore*, Ringwood, 1987 (1970).

Wannan, W., *Bill Wannan's Great Book of Australiana*, Adelaide, 1977.

Wannan, W., *Come in Spinner*, (1964 as *Fair Go, Spinner*), Melbourne, 1979.

Wannan, W., *The Australian*, Sydney, 1954.

Ward, R., *The Australian Legend*, Melbourne, 1958.

Welborn, S., *Lords of Death: A people, a place a legend*, Fremantle, 1982.

White, R., *Inventing Australia*, Sydney, 1981.

Winter, D., *Death's Men: Soldiers of the Great War*, London, 1978.

Winter, D. (ed), *Making the Legend: The War Writings of C.E.W. Bean*, St Lucia, 1992.

Winter, D., *25 April 1915: The Inevitable Tragedy*, St Lucia, 1994.

Young, M (ed), *'We Are Here, Too': Diaries and Letters of Sister Olive L. C. Haynes No 2 A.G.H. November 1914 to February 1918*, Adelaide, 1991.

Zumwalt, R., *The Enigma of Arnold van Gennep (1873–1957): a master of French folklore and hermit of Bourg-la-Reine*, Helsinki, 1988.

Articles and Book Chapters

Alomes, S., 'Parades of Meaning: The Moomba Festival and Contemporary Culture', *Journal of Australian Studies* 17, November 1985.

Anderson, H., 'On the Track with Bill Bowyang', *Australian Folklore* 6, Sept. 1991.

Anon., 'Our First Dawn Service', *Willoughby* (NSW) *Legion Club News*, April/May, 1989.

Barlow, A., 'Festivals' in Davey, G. and Seal, G (eds), *The Oxford Companion to Australian Folklore*, Melbourne, 1993.

Barrett, J., 'No Straw Man: C.E.W. Bean and Some Critics', *Historical Studies*, 23:89, April 1988.

Bazley, A., 'C.E.W. Bean', *Historical Studies*, October, 1969.

Bean, C.E.W., 'Sidelights of the War on Australian Character', *Royal Australian Historical Society Journal*, 13:4, 1927.

Bennett, B., 'Wartime Culture: The Westralia Gift Book 1916', in Layman,

L. and Stannage, C.T. (eds), *Celebrations in West Australian History*, Studies in West Australian History X, April, 1989.

Bennett, G. and Smith, P., 'The Birth of Contemporary Legend', Introduction to Bennett, G. and Smith, P. (eds), *The Questing Beast: Perspectives on Contemporary Legend*, Vol. IV, Sheffield, 1989.

Buchbinder, D., 'Mateship, *Gallipoli* and the Eternal Masculine', in Fuery, P., (ed), *Representation, Discourse and Desire*, South Melbourne, 1994.

Caplow, T., 'Rumors in War', *Social Forces* 25, 1947.

Carroll, J., 'Mateship and Egalitarianism: The Failure of Upper Middle-Class Nerve' in Carroll, J. (ed), *Intruders in the Bush: The Australian Quest for Identity*, Melbourne, 1982.

Clarke, D., 'Rumours of Angels: A Legend of the First World War', *Folklore*, 113:2, October 2002.

Cochrane, P., 'Deliverance and Renewal: The Origins of the Simpson Legend', *Journal of the Australian War Memorial*, 16 April, 1990.

Cochrane, P., 'Legendary Proportions: The Simpson Memorial Appeal of 1933', *Australian Historical Studies*, 24:94, April, 1990.

Cole, D., 'The Crimson Thread of Kinship: Ethnic Ideas in Australia 1870–1914', *Historical Studies* , 14:56, 1971.

Davis, N.Z., 'The Possibilities of the Past', *Journal of Interdisciplinary History* 12, 1981.

Degh, L. and Vazsonyi, A., 'The Hypothesis of Multi-Conduit Transmission in Folklore', in Ben-Amos, D. and Goldstein, K. (eds), *Folklore: Performance and Communication*, The Hague, 1975.

Edwards, R. 'Yarns and Contemporary Legends: A Reassessment', in Edwards, R. (ed), *Proceedings of the 3rd National Folklore Conference*, Canberra, 1988.

Ely, R., 'The First Anzac Day: Invented or Discovered?', *Journal of Australian Studies* 17, 1985.

Evans, R., ' "Some Furious Outbursts of Riot": Returned Soldiers and Queensland's "Red Flag" Disturbances, 1918–1919', *War and Society*, 3:2, 1985.

Fewster, K., 'Ellis Ashmead Bartlett and the Making of the Anzac Legend', *Journal of Australian Studies* 10, 1982.

Fewster, K., 'The Wazza Riots, 1915', *Journal of the Australian War Memorial* 3, 1984.

Finnegan, R., 'A Note on Oral Evidence and Historical Evidence', *History and Theory*, 9:2, 1970.

Firth, S. and Hoorn, J., 'From Empire Day to Cracker Night', in Spearritt, P. and Walker, D. (eds), *Australian Popular Culture*, Sydney, 1979.

Flaherty, C. and Roberts, M., 'The Reproduction of Anzac Symbolism', *Journal of Australian Studies* 24, May 1989.

Fox, L., 'Early Australian May Days', *Bulletin of the Australian Society for Labour History* 2, May 1962.

Gailey, A., 'The Nature of Tradition', *Folklore*, 100:ii, 1989.

Gammage, W., 'Anzac's Influence on Turkey and Australia', paper presented at the Australian War Memorial History Conference, July, 1990.

Gammage, W., 'Anzac', in Carroll, J., (ed), *Intruders in the Bush: The Australian Quest for Identity*, Melbourne, 1982.

Gammage, W., 'The Crucible: The Establishment of the Anzac Tradition, 1899–1918, in McKernan, M and Browne, M. (eds), *Australia Two Centuries of War and Peace*, Canberra/Sydney, 1988.

Gerster, R., 'War Literature' in Hergenhan, L. (ed) *The Penguin New Literary History of Australia*, Ringwood, 1988.

Goody, J. and Watt, J., 'The Consequences of Literacy' in Goody, J., (ed) *Literacy in Traditional Societies*, Cambridge, 1968.

Henderson, G., 'The Anzac Legend After Gallipoli', *Quadrant* 26, July 1982.

Heseltine, H., 'Australian Fiction Since 1920' in Dutton, G. (ed), *The Literature of Australia*, Ringwood, rev. edn. 1976.

Hirst, J.B., 'The Pioneer Legend' in Carroll, J. (ed), *Intruders in the Bush: The Australian Quest for Identity*, Melbourne, 1982.

Howe, A., 'Anzac Mythology and the Feminist Challenge', *Melbourne Journal of Politics* 15, 1983.

Inglis Moore, T., 'The Meanings of Mateship', *Meanjin*, 24:1, 1965.

Inglis, K., 'A Sacred Place: The Making of the Australian War Memorial', *War and Society*, 3:2, 1985.

Inglis, K., 'Memorials of the Great War', *Australian Cultural History* 6, 1987.

Inglis, K., 'Remembering Australians on the Somme, Anzac Day 1988', *Overland* 115, August 1989.

Inglis, K.S., 'The Anzac Tradition', *Meanjin*, 24:1, 1965.

Inglis, K.S., 'The Australians at Gallipoli', parts 1 and 2, *Historical Studies*, 14:54, 1970–14:55, 1970.

Johnson, Lesley, 'The Study of Popular Culture: The Need for a Clear Agenda', *Australian Journal of Cultural Studies*, 4:1, June 1986.

Johnson, R., 'The Story So Far: And Further Transformations?' in Punter, D. (ed), *Introduction to Contemporary Cultural Studies*, London, 1986.

Joyner, C., 'Reconsidering a Relationship:Folklore and History', *Kentucky Folklore Record*, 32:1–2, Jan–June 1986.

Kent, D., 'From the Sudan to Saigon: A Critical View of Historical Works', *Australian Literary Studies* 12, 1985.

Kent, D., 'The Anzac Book and the Anzac Legend: C.E.W. Bean as Editor and Image-maker', *Historical Studies*, 21:84, April 1985.

Kent, D., 'Introduction' to *The Kia Ora Coo-ee*, Sydney, 1981.

Kent, D., 'Troopship Literature: A Life on the Ocean Wave', *Journal of the Australian War Memorial*, 10, April 1987.

Kitley, P., 'Anzac Day Ritual', *Journal of Australian Studies* 4, 1979.

Lake, M., 'The Power of Anzac', in McKernan, M and Browne, M. (eds), *Australia Two Centuries of War and Peace*, Canberra/Melbourne, 1988.

Linton, R., 'Totemism and the AEF', in Lessa, William A. and Vogt, Evon Z. (eds), *Reader in Comparative Religion*, (2nd. edn.), New York/Evanston/London, 1965.

Long, G., 'The Australian War History Tradition', *Historical Studies*, November 1954.

Ludtke, Alf, 'The Historiography of Everyday Life: The Personal and the Political', in Samuel, R. and Stedman Jones, G. (eds), *Culture, Ideology and Politics: Essays for Eric Hobsbawm*, London, 1982.

Mansfield, W., 'The Importance of Gallipoli: The Growth of an Australian Folklore', *Queensland Historical Review*, 6:2, 1977.

McKernan, M., 'Clergy in Khaki: The Chaplain in the AIF, 1914–1918', *Journal of the Royal Australian Historical Society*, 64:3, 1978.

McLachlan, N., 'Nationalism and the Divisive Digger', *Meanjin*, 27:3, 1968.

McQueen, H., 'Emu into Ostrich: Australian Literary Responses to the Great War', *Meanjin*, 35:1, 1976.

McQueen, H., 'Gallipoli to Petrov' in McQueen, H., *Gallipoli to Petrov: Arguing with Australian History*, N. Sydney, 1984.

McQueen, H. 'Sentimental Thoughts of "a Moody Bloke": C. J. Dennis', in McQueen, H., *Gallipoli to Petrov: Arguing With Australian History*, N. Sydney, 1984.

Millar, A., 'Gallipoli to Melbourne: The Australian War Memorial, 1915–19', *Journal of the Australian War Memorial* 10, April, 1987.

Moroney, J., 'Fremantle War Memorial: Patriotism or Civic Pride?', in Layman, L. and Stannage, C.T. (eds), *Celebrations in West Australian History*, Studies in West Australian History X, April, 1989.

Murphy, J., 'The Voice of Memory: History, Autobiography and Oral Memory', *Historical Studies*, 22:87, Oct. 1986.

Newall, V., 'The Adaptation of Folklore and Tradition (Folklorismus)', *Folklore*, 98:ii, 1987.

Nile, R., 'Orientalism and the Origins of Anzac', in Nile, R. and Seymour, A. (eds), *Anzac: Meaning, Memory and Myth*, London, 1991.

Nile, R., 'Peace, Unreliable Memory and the Necessity of Anzac Mythologies', in Nile, R. and Seymour, A. (eds), *Anzac: Meaning, Memory and Myth*, London, 1991.

Nile, R., 'War and Literature: Imagining 1914–1918' in Nile, R. and York, B. (eds), *Workers and Intellectuals: Essays on Twentieth Century Australia from Ten Urban Hunters and Gatherers*, London, 1992.

Nkpa, N.K.U., 'Rumor Mongering in War Time', *Journal of Social Psychology* 96, 1975.

Oring, E., 'Totemism in the AEF', *Southern Folklore Quarterly*, 41:1–2, 1977.

Pearse, A.E., 'Soldiers' Songs', *Stand-To*, July–Aug., 1956.

Pollard, A.F., 'Rumour and Historical Science in Time of War', *Contemporary Revue* 107, 1915.

Robson, L., 'Behold A Pale Horse: Australian War Studies', *Australian Historical Studies*, 3:89, April 1988.

Robson, L., 'The Australian Soldier: Formation of a Stereotype', in McKernan M. and Browne M. (eds), *Australia Two Centuries of War and Peace*, Canberra/Sydney, 1988.

Robson, L., 'The Origin and Character of the First AIF, 1914–1918: Some Statistical Evidence', *Historical Studies*, 15:61, Oct. 1973.

Roe, M., 'The Australian Legend', Davey, G. and Seal, G. (eds), *The Oxford Companion to Australian Folklore*, Melbourne, 1993.

Roe, M., 'Comment on the Digger Tradition', *Meanjin*, 24:3, 1965.

Roper, M., 'Inventing Traditions in Colonial Society: Bendigo's Easter Fair, 1871–1885 *Journal of Australian Studies* 17, November 1985.

Russell, I., 'Parody and Performance' in Pickering M. and Green, Tony (eds), *Everyday Culture: Popular Song and the Vernacular Milieu*, Milton Keynes/Philadelphia, 1987.

Sackett, L., 'Marching into the Past: Anzac Day Celebrations in Adelaide', *Journal of Australian Studies* 17, 1985.

Schwartz, B., 'The Social Context of Commemoration: A Study in Collective Memory', *Social Forces*, 61:2, Dec. 1982.

Scott, A., 'Parody and Beyond', in *Proceedings of the 3rd National Folklore Conference, National Library, Canberra, 1988*, Canberra, 1988.

Seal, G., 'Two Traditions: The Folklore of the Digger and the Invention of Anzac', *Australian Folklore* 5, 1990.

Seal, G., 'Written in the Trenches: Trench Newspapers of the Great War', *Journal of the Australian War Memorial* 16, April, 1990.

Serle, G., 'The Digger Tradition and Australian Nationalism', *Meanjin*, 24:2, 1965.

Shaw, B., 'Bush Religion: A Discussion of Mateship', *Meanjin Quarterly*, 12:3, 1953.

Shute, C., 'Heroines and Heroes: Sexual Mythology in Australia 1914–1918', *Hecate*, 1975.

Stanley, P., 'Paul the Pimp re-considered: Australian "G" staffs on the western front and the "Kiggell" anecdote', paper presented at Australian War Memorial History Conference, July, 1987.

Stubington, J., 'Songs of War and Songs of Peace', unpublished paper presented to Symposium of the International Musicological Society, Melbourne, Aug–Sept., 1988.

Taussig, M., 'An Australian Hero', *History Workshop Journal* 24, 1987.

Thompson, E.P., 'Folklore, Anthropology and Social History', *The Indian Historical Review*, 3:2, January 1977.

Thomson, A., 'A Past You Can Live With: Digger Memories and the Anzac Legend', in Nile, R. and Seymour, A. (eds), *Anzac: Meaning, Memory and Myth*, London, 1991.

Thomson, A., 'Anzac Memories: Putting Popular Memory Theory into Practice in Australia', *Oral History*, 18:1, Spring 1990.

Thomson, A., 'Steadfast until Death? C.E.W. Bean and the Representation of Australian Military Manhood', *Australian Historical Studies*, 23:93, Oct. 1989.

Topperwien, B., 'The Word "Anzac"', *Sabretache*, vol XXXVIII September 1997.

White, R., 'Europe and the Six-Bob-a-Day Tourist: The Great War as a Grand Tour, or Getting Civilised', *Australian Studies* (BASA) 5, April 1991.

White, R., 'Sun, Sand and Syphilis: Australian Soldiers and the Orient Egypt 1914', in *Australian Cultural History* 9, July, 1990.

White, R., 'The Soldier as Tourist: The Australian Experience of the Great War', *War and Society*, 5, May 1987.

White, R., 'War and Australian Society', in McKernan, M and Browne, M. (eds), *Australia Two Centuries of War and Peace*, Canberra/Melbourne, 1988.

Wilson, Mary, 'The Making of Melbourne's Anzac Day', *Australian Journal of Politics and History*, 20:2, August 1974.

Bibliographical Works, Theses, etc.

Australian Literary Studies, 12:2, Oct. 1985. 'War in Australian Literature — Special Issue'.

Australian National Dictionary Centre Newsletter

Dewar, S., '"Having A Lively Time": Australians at Gallipoli in 1915', La Trobe Library, Melbourne, 1990.

Fielding, J. and O'Neill, R., *A Select Bibliography of Australian Military History 1891–1939*, Canberra, 1978.

Hults, D., 'A Bibliographic Guide to Australian Folklore', in Davey, G. and Seal, G. (eds), *The Oxford Companion to Australian Folklore*, Melbourne, 1993.

Hults, D., *Bibliography of Australian Folklore, 1790–1990*, Perth, 1995.

King, T., 'On the Definition of Digger: Australia and its Returned Soldiers, 1915–1920', PhD thesis, La Trobe University, 1988.

Laird, J.T., 'Australian Literature of the First World War', *Australian Literary Studies*, 12:2, Oct. 1985.

Laird, J.T., 'A Checklist of Australian Literature of the First World War', *Australian Literary Studies*, 12: 2, Oct. 1985.

McLeod, F., *The Gallipoli Campaign: A Select Bibliography*, Duntroon, 1990.

Seal, G. (ed), *Australian Folk Resources: A Select Guide and Preliminary Bibliography*, Canberra, 1983. Rev. edn. with Edwards, R., 1988.

Index